D0201337

REMINISCENCES

A Memoir

H. J. Daniels, PhD

REMINISCENCES
A MEMOIR

iUniverse books may be ordered through booksellers or by contacting:

iUniverse
1663 Liberty Drive
Bloomington, IN 47403
www.iuniverse.com
1-800-Authors (1-800-288-4677)

ISBN: 978-1-4917-8982-7 (sc)
ISBN: 978-1-4917-8983-4 (hc)
ISBN: 978-1-4917-8984-1 (e)

Library of Congress Control Number: 2016902760

Print information available on the last page.

iUniverse rev. date: 4/12/2016

In memory of Mother and Father.
They left indelible fingerprints of
personal refinement on my life.

PREFACE

The author often saw a funny side to what goes on around him, and has had a propensity for further spicing up events with an unusual satiric cartoonist twist. With this in mind and relying upon an aptitude for remembering minute details of events, coupled with an affable personality and effective interpersonal communication skills, he ventured into writing up past incidents in his life.

In essence, this work is biographic molded in a story-telling framework; life itself is but a book, anyway, the chapters of which, some people religiously believe, have been written in their entirety and in the minutest details beforehand. Narratives of the author's life happenings are presented in chronological order; however, some stories have properly fitted better where subject and topic were more important than chronological sequence. Taken as a whole, those stories tell quite a lot about the author, not only in 'historical' context, but also in personality. All names mentioned herein are not real, unless by explicit consent.

The author holds a PhD degree from Bristol in the United Kingdom; he has vastly enriched his English-language vocabulary and improved sentence structure by reading a wide spectrum of classical English literature augmented by forty years of scientific report writing. During early university years, he indulged in visual art, painting in particular, a trait that he was fortunate to be able to cultivate later on in life. The antler's silhouette, superimposed on a forest on the cover, reflects the author's deep love and respect for nature.

TABLE OF CONTENTS

(Selected Subtitles: Best Reading Where Bolded)

A LIST OF IMAGES

The Children
Map of Aramean Migration Route
The Captain (an oil painting)
Friends Haney and Kays
The Flower Arrangement
The Cat
The Doggie

PART ONE: HOME-COUNTRY STORIES / CHILDHOOD - ADOLESCENCE (PRE-1958)

THE SPECTRE

I have an overwhelming urge to start this book with one of my earliest memories, one that has had a profound, inerasable imprint on my psyche for much of my life, a singular recollection that has, to a great extent, even influenced my religious beliefs.

When it comes to supernatural manifestations, people are divided into two categories: *believers* and *non-believers*. Inquisitive people of education are inclined to fall into the latter group; believers, on the other hand, tend to be those who are deeply influenced by religion and also those *who have had 'certain encounters'*. I have heard so-called 'witnesses' on television talking about ghosts and UFOs, and wondered about the accuracy and even the authenticity or credibility of their accounts, only to remember the following personal incident and wonder no more.

I was about six years old when the heavenly, peaceful times directly following the end of World War II (on the European 'theatre') had just started, though unfortunately for a relatively short duration only. **Location**: Our family lived in al-Ma'qal, Basra, in (then) the **Kingdom** of Iraq up to 1958. Many of the houses in that small town, all being the property of the **Iraqi Ports Directorate**, were built with flat roofs, on which people slept at night during the exceptionally hot and humid months of the summer season. So, 'preparing the beds' (unfolding mattresses and arranging bed sheets) was a daily chore performed after sunset, when the heat subsided considerably; that task was decidedly my mother's responsibility, not that anyone had any proclivity to contest it.

One late evening, around dusk, my mother told my father who was sitting in the 'front' yard that she was going to work on the beds, after which she asked me if I wanted to accompany her. I followed her into the house and then out to the back yard, where a wooden staircase leading to the roof was mounted. She was halfway up the stairs when I turned to my left and started ascending in an opposite direction to where came from. As I did so, something, in the form of light, contrasting with the progressively darkening sky, attracted my attention. I turned sharply sideways to my left and looked upwards towards the sky; there, I saw a sedentary, bright and sharply outlined *Spectre* of a tall old man with a solemn face and a long beard facing where we were. The *Spectre* held a 'bucket' in each hand, with arms extended downwards close to its form towards a flat ground-like base, on which 'it' stood; the 'base', about one-third in width as the height of the *Spectre*, faded out rather sharply towards an irregularly-shaped edge. The entire apparition was in unadulterated white; it matched in height a neighbouring brown house above which 'it' stood.

In an excited voice, I called my mom, at the same time telling her what I saw and pointing to where the *Spectre* was. Following a glance, she instantly called my father, asking him to come quickly, after which I heard his unhurried footsteps approaching us. As soon as I heard him coming towards us, the *Spectre* started to fade out with every step. By the time my father was in a position in the yard to look where my mother pointed, the *Spectre* had already vanished; my father saw absolutely nothing, other than a dark sky! In response to his inquiry, my mother related the story, exactly as has been outlined above with a little variation, the latter being that the *Spectre* was holding 'suitcases', rather than 'buckets'. Both my mom and I have had vivid visions of these details for many, many years thereafter. The next day we asked some of our neighbours if they had seen anything; all responses were in the negative.

About sixty years following that exceptional incident, I visited my mother and sister's family in Copenhagen (Denmark); my very old mother was sick and in hospital. She died within two days of my arrival, and her body was taken to a Catholic church. Two days later, all relatives (my brother, two sisters and their families) congregated at the church attending the 'mass for the dead'. When the mass was over, we carried her coffin to the sextant's car. My older sister, Hind, and I then stood, separate from others, on the walkway waiting for everyone to get in their respective cars on our way to the cemetery. I was standing by that car's front end, on the passenger's side, about a yard from it; my sister stood next to me on my right. There was sombre ambient silence and overwhelming serene tranquility, as though time stood still for a moment. Suddenly, I became mystically aware of the presence of someone beside me on my left; I instinctively turned sharply, only to see my mother standing there and looking pensively at a large tree on the other side of the road past the sextant's car. She looked as I had seen her on my previous visit, when she was in good health, not this last one. The apparition took about a second; I turned to my sister and mumbled something about what I had seen. She later told me that she didn't understand what I had said at the time. My relatives, including my old aunt, told me later that my mother had loved me a lot during her life, more than the rest of my siblings, a statement I had heard several times during my life.

CHEERS!

In later years, following the former story (appearance of the Spectre), when I got to an age where memory started to actively kick in, I oftentimes heard this next story from my father as he related it to friends of the family during mutual visits. I was two years old, when he was transferred on a temporary basis to al-Faw, a town at the southern tip of Iraq, where the country's borderland touched the waters of the Arabian Gulf.

He, my mom and I were taken on board a small ship (the *Yenen*) sailing down the Shat al-Arab River to a location at its southernmost part, where we were supposed to disembark and reach al-Faw by car. The story goes that during that trip I disappeared by wandering around *(well, everything was so exciting; a ship! I never saw anything like that the **whole of my life!**)*. It didn't take my parents long to find me; I was then holding in my tiny hands a small can from which I was drinking **kerosene**; was it ever yum-yum; *cheers/cheerio and, as the Chinese say: 'Gam Bay!'* **I herein honestly and solemnly declare that I didn't consume enough then to cause any subsequent fuel-price hikes, be it on the short or long run.**

UNINTENDED STOMACH CLEANSING

With this story, I go back to a curious event (around 1950). One day, we had two visiting families. After chatting and presenting tea with cake, it was time to serve a homemade sweet in the form of marmalade jam.

The latter closely resembled orange marmalade; instead of orange peels, however, Iraqis had the advantage of having another kind of citrus called 'Ttringe', resembling pomelos. That fruit, quite larger than an average orange, had a peel that was rugged and close to 1 centimeter thick, thus being ideal for such jams. The peel of each fruit was cut vertically into four or five pieces, then boiled and simmered with sugar.

We had during those days an epidemic related to infected vegetables, so sanitization was meticulously followed; at that time, people used diluted solutions of 'potassium permanganate' as an anti-bacterial agent to kill germs on vegetables and kitchen utensils; it came as black crystals, a small amount of which was dissolved in water, turning it into a medium-to-deep violet solution. Following my father's instructions, my mother brought in a tray bearing a wide plate that had several mouth-size marmalade pieces, arranged like a flower (nice to look at!). There also was a fork and a glass containing that antiseptic solution. My father asked the visitors to dip the fork they were using in that solution before sampling the marmalade.

Starting from the right, as custom implied, the gentleman took a sample of the jam, returned the fork on the plate and, after slight hesitation, took a sip from the glass! Quickly, and under my father's incredulous stare, the next visitor did the same, this time without any hesitation!

After that, it was far too late for my father to correct any misapprehension; all enjoyed both of those two 'servings'!

THE SAVING OF MY SISTER

One day, only a few years subsequent to the narrative on the *Yenen* trip, above, and around the time of the Spectre story, my sister, Hind, and I were playing outside our house's front garden; she was not even three years old then, fair complexioned, blue-eyed and blonde-haired. A dark-skinned local man passed by us, and as he did so he gazed at her, then picked her up and walked away. I ran indoors and breathlessly told my mom what had happened. She jumped out to the front yard, hysterically calling our gardener, who was a stout man, and begging him to do something. After I indicated to him the direction where that man was headed, he ran that way. A few minutes later, he brought my little sister back; he said that the kidnapper, hearing someone running behind him and yelling: "stop!" dropped her and ran away.

Our gardener told us then that the kidnapper likely planned to have her grow up with a group of gypsies, who would later turn her into a belly dancer, and that such nomads were in the habit of kidnapping kids! We certainly would have lost her if it wasn't for that chivalrous and courageous gardener! (How many of that type do exist these days!)

The Author
(A 'few' years earlier)

My little Brother; not so little now
(with his protruding belly, that is)

The kidnapped
Sister

There is **another one** (the youngest), who is
not represented in this photo (too young)

FATHER

The courses of thought outlined above bring to my
mind the following memory: My father was only thirteen
when his father died (1912). He had, then, to leave school
and work in order to make ends meet for his family (mother,

aunt and four siblings). He readily found a mediocre job that earned him a small salary. One day, he went to the bank to withdraw **2 dinars** (US$7). The money was given to him in small change (which was not small at that time, considering the value of the local currency; example: one Iraqi dinar could probably have brought 50 chickens; now, after the 'blessings' of all the *coup de tats* and wars following 1958, a chicken is worth 2000 dinars. After receiving the money, my father stood not too far from the cashier's till, in order to carefully count his money which was in the form of 'change'. As he was absorbed in that process, he heard a man (who had been in line just behind him) asking the cashier to give him **100 dinars**.

My father was astounded, to put it mildly, and as the gentleman had collected that huge sum and turned to leave, my father approached him with a smile and both politely and humorously asked: "Sir, can you please tell me why I can only withdraw 2 dinars when you collect 100?" Lowering his head, in order to be able to see the person addressing him closely over the edge of his eyeglasses, the gentleman looked probingly at my father who was light-complexioned, in contrast to the commonly 'tanned' general populace, and asked: "You are Christian, *'ma'* (isn't that so)?" After a response in the affirmative, the gentleman said: "Look, it is simple; when you Christians pray to God, you ask for **enough subsistence for the day**; whereas we, the Jews, **ask God to give us a lot of money**! He gives us what we ask for!" This happened when Iraq still was civilized enough to embrace people of different religious faiths, including Jews.

The job my father had then did not bring enough income to satisfy the needs of the family, so he decided to learn typing in English, which was a scarce commodity in Iraq in those days, since many Iraqis could not even write their own name in Arabic. There were a few English companies in Basra involved in international maritime trade and services (imports of manufactured goods, exporting barley and passenger travel), and a job with one of those companies was expected to be exceptionally rewarding. However, there was no way to get help getting education and training on such a profession as 'typist', since typewriters weren't even available there, except at a few select offices. One day he had an opportunity to be in the presence of one of those *enigmatic and 'majestic' machines*. There were letters and numbers built in a step-like lay out, and those letters moved down, when pressed, a process that resulted in letters appearing on a sheet of paper; there were other features like a space bar and shift key. After observing how different parts of the machine worked, he hurriedly looked for and soon found a board on which to draw a facsimile of what he saw, paying attention to the actual and relative positions of the letters. Driven by ambition, he enthusiastically took that board home and spent quite some time trying to memorize those arrangements, while moving his fingers around over it.

A few days later, he went to the largest of those English companies (Strick Ellerman Lines) and asked if they needed a typist in English. The person in charge of the office looked at him quizzically and asked if he could type; after replying in the affirmative, that person brought a typewriter, handed him a sheet of paper and asked him to type a paragraph from a book. At that juncture, my father, with some obvious embarrassment, asked the gentleman if he would kindly insert the sheet in the typewriter for him, in response to which the surprised gentleman said: "But you said you knew how to type!" My father boldly responded: "Yes, yes, I can; but please put the paper in there". To satisfy his own curiosity and bemusement, the gentleman got that done and stood aside waiting. After slight hesitation, my father started typing, awkwardly but fairly well. Soon after explaining, as he was bid, that gentleman gave him the job. Later in life, he held another (supplementary) part-time job with them for several years; his younger brother worked for that same company 42 years.

With time, and pushed by strong ambition, my father acquired a small cigarette-making machine and started a good business, based on two or three brands. As a consequence, he was able to buy four houses. With time, that machine broke down, and he had to buy another one from overseas, because there was no one there who could repair it. After a long wait, the new machine finally arrived by sea. As it was being loaded on a cart, it fell down and broke: no more cigarette-making business! At one time, thereafter, he started

importing kitchen china from England, but didn't succeed
because most buyers could not afford the merchandise.

THE 'DENTIST' OF OLDEN-TIMES

I was at a delicate age then, probably five to six years old
(circa 1945), when my parents and siblings visited Baghdad,
the capital of the country, where my mom's parents lived.
One day, my father took me with him to visit my grandfather,
whom I knew was a dentist, at his work place. We arrived at
an old building (called "khan") which was square and two-
storied, and had an inner courtyard in the middle that was
open to the sky; that courtyard was surrounded by rooms on
two levels. Khans were precursors of present-day hotels, and
they had acted as such for centuries, catering for travelers on
what used to be known as the "Silk Route" between Europe
and India-China, and vice-versa.

We went up a wooden staircase to the upper floor,
then walked over an inner courtyard's wooden walkway
surrounded with a wraparound railing and proceeded towards
my grandfather's 'clinic'. Halfway there, we heard horrid
screaming emanating from that office, then saw a large man
with bloodshot cheeks and drooling mouth dashing out of
that office; he rushed madly towards the staircase, as though
being chased by the devil, himself. Soon after, my grandfather
emerged from his clinic's doorway opening holding a pair of

pliers (resembling those used by barbers/'dentists' shown on Western movies) up in the air and pleading in a loud voice to the runaway patient: **"Come back, come back, there still is a tooth fragment in there!"** Well, he couldn't catch him! It is relevant to explain that in those days, there were not many university-graduate dentists in that region of the world. As we were just about to enter his office, I could, with difficulty, read a sign saying: **"TEETH OVERHAULER."** (!)

YOYO

Presentation of bygone incidents would be lacking a pivotal personality, without an account of 'Yoyo'. He was an old beggar, tall and wiry; he had a long boney face 'adorned' with a long and rather narrow white beard. He wore decrepit nondescript cloths, which at sometimes may have shown distinct colors; his head was always covered with a short blanket (or a jacket) matching the rest of his tattered outfit, lending him an unfathomable enigmatic appearance. As far as I can remember, and this could possibly be imaginary on my part, but likely true, he had a sharp penetrating look that scared both my brother and me out of our wits. We were then about five and seven years old, respectively, and still living in that same house where my mother and I saw the Spectre (story above).

I remember once that I went outside our house to play and saw him at a distance, but moving away; he had just passed by our house, so I had no fear staying out. On another occasion, however, I wasn't that lucky with regard to timing. One late afternoon around dusk, my brother and I, both still kids of about the ages listed above, were outside at a time when my father was expected to come back home from his part-time job with Strick, above. As we opened the small wooden front-garden gate and went out, there it came, a small car (probably an English-made Consul) stopping right in front of our house. As I saw my father getting off, I ran across the road to meet him. At that point, I heard my brother screaming: "Haney, Yoyo!" I turned to look and there he was on my right, just a few steps away from where I was. It took me only a split-second to reverse direction of movement and zoom backwards towards my brother; within a second, we were both inside the house, father or no father!

THE MYSTERIOUS HOLE-DIGGING
(Presented by my brother Owen)

"Haney, I don't know if this real incident is worth mentioning in your book, but I'll tell it as it was about seventy years ago. At that time, we were living in our small house near Ashuriyeen Church on a street called Ethel Road. We had only one bedroom; so dad, mom, you, Hind and I were used to sleep in that bedroom. My age at that time was four or five, and when the night comes and everyone is sleeping, I start hearing a sound of digging just outside our house's bedroom, in that open space between our house and the church. This digging happened almost every night, and took a long time, too.

At that time, I thought there was a mysterious scary man outside digging the ground. The next day when checking the area, I did not find any holes. I did not mention this to anyone at that time; maybe I was scared. I forgot about this when I grew up, and did not resolve this until one day (maybe in university or high school) I suddenly and intuitively realized that the digging noise was our dad snoring! (I hope you didn't pee in your pants from laughter!)"

TTANTTAL

I remember that I was about five or six years old (around 1945) when my father took me, sometime in the morning, to the small church in al-Ma'qal (a present from the British-run Iraqi Ports management to its Christian employees; those were the days!). That day, my father, together with others, had a meeting with the priest. Other children were there as well; all kids were to play quietly outside the church building itself, but had to stay within the limits of the church's courtyard.

The church had a guard then. In order to prevent us from crossing the road and wandering in an uninhabited area close by and getting lost, the guard told us not to cross that road, because there was a *'Ttanttal'* roaming around in the area! When we asked him what that thing was, he said that 'Ttanttal' was a giant as tall as a palm tree! No one dared to go anywhere but stayed close to the guard! Years later (around 1962), I was reminded of that story when I had a chance to read *Tall Tale, America* at the American Library in Baghdad and came across *Paul Bunyan*; my thought then was: "Oh, they have a 'Ttanttal' too!" I believe most, if not all, cultures do. Canada has Bigfoot/Sasquatch and Tibet is well known for its Yeti; and how about the Yeren in China!

The mention of the big humanoid creatures, above, reminds me of something else; something that is related to unfairness in this world of ours, one which specifically concerns the wide disparity in people's sizes. At primary school, I remember having a huge teacher who was partly of Indian descent. When he sneezed, he went: "atseu"; by unfair comparison, I, then 1/8th his size, produced room-rattling clamour when I did so. Once, I remember seeing him giving me a 'dirty' look after I had sneezed; I wondered then whether he was protesting the uproar, or envying me the ability to generate sneezes that were powerful enough to befit his own enormous size; it was like he was saying: **"That is not at all fair; what is happening to this world!"**

THE WAR IS OVER!

One day in early May, 1945, I was playing in our front-yard at around six o'clock in the afternoon; our family then had a mediocre-sized garden including several banana trees and grape vines. I remember that a banana tree bore fruit only once, after which it was cut right at its base. Soon, thereafter, several new shoots emerged around the stump, which were then subdivided into as many individuals, each with some roots from the parent tree, and transplanted.

Our town of al-Ma'qal (meaning the stronghold) as usual then was quiet that afternoon; all of a sudden, however, I heard footsteps approaching. I looked at the garden's small wooden gate and saw a man coming from the road towards it; I recognized him as being one of our neighbors. As he got to the gate, he said, with a tired but content smile: "**Tell your dad that the war is over**". That is all of the Second World War I was aware of; I was six years old then. The German armies surrendered to the Allies and the Russians on May 7 and 8 of that year; let us hope that the number of world wars remains at two forever!

THE THING

Soon after moving into that house (story above) I remember that one afternoon my father, brother (then 5 years old) and I (7 years old) were in our garden enjoying the presence of the plants and flowers we had then. I quickly noticed that one of the flowers was white and that there was a tiny white thing on top of it; the whole plant was about one foot high. At that age kids are endowed with sharp eyesight, so I could visually discern its presence quite readily. Out of natural child's curiosity, I asked my father, who was standing beside me, what that little thing was.

At around fifty-five and, with eyes being at quite a higher distance from the flower than I was, he couldn't see anything there, except the flower itself. He casually told me it was a flower; at that I pointed to it and said: **"This thing"**. He then looked at it again and said: "That is a white flower". I repeated the question once more, only to get the same answer.

By that time I had lost any little patience, which is a rare commodity in kids, I had had and shouted: **"This thing; what is wrong with you; are you blind?"** (Oops; during those days youngsters normally didn't dare look their father or mother in the eye, but kids are kids!) He bent down to the flower's level and gave it a scrutinizing look, and as the thing became discernable, he said, while exuding genuine merriment in response to an unexpected torrent of abuse on my side: "Oh, this; this is a spider". It was a 2 millimeter-long/across white spider that had blended intricately with its surrounding. *Lesson: Do pay attention to what kids say, even if they were a Haney; it could be something important to grown-ups as well.*

USE THE OTHER ONE, STUPID!

I still remember my father, who was a great storyteller, recount this one even at my young age of seven. One day, in the **Kingdom** of Iraq, he went to a doctor to seek his advice with regard to a certain ailment. I still remember that doctor as being from the sub-continent, old, completely bald, tall and wiry, stern looking and decidedly self-assured. His office had dark furniture and wasn't very well lit. My father's turn came when a patient left that office followed by the doctor saying: "Next".

The door's opening to the office was always open, but regularly obstructed by a heavy dark brown curtain. My father approached and tried to make an entrance from the left side of the curtain, as he faced it, which was closer to him. He soon heard the doctor saying in his distinctive Indian accent: "Not from there". My father was perplexed and, trying again, heard the doctor say: "Use the other one", but this time with clear irritation. At that, my father retraced his steps and looked around; he couldn't find another door, so he went out of the clinic looking for another entrance to that office, but failed to do so. He went back and tried again! This time, the doctor shouted: "The other side, stupid!" (I assure the reader that my father was anything, but that!). Then, the gist of what the doctor had actually meant started to emerge; but my father still wasn't quite certain, and he had to be careful with the owner of that menacing voice. Because he knew the doctor's temper, he slowly, lightly and stealthily moved the right hand side of the curtain and waited for a reaction, before fully committing himself to such a perilous endeavor, and heard: "Yes, yes, that one!"

HANDOUT

My parents, siblings and I were visiting another family (around 1952/53). It was a pleasant moonlit summer evening, and everybody was sitting in that family's garden. After a while, everyone was handed a cup of tea and offered a generous slice of patchy, light and dark home-made 'sponge cake'. It happened that I was sitting next to the other family's sixteen-year old son and facing my father.

As we were enjoying what we had, I noticed that my father was looking towards that young man in a curious way, which attracted my attention. So, I glanced sideways and saw the young man having a bite from his cake; then his hand brought the rest of it all the way down at his side, where the family's small dog was sitting motionless. As the cake reached the level where its head was, it gently and delicately took a bite (must have been a female!). After a short while, the cake went up to the young man's mouth again and then back to that of the dog. **At the end, both were happy and content, and one of them was wagging a tail!**

OUR AFFECTIONATE NEIGHBOUR

While living in that house (white spider), which was a half-duplex adjoining another (the spectre story, above), we had a large family living next to us. That family comprised a stout-built couple, two older close relatives and five children whose ages fell between six and eighteen, four sons and one daughter. The latter was a genuine redhead, and as for the boys, one was slightly cross-eyed, another stuttered a little and a third whose hearing was slightly impaired, with the last being another redhead.

The two sides of that duplex were mirror image of each other and overall small in size, having only two bedrooms, each. So, that house was overcrowded, especially in summer when all kids were on school vacation. During summer days, marked by being hot, tempers of the older folks flared rather quickly, particularly with the noisy small ones running here and there and sometimes getting in between the legs of the larger people. At times, the mother, who had a lot on her hands in terms of cooking for a large family and cleaning, got angry with her kids and at such instances, her yelling could have reached two miles away. During such dark times, it was not difficult for us to tell which kid was the unforgiven culprit, since she unceremoniously identified them as: *Tomato, Blind, Mute* and *Deaf, all yelled in non-musical rhyming pronunciation ending with an extended 'O'!* We had, though, some uncertainty regarding who the impertinent redhead actually was; however, knowing that, in general, boys are demonstrably more mischievous than girls, we tended to blame the male redhead, rather than his sister.

OUR HOUSE ON TRAIN-STATION ROAD

In the late spring of 1953, our family moved to a two-storey duplex, with a double-pitched roof, on Mahatta (railway station) Road, and stayed there until the middle of August 1958. The al-Ma'qal railway-train station was situated right across the road from where we lived, so we often watched the passenger train leaving in the evening at 6:30pm and (during summer) arriving from Baghdad in the morning at 7:30am. Three hours later, a freight train brought fruits from the same town; the central part of Iraq, where the capital is, encompassed large 'bistans', which are known for copious, high-quality fruits. Such produce came in improvised boxes made of palm-tree leaves. As those boxes were taken off the train, my brother and I could easily peek through openings and discern their content of snow-white apples (with a red patch), deep yellow nectarines, greenish-yellow and black 'Turkey' figs, red-seed pomegranates and others. Both the apples and smooth yellow-skinned nectarines are indigenous, the likes of which I haven't personally encountered elsewhere; but I realize that the former do exist in other places. On rare occasions, my brother and I 'sampled' the merchandise with the explicit approval of the fruit handlers.

During that period, we made trips to the capital Baghdad during every summer vacation. Such events were the most remarkable and enjoyable, and all of the family waited patiently for them! Such trips started with **boarding the steam-engine train**, which was exquisitely built in England and ran on what was called 'narrow tracks'. We always had a private train **sleeper compartment** comprising two large comfortable leather-clad sofa-chairs facing each other and separated by a folding table with a washbasin where it joined the base of a window. There were two overhead bunks, which were lowered during bedtime; bed sheets were perfectly washed and ironed *(that is when the nation was a kingdom)*. All of the surroundings in those passenger compartments were exquisitely made of shiny deeply stained wood. Each of those compartments had a fairly large window fitted with three layers of curtain, glass and shutters, all of which could be raised, allowing the wind to roam inside; I remember that my brother and I stuck our heads out several times during those magical trips, in order to watch the train as it turn to the right.

The train left al-Ma'qal, heading west for about twenty kilometers, then veered towards the northwest. As the train crossed a stretch of wasteland, at the edge of reed-marshes (Ahwar), it went over a bridge (about 200 meters-long) built across low terrain that was flooded during springtime with water brought in from the north by the Euphrates River, after connecting with those marshes. We were lucky to go over one of those floods once; the train, then slowing down to a 'crawl', was more akin to a huge worm-like motorboat; that experience was enthralling and a memorable once-in-a-lifetime treat!

The train had several stops during the trip to Baghdad; after three or four such stops, we normally had our supper, an oven-baked chicken, after which we went to bed. At 12:00am, the train stopped in the middle of the route (Samawah) for a whole hour. I never could sleep on the train, but enjoyed its sideways swaying while continuously listening to the blissful sound of: 'te-tuk, te-tuk' of the train's wheels as they crossed the gaps between rails, a sound I still very much enjoy when I hear it on some of the "film noir" movie treasures.

Early in the morning, my father ordered **tea**! It came in a **heavy white teapot**, with matching **cups** and **plates**. The tea was timed to be served when the train stopped at a certain train station (Hilla), where black-clad village women sold yoghurt and 'Qaimer'; the latter is a thick, delicious 90%-fat white mass, skimmed from boiled fatty milk coming from huge 'water buffaloes'. Those ladies also sold yoghurt, which was fatty and thick, made from the same milk. Selling and buying was done through open train windows. On one occasion, a young woman approached the window where we were standing. My father bought Qaimer for our breakfast, and then asked her if the yoghurt she carried in thick-walled, rounded and tapered brown clay pots was 'good'; she turned one of those pots upside down, without uttering a word; the thick and firm yoghurt stayed where it was! He bought a couple of those right away.

EATING FISH IN THE GARDEN

Basra has a wide river (Shatt al-Arab) forming at the confluence of two large rivers (Tigris and Euphrates, both flowing from the north) not too far away from that city. That river's mouth, where it joins the Arabian Gulf waters in the south, is not far from that city, either. In this regard, Basra has been lucky to be rich in both fresh-water and sea fish varieties, the latter entering the river in spring and migrating northwards against the natural water current; several kinds of fish were always available and abundant. For quite a long time, fish was cheap, thus constituting an affordable staple food for the poor. To my knowledge, nowadays that commodity is not as affordable in Basra as it used to be, since, with refrigeration, fish can be transported anywhere in the country, thereby suppliers are asking higher prices because their fish crop is widely distributed and more readily sellable. Anyway, those times were quite different.

Living in that train-station road house is all I want to remember about Iraq for all the time I had lived in that country; *five years of peace, tranquility and valued human life,* only to be ended abruptly by a *coup d'etat.* In addition to being truly pleasant, that house's garden had two barrel-like 'tenoors' (a cylindrical clay oven tapering at both ends, with a baseball-sized opening at its base allowing air/oxygen to get in and keep the fire going on). One of the two was wholly encased with bricks. Those 'tenoors' were heated up with burning wood until they became 'white-hot', a process taking between twenty and thirty minutes; at that stage of heating, most of the fuel would have been consumed and hardly any smoke left.

Barbequing was, and still is, the most popular method of cooking fish in Basra; so, it was convenient to have those 'tennoors'. During spring, most people in that city looked for a fish variety called **'suboor'** (also known as *hilsa shad/river shad/hilsa herring*; scientific name *Tenualosa ilisha*); that fish is uncontestably the most delicious of all fish anytime, anywhere (and here I don't say believe it or not!). I had a cousin who sometimes ate it at breakfast, lunch and supper, all three meals in one day. Our family too looked forward to those days when that specific variety of fish came on the market, which some people, including us, covered with a thick pre-prepared mix of diced onions, curry, tomatoes (or tomato paste), parsley and tamarind before barbequing. Some female 'suboor' came with two large off-white sacks of roe, which were barbequed whole too, until they turned brownish-orange in color (flavour? heavenly!).

So, after wandering in the wondrous realm of flavour, I go back to my story. When the fish was taken out of the 'tennoor', it was served, while still hot, with 'basmati' or 'umber' rice. That meal my mom served in the shade of a tall, spear-like pine-tree (rare in that area) on a rounded 'mat' made of interwoven palm leaves. That spectacle was fit to be a **Renoir painting subject**! It also reminds me of a certain **Frederick Daniel Hardy's** painting depicting a humble gathering of a family having dinner. After the meal, sweetened black tea was a must. I still cook fish that way, using what fish is available (large trout, white fish!) There is another *'yum, yum'* way of barbequing fish. Make deep cuts in the meat and fill with a mixture of garlic paste and margarine, and wipe that surface generously with vegetable oil (the latter preserves fish and garlic mixture from excessive drying). Sprinkle with salt, black pepper and quite a bit of **'fish masala"** *(the latter, a must, is available at Indian stores);* cook face down (spiced surface) on high temperature (until brown and/or crispy, about 5 minutes), then turn over and cook on low temperature (5 – 10 minutes; less for juicier). When done, let it cool for a couple of minutes, then generously sprinkle it with lime/lemon juice; use fingers to eat (avoid munching the latter). This recipe works well with salmon (Atlantic variety is best), as well.

Barbequing river fish along the Tigris River in Baghdad, certainly a treat in its own right, was done, and still is, in a different way. The fish is cut *along the length of its ulterior (backbone)* and cleaned; then it is laid flat with its skin-side down, thus exposing the meat. After having been lightly salted, two pointed palm-leaf sticks are inserted across it, and the other ends stuck into the ground, with the meat facing a small fire. The person in charge of cooking makes sure that the fish is positioned in such a way that the wind generally blows the smoke away from it; that way it gets cooked and lightly smoked. Such a meal, called 'mezgoof', is normally eaten with pitta bread, instead of rice, and pickles. Strong black Ceylon tea after such a meal is served!

KHUBIZ TENNOOR

Now and then, an older great-aunt (on my father's side) used to visit us for a day at that location. Being very good at making bread, commonly known there as 'khubiz', she baked some every time she visited us. [Bread in that part of the world is 'holy' and considered a gift from God. When one saw a piece of bread on the ground, particularly where people normally tread, he or she usually, if not all the time, would bend, pick it up and put it on anything that is higher than the ground, so that it wouldn't be stepped on!]

The bread that our great-aunt baked for us couldn't be found in the Basra markets. Its recipe(s) originated in the **northern part of Iraq; that is where my father's and mother's grandparents came from** (Ancestral Heritage, below). She used two kinds of flour, 'barley' and all-purpose white. The former type she used to make thick (1 inch), brownish, rounded and mildly 'salted' bread resembling the edge of a thick and solid pizza crust. Both breads, particularly the latter type (all-purpose white), which was sweetened and a little oily, were good to eat by themselves in the afternoon, while having a cup of tea, a true reflection of simple life and habits!

GRAPES? NO PROBLEM!

The Iraqi-Ports house, situated opposite the railway-train station in al-Ma'qal where we dwelled, had a comparatively huge garden. There were several trees, including three, which were lime bearing and producing a profusion of fruit. The limes were medium-sized and dark green on the outside but orange-yellow inside; they were sweetish-sour and delicious to eat by themselves; we used to put a hole in them and squeeze them in our mouths! There were several white-seed pomegranate shrubs and fig trees, as well, the latter producing small but sweet fruits *when available*; the sparrows beat us to them every day, as they woke up two hours before we did in the morning!

In addition to palm trees, that garden also had a large metal-wood arbor, which was approximately two yards wide, and twenty long. It held several very well established vines; so, we had a fair grape-crop, amounting to about thirty pounds during summer. One summer, around 1957, we visited our cousins (my father's youngest brother), who were living about a ten minute walk away from where we were. We all gathered in their living room, when Father, an excellent conversationalist in his own right, talked about that yard and the grapes. At that point, my uncle's wife, who was an astute woman waiting for an opportunity to prove superiority over someone whom people, in general, thought was knowledgeable and smart, asked my father with a sly smile if he would send her a few bunches as a family gift. To that, my father answered: "Certainly; send me a **basket**".

The next day, two of those cousins arrived with a **'zembeel'**, instead of a basket. Both were made of interwoven palm leaves and intended to carry food, mostly vegetables and fruits, during shopping; while baskets were a foot long and half a foot deep, 'zembeels' were a yard long, both in diameter and depth! When they arrived, those cousins told my father that their mother said hello. My father looked at the 'zembeel' and thought: "I told her a basket; all the grapes in our garden wouldn't fill this thing! What does she think, I have a vineyard!" Being quite smart, he called our gardener right away and asked him to bring several banana leaves; we had plenty of those subtropical trees in that garden. He asked him to lay them on top of each other in the 'zembeel'; when the 'zembeel' was almost full with worthless leaves, he put a few bunches of grapes in the middle and covered them with a few more leaves. He then gave that 'zembeel' to the cousins and said: "Tell your mom she is welcome!"

KAYDEE, THE POSTMAN

My brother, Owen, then about fifteen years old, was riding our green Raleigh bicycle, while having his friend sitting in front of him on that part of the frame between the saddle and the handlebar, called the *top tube* (This practice was common then, since only a few children could afford bicycles of their own).

In those times (times in Iraq that I have always resolutely relished as being golden), there were hardly any cars on the streets where we lived. However, at that particular time when my brother was cycling, it happened that there was a car parked only a short distance ahead of the bike. As he approached it, my brother, by chance, noticed Kaydee, an immigrant postman, on his bike on the other side of the road. In those days, both my brother and I were collecting international postage stamps *(kids then were interested in such hobbies, rather than indulging in consuming drugs and partying)* and, accordingly, were corresponding by letter with others residing overseas who had the same hobby and were interested in exchanging stamps. My brother hollered excitedly: **'Kaydee; do you have a letter for us?'** In response, Kaydee jovially answered: **'Yes, yes, come!'**

Just then, and while my brother had his head turned towards the postman, the bike veered to the right towards the parked car. The bike went bumping into it, with my brother's friend flying in the air like a basketball and landing hard on the trunk of the car! After a quick check, it was evident that no harm was incurred and that all body-parts of the spontaneously-initiated human-projectile were retrieved intact and correctly assembled in the same natural manner in which they were set (by God, of course, not C. Darwin, as many honorable learned scholars have in the past/present unequivocally maintained) before that unforeseen bump. My brother, still **thrilled and full of undiminished anticipation**, anyway, went to the postman and, undaunted by the recent mishap, excitedly asked: *'All right Kaydee, where is our letter!?'* Kaydee went through his postal bag quickly and, finding none, said in a broken accent: *'Maku', (meaning there isn't any! Really, after all the hassle)!*

OF READING AND WRITING

The duplex where we resided on the train-station road, had a huge covered wooden balcony, with green wooden railing, built in continuation with the second floor (ground floor there was identified as 'first' floor). That balcony extended continuously along the front of both attached houses, but was split in its middle, where a densely-patched, double-sided wooden wall had been built; that wall separated the two dwellings discretely, following the traditional norm there. That balcony faced north and thereby was *cool in summer.*

Our neighbours had four children, the oldest (Achmedi) being a boy of my age; we quickly made friends, meeting often to chat. One day in May, close to the final yearly school examinations, both of us 'happened' *(just by the purest forms of chance and honest intentions)* to have our necks extended forward on either side of that separating wall, enjoying an immeasurably 'short' reprieve from the unwelcome burden of studying for the exams by talking to each other. Actually, in such situations, any talk subject was welcome and of unparalleled interest, as though the future of the world depended on it (anything, but those darned schoolbooks)!

Of course, the following disruption was irreversibly destined to happen! After a 'significant' length of chatting that could not be qualified as 'short' by any time scale, our neighbour's door opened and Achmedi's father appeared in the ensuing opening. In a firm tone, he asked his son: "Achmedi, what are you doing?" The young man quickly answered: "Dad, I am writing". The father's voice suddenly erupted (like a volcano) in an unbridled spasm of anger: *"Are you stupid, or what?! For writing, you need a table, a chair, a notebook, a pencil and an eraser, which obviously you don't have with you. You could more logically have said 'reading', instead; for that you only needed a book!"*

MY BELOVED COUSIN AND THE TRENCH (1)

There were four of us: my brother (Owen) two male cousins (Nebeel and Na'il), residing in the town of al-Ashar, and myself having the chance of being together (around 1957); our ages then ranged between 15 and 17. Because of the travel cost involved, those cousins rarely came to visit us in our railway-station road dwelling; and when they did, we played around, sometimes roughly, as in wrestling, chasing each other and so on. We had then a fairly high brick fence in the backyard of that house separating the house and its garden from a deep trough (about three meters wide and one meter deep). That trench served as drainage of waste derived from houses in that area. Its relative level above seawater was such as to cause it to retain part of the sewage, mostly murky and filthy water with various kinds of waste; as such, it was half-full all the time.

After exhausting several kinds of physically-exacting games, we decided to jump that fence; height, no problem. All climbed it and landed safely at the trough's side. At that location there was a metal pipe, about 12 inches in diameter, connecting the two sides of the trench, presumably placed there for workers to cross that trench. All four of us had no difficulty in using it to cross to the other side of that trench, which was considerably wider. We walked along that trench and met several *'oleander'* shrubs, about 12 feet high, each bearing large (approximately10 centimeters-across) fragrant pink to deep reddish-pink/red single petal-layered flowers.

All, or most, of the stems originated from the base of those plants. At that age we weren't much concerned with those flowers but were interested in the stems, which were about one centimeter in diameter and fairly straight and long; they conveniently served as 'swords', especially when the bark was removed (except for a handle section) and dried in the sun. That day every one acquired a 'sword', after which we started to go back home to fence. I was the first to cross over that pipe, followed by my older cousin, Nebeel. By the time I was on the other side, he had reached the middle part of the pipe.

At the time, fencing there and then seemed a great idea, something out of the movies (after all, Errol Flynn's exploits were fresh on my mind), irrespective of potential disagreeable consequences. I lifted my sword, and my cousin did the same, and, after the proper en garde, we fenced resolutely, but only for a short while. He lost his balance and fell into the trench; the sewage water being only about half a meter deep, he managed to stay upright on his feet. We all rushed to help and got him out. He was soaked from the waist down, a true picture of a perfect mess. As soon as we were back in our backyard, we went straight to the water hose and took turns in hosing him down, as that was an intricate and protracted process—the mess that came down! The laughs we had!

After staying under the hot sun for about half an hour, his pants were dry again, but he still smelled awful. Soon, we were called to have lunch! We had to go then, since my father was there, and we wanted everything to look normal. We quickly agreed that, in order to achieve a semblance of normality, the 'victim' was to sit at the end of the table opposite to where my father sat, that is as far away from him as possible. Alas, that wasn't good enough! My father had a keen sense of smell, almost as good as that of a dog, which I inherited (sense, not dog); even with the deliciously aromatic dish wc had on the table then, we all could see his nostrils opening wider and taking a sizeable sample of some odour other than food. Right away, he forcefully said: **"What is that stinking smell?"** We (that is the culprit, victim and two witnesses) were thrown into inexorably bewildered silence. He soon learned what had occurred but thankfully wasn't angry with us, since the incident, in its own merit, was hilarious.

THE PILOT AND HIS COUSIN (2)

During the 1950s, Nebeel worked for the Iraqi Ports Directorate, starting at the tender age of fifteen as **'prentice'**, on his way to become a **'harbour pilot'**; he quickly learned enough of the profession to 'graduate'. His job was to guide ships from the northern tip of the Arabian Gulf, up the Shatt al-Arab River, to the city of Basra where they unloaded, and were reloaded with imported merchandize. Shortly after training, commercial activity with the outside world increased tremendously, and soon my cousin found himself in the middle of working long hours.

The pay was fantastic, based on the number of ships piloted; it beat the average national pay by many folds, and money was, as always is, an exceptional incentive to work harder. Soon, long work hours became very long, and Nebeel had to be at his job for several days at a time, with only short breaks. One day, marking Easter, all of us cousins met again, and Nebeel was full of stories regarding his job; one of those stories that I remember very well was about a long stretch of work he had to endure. My cousin then had to work three days and nights uninterruptedly, without sleep; he reached a stage where it was impossible to fight that natural urge and physical requirement, so he forced himself to walk on the ship's deck, in order to stay awake. Being the pilot, he was fully responsible, and the ship was on its way to Basra. Then suddenly he experienced the jolt of his life; he slept while walking and bumped his head against a metallic post. He was thus unceremoniously **shocked back into the grim realm of reality**, after which he stayed awake for another week!

SOME OF MY COUSIN'S STORIES (3)

During his long stay with the Iraqi Ports Directorate as 'pilot', my cousin had to work in a rough environment, and 'rough' here is only put mildly; pilots were virtually awash

with whisky that was bought cheap on ships, and my cousin
was one of those.

Once, he boarded a ship with a Greek captain.
Because of heavy traffic, there was a period of several
hours of waiting for that ship before it was given permission
to enter Shatt al-Arab River from the Gulf and navigate
towards Basra. After a while, both my cousin and the captain
got bored; the latter suggested a game of backgammon, a
game which my cousin played very well; they bet a bottle of
whisky to be provided by the loser for their joint drinking
enjoyment after the game. The captain lost, after which he
took leave to go and bring a bottle of that mystic elixir. Ten
minutes later, he came back with an expensive one, a brand
that my cousin immensely loved. The latter was so happy
(understandably so after winning and having another chance
of enjoying that marvellous drink); they emptied that bottle
in a couple of hours. When done, both rose to go to their
respective quarters; at that point, my cousin thanked the
captain for the drink. The captain answered: *"Come on,
there is no need to thank me; I stole it from your own bag
in your cabin!"*

Nebeel was, and still is, a good backgammon player.
However, he invariably lost against his brother Na'il (God
rest his soul), not because the latter played any better, but
since the latter 'talked to the dice', asking it for 'du-shesh'
or 'besh-dort' (two sixes and five-four, respectively), or 'kie-
beer' (two-one) for that matter, according to what exactly

he needed at the time. I had watched them play many times and, more often than not, the younger cousin got what he asked for. Thus, he frequently got out of difficult situations that were deemed hopeless at the time, and went all the way to win the game. That aptitude wasn't only annoying, but maddening, with Nebeel expecting an almost assured win, only to be thus frustrated. But what really made the whole situation immensely worse was that every time Na'il got what he asked for, he would laugh his head off, and that was irreversibly infuriating; if such instances had occurred once or twice, they could easily have been brushed off as 'fluke', or luck, as some may judge it, but happening so often! Those situations invariably enraged Nebeel, especially in the presence of onlookers who never failed to find such thwarting singularly hilarious. I remember one such incidence when Nebeel became so angry, he slammed the two halves of the backgammon box shut, raised it in the air and threw it ten yards away, after which he left the scene of misery while swearing profusely at this and that. *[Here is another instance when Nebeel got angry. At age fifteen, he and I weighed about 50 kilograms; I still do, while he doubled in weight and size, with a belly protruding quite a bit forward. While visiting, I had their TV on, but barely audible; all of a sudden I heard him swear under his breath, while leaning this way and that way against a sofa. When I asked him what was wrong, he blurted something about him trying for ten minutes to wear a pair of socks!]*

Pilots only worked when guiding ships; so, sometimes they had a lot of extra time on their hands. Since they had excellent salaries, some of those pilots often indulged in playing poker and, of course, drinking. Once, after successive poker games stretching over two days, my cousin was contacted by his superior at the Ports and was ordered to board a certain ship immediately and pilot it to the Gulf; he had no alternative, but to comply, even though he was both drunk and heavily sleepy. After arriving at Basra Port and boarding that ship, he sluggishly took his position in the ship's wheelhouse. A few minutes after arriving there, however, the captain of the ship, who over the years my cousin had known very well, approached him slowly and said jokingly: "Tell me, Nebeel; **how are you going to pilot the ship out with your ass facing the front of the ship!?**"

My cousin also related the following narrative. It was one of his fellow pilots' turn to guide a ship into the port. That day in mid-summer happened to be very hot. The guy was very fat, so he only wore a light shirt and short trousers without bothering about any underwear. The shuttle motorboat took him to the ship's side, after which he stepped over a ladder that was electrically driven and was to be hoisted towards the ship's deck. Halfway there, the motor driving the ladder broke down, and he was left hanging midway. He became so scared that he clung hard to the ladder, while both swayed erratically in the air. Within a minute, his shorts slipped down! Both the Iraqi hands on the motorboat below and

Italian sailors on the ship's deck had a good look and started laughing boisterously. With the little Italian he knew, and in Arabic, he started shouting and cursing angrily, upwards at the ship's Italian hands and downwards at the Iraqi sailors on the boat; he screamed in those two languages alternatively, while moving his head up and down: **"You bastards; don't look, stop staring!"**

A SIMPLE MATTER OF MISINTERPRETATION

It was around five o'clock of a hot early summer afternoon, sixty years ago, in al-Ma'qal when I visited a close friend (Newadir), who was of my own age and a schoolmate. I chose not to enter his house; instead, we moved a few yards away to avoid the blistering sun and stood chatting in the shade of a palm tree.

After a few minutes, the door of one of the houses opened and a huge woman, in her late forties, emerged. She looked around, then her gaze rested on us; soon, she came forth with a torrent of abuse, starting with swearing vehemently like: "You shameless ass-hole, street lover…" My friend and I looked at each other, spellbound to say the least; all the sin we had committed then was to be out in the heat, not indoors, and that, Sir, wasn't any of her business. *Soon, however, we were instantly relieved, as we saw a small white dog scurrying beside us and heading towards her!*

'ANEE HATTA TIETHEE IETHOOF!'

Newadir and I went into high school together; the school was in al-Ashar, which was about fifteen minutes by car from where our homes were in al-Ma'qal. We went on the same school bus, sat together in the same classroom desk (designed for two students), ate lunch together and walked around during recess.

One day, the two of us decided to eat out, instead of our usual homemade sandwiches. We went to a small cafeteria, where they had several kinds of sandwiches to choose from. I quickly chose one; Newadir, by contrast, couldn't make up his mind but finally he wavered between two items (A and B) only. He asked the server one question about item A, then another and another regarding item B. At the time, and after starting to feel somewhat uneasy because he asked so many questions relevant to the latter, I thought he was heavily inclined to choose item B; he inquired enthusiastically about ingredients and method of preparation, in detail. After long minutes of dialogue, he jubilantly said: **"OK, give me a sandwich of item A!"** (What)!

We ate our sandwiches there and left. On our way back to school, we stopped at a small food store/delicatessen shop, which was open to the road (no glass or any other barriers), as most stores there did; there was a wide variety of sweets spread on a large tray at the front. We asked the owner, who was an older guy with obviously poor eyesight, for an item, which he said he had in the back of the store. He then turned to fetch it. He took only a few steps, however, turned around sharply and angrily said: *"Are you trying to steal something? Anee hatta tiethee iethoof"*, which in Arabic meant: **"even my ass sees!"** He then continued walking towards the back. Both Newadir and I were flabbergasted (us, Christians, stealing?), but he kept his wits around him; *his hand, which was hanging by his side, moved like lightning, snatched a pack of chocolate and slid it into his pants pocket as if by magic!* He then stood there like a statue. The owner brought the item, which I paid for and we both left. As we walked a few steps, I turned to Newadir and said: "Deplorable, but he deserved it!"

IN THE HIGH SCHOOL CLASSROOM

The two of us shared the same desk, with him usually sitting next to the wall, and I taking the aisle seat. One day, the math teacher entered the class slowly, flashing a huge smile reflecting 'pure' gratification with life (he must have just had a hearty meal)! That majestic smile, however, unmasked a set of teeth protruding unevenly from both jaws.

That was all right, since everyone else has them. In that unique case, however, his teeth were heavily stained with nicotine! The teeth edges were yellow, while the rest bore irregular patches of brown and green following the gums' contours, alas not artistically; they were an absolutely comical spectacle! Under my breath, I whispered: "Look at his teeth; they are green and brown", which was just a **factual** statement describing their appearance at that time (partly correct, since I said that **sarcastically**). Right then, I felt the seat of the desk we sat on shaking. I turned towards Newadir; he was convulsing uncontrollably with subdued hysterical laughter; with his head bent low, tears came down from his eyes, dripping profusely onto his notebook. I quickly moved the upper part of my body forward, thus obstructing a direct line of sight between him and the leisurely advancing, smiling and unsuspecting gentleman; in anger, that *'gentle' man* could have chewed both of us!

Newadir was so ticklish! One day, at lunch break, we just had our sandwiches and sat in the classroom, each in a desk, this time waiting for the other students to come back from recess before the start of the afternoon session (2 hours). One thing led to another, and I remember that at one point I was sitting on top of him (lying on his back) and tickling him. He laughed out of control and started to have a problem breathing regularly. I then quickly moved away from him fearing that he might choke in laughter; I could then have unfairly been accused of '**murder**'! **Also, frankly, he was a dear friend and I was anxious to keep his company!**

THE PORT-CLUB SWIMMING POOL

While living at the train-station road house, we had access to the outdoor swimming pool of the Ports Directorate (Port Club), which Owen and I frequented during the hot mornings of summer, especially as it was close to where we lived, immaculately clean and used by only a few 'privileged' employees of the Ports and their respective families.

That swimming pool was lined with square white tiles and filled with circulating chlorinated water; I loved to watch the surface of the water shimmer in the bright mid-day sun-light! It was intriguing, however, how different the pool appeared in the late morning sun and in the late afternoon, a variance that some people are more likely to perceive than others. While in the morning it was pleasant, it appeared dull and sad in the afternoon, while in the evening it was almost scary (for me personally; I still dislike the afternoon sun, while exulting in that of the morning! The same goes for the happy spring sun, in preference over that of sad autumn; I guess I am a sun-sensitive guy and, frankly, what is our Mother-Earth without its patron, the Sun!).

The swimming-pool area was lined with fairly young palm trees, and had covered shaded areas on both sides along its whole length; a high brick wall separated its deeper end from the Ports summer-time open-air cinema. Most of the time there were only friends around. The first time I jumped in the water, under supervision, it struck me as being a wholly singular world! That recreational facility was typically tranquil and inviting, with kitchen service (sandwiches, tea and soda soft cold drinks, including two types of German 'sinalco') being available.

Swimming in that pool was so enjoyable, especially with friends around, except for one thing; I quickly developed an allergy to chlorine (pool sanitizer). The latter caused me to sneeze profusely and incessantly, thus attracting the attention of other people in the pool area. As cover up, my brother sometimes used to splash water vigorously with his feet, in order to generate enough clamour to drown the unwelcome fun-disrupting noise (my sneezing, that is). One of that pool's memories, still entrenched in my mind, is related to a particular 'incident'. One morning, when I had only little swimming experience to boast of, I saw friends coming in, heading for the 'changing room'.

Their presence, though not close at hand at that particular moment, gave me a false sense of security and fueled illogical, ill-placed and unwarranted bravado. Although alone in that swimming pool, I, then and there, **decided to conquer** it by swimming its whole length; yes, all by myself! In response to that valiant decision, I somehow had an indescribable feeling that the pool, in its turn, laughed silently at me! I was smart enough, though, to start my venture from the deeper end, just in case there was any untoward danger lurking there, since I could sense the pool's silent acrimony and possible veiled antagonistic design against me.

After bravely embarking on that risky mission, I went splash, splash and more splash, with my eyes closed (a bad habit). However, after all that Herculean effort, and expecting to be laughing at the other (shallow) end, I opened my eyes only to find myself having swam obliquely and had not even covered half of the pool's length. By then I was exhausted, and there was no immediate help around; I had the presence of mind, however, not to panic. After taking a deep breath, I let my body drop to the bottom of the pool, and with determination I pushed myself back up to the surface and, after pumping a large volume of oxygen fuel into my lungs, started with renewed vigor to splash, splash again! By the time my friends appeared, I was safely at the shallow end and triumphantly elated; Olé. Moral: **Keep trying, until you get it**, but not before intelligently and wisely evaluating the risk involved!

ON THE WOODEN BRIDGE

Al-Ma'qal's international airport was only two minutes (by car) away from the railway-train station; that route went through maiden land that wasn't only pleasant to walk through, but had an ancient ox-bow lake (cut off from the main stream thousands of years ago), which was as salty as the sea itself, some said. Just past the airport terminal, a solid military-grade British-constructed wooden bridge, built over a tributary, was then a marvelous piece of architecture. During summer, a friend of mine and I occasionally walked around there, after arriving on bicycles, in order to enjoy the view of the river and date palm tree-studded banks. Sometimes, however, we did more than that; we walked over huge horizontal cross-beam timbers (12 x 12 inch) bolted to posts of the same material, with both components forming part of the bridge's solid support structure.

Those beams extended three to four yards across the bridge into the river. At the young age of about sixteen, we found nothing abnormal, or perilous, in walking over them to their very end, although one slip and a fall in the river would have meant certain death. There we sat down with our legs dangling on either side of a beam and watched fish swim across the current underneath us. One kind of fish is still sharply imprinted on my mind; they were about one and a half foot-long, cylindrical and narrow resembling a spear. What was striking about them was that they were translucent between the back of their pointed heads and posterior half, thereby showing some details of their insides (intestine, etc.). Sitting at those beam-ends served another peculiar purpose, as well. We developed the habit of gazing incessantly and absent-mindedly at the running water flowing below us until we had the false sensation of our own movement (together with the bridge) in a direction opposite to that of the current; as such, we had the luxury of enjoying a free boat-ride experience fantasy!

BASRA'S 'GONDOLAS'

During summer in the 1950s, my father took the family on a boat ride on Shatt al-Arab waterway in al-Ashar, Basra. Those boats, resembling gondolas, were narrow with raised curved front and back ends; they were steered across the water with paddles and redirected by a long wooden pole, where it was shallow enough. The middle part of those boats, where guests sat on low seats and leaned against colorful cushions and side pillows, was fairly wide and spacious; thus, rides were both comfortable and enjoyable. The gondolier steered the boat on a pre-prescribed route, based on water currents and scenery. While the latter wasn't as colorful and captivating as those of **Canaletto's** (Venice-born **Giovanni Antonio Canal**) paintings, there were diverse warm sceneries of 'bistans', the local term for palm and other fruit farms. The tour took us to the huge "Sheikh Khaz'al's Palace", which was characterized by the presence of two large, well-sculptured yellow statues of a lion sitting on either side of a brick stair-case leading down to the river.

The gondola's tour always included a 'touch-a-ship' event, whereby on our way back, the 'gondolier' took us to the side of one of those hulking ships, which were then anchored in the river. When we landed back on shore, my father used to open his hand, full of money, and offer the latter to the 'gondolier', while asking him to take as much as he wanted. Those gondoliers never took anything more than their regular fare; **those were the fifties!**

Just recently, an illegal alien-running agent had several immigrant/refugee Syrian families, escaping the miserable war in their country, on a boat on the understanding that he took them to Italy. After charging them about $100,000, practically all they had had, he took them from Turkey on an unscheduled 'round trip' in the Mediterranean sea and brought them back to a different location on Turkish soil; after telling them that they had reached their destination in Italy, he landed them and sailed away! *Moral: Honesty and conscience are rare commodities in this world of ours; more and more people now have to look over their shoulders to see if someone is about to deprive them of something.*

DATE PALMS AND THEIR FRUIT

Dates have been cultivated for millennia, a process that can probably be evidenced as far back as 9000 years ago; however, fossils records indicate a very long history and survival for millions of years. *[Recently the Israelis were able to grow a palm plant from a 2000 year-old seed they had found decades ago during archeological excavations (www.treehugger.com › Science › Natural Sciences).]* Palm trees are now widely distributed along a belt spanning the Middle East, including northern Africa, and extending all the way across southern Iran and the northern part of the subcontinent to Malaysia and Indonesia; they also have been transplanted in Spain and Baja California/southern California.

Present-day date-palm trees may be traced to an origin around Mesopotamia, the area in what now geographically is Iraq. There are three major date groups; as I am writing this section, I am enjoying a **semi-dry variety called 'Deglet Noor'** from Algeria, and a few months ago had soft varieties called **'Berhi'** and **'Madjool'**, both from California; there is also a rather rare and famous dry variety in Iraq called **'Eshresi'** which is preferably eaten stuffed with walnuts.

Tiny white female flowers, clumped like a broom, break out of slightly bent, smooth and stout, and light greenish –to– brownish scabbard-like wooden casings, which are narrower at their base, in late spring. Those flowers are pollinated by farmers using a primitive, but efficient, climbing contraption consisting of a flexible cloth-pad, which is firmly attached to a stout rope, one end of which is in the form of a noose, while the other end is tightly attached to a two-ended wooden handle. The climber, typically bare footed, winds the latter end of the rope around the tree trunk and into the noose on the other end, while positioning the pad comfortably around the small of his back for support. The next step involves raising the rope to a position above his shoulders and getting hold of some of the several knotty bases of previously cut leaves on the other side of the trunk. Then, as he faces the tree, he pulls on the rope to tighten the noose's grip around the handle and starts to ascend one foot at a time until his shoulders are quite a way above the rope on the other side of the tree. At that point, the climber leans forward to give slack to the rope and thus be able to flip it upwards on the other side once more, after which he tightens it and climbs again. This manoeuvre is repeated until he reaches the female flowers, which by then would have broken out from their wooden scabbards through naturally opening cracks; he then would brush them with a bunch of male flowers. When done, he reverses those movements climbing down, and that could be faster than a monkey.

Female flowers taste bitter, in contrast to male flowers, which are slightly sweetish and aromatic (food for thought!). The scabbards housing male flowers, which are straight and fairly wide at base, are used to keep drinking water and hung in a cool shaded part of the garden, where the water cools off by the wind; that water becomes both fragrant and tasty.

In Basra, palm-trees have been extensively planted along both sides of wide and deep trenches cut across the Shat al-Arab riverbank deep into land, allowing river water to reach all trees; thus, farmers have been able to cover extensive expanses of fertile land that is contiguous with the river. As a result of abundant fresh water and nutritional soil, those palm trees are characterized by having huge trunks and healthy deep bluish-green leaves (about 2 meters long), and producing generous juicy-fruit crops.

Iraq in the 1950s had around **30 million** palm trees and boasted a wide range of variety, in terms of fruit size, shape, color, texture and firmness, and also sugar content; each variety, or cultivar, has its own distinctive name. Following pollination, dates start as a tiny knob and go through stages of growth and maturation, each of which is identified by a distinctive term ('hababok', 'chimry', 'khllall', 'rittub' and 'temur'). With time, dates turn from green and woody to yellow and somewhat juicy, and then fully ripen to brown, soft and sweet 'temur'; most people like them when they are at the stage of turning from yellow to brown ('rittub').

With superb quality and variety, the potential income Iraqis could have garnered from international sales of dates was huge. However, during an eight-year war with Iran in the 1980s, 'wise' Iraqi rulers decided that destroying **10 million palm-trees** covering large expanses of the war zone in the southern part of the country, was a marvelous idea. They considered such a plan a **military stroke of genius that was of historical proportions** equaling, in the annals of military history, to that of the 1967 Middle East feat! Thousands of neglected remnant palm-trees now are being reported to have been reduced to 'a sorry state of affair', because of both uncontrolled widespread diseases and an upstream influx of saline water from the Arabian Gulf, the latter being a consequence of dwindled fresh-water supplies [Turkey in the north controls, through many dams, water-resource supplies of the Euphrates]. By stark contrast, a tiny country in that region, Israel, caring for only a 'couple hundred' palm trees, in part brought in many years ago from Iraq by emigrating Jews (fleeing persecution), is now exporting dates ('Berhi', 'Medjool', 'Diglet-Noor' and six more varieties) reaching all the way to Canada! *There is even a rumor floating around* *nowadays, the authenticity of which I cannot confirm, that there are secret high-level negotiations between the two countries (Israel and Iraq) to export some of those dates to the latter, as well!*

This next account serves as an antithesis to the above issue, and thus fits in here very well. One day, a very long time ago, the 'Ameer' (ruler) of a state in Iraq was travelling with his entourage when he saw a hunched old man planting a 'baby' palm tree. He stopped right away and, in bewilderment, asked that man why at his age he would want to plant that tree, since he had a little chance of eating its fruit that could only be produced in several years to come. The old man answered: "Mawlana, they planted palm trees so that we could eat; by doing the same, I am paying my debt to the next generation".

Moral: This is obviously a disheartening joke, but one that exposes the immensity of the deliberate destruction of a vital facet of the natural assets of a country by unscrupulous power-hungry and greedy delinquents operating within an undemocratic system. Within such a system, a small number of powerful political figures do not have to answer for anything, and are immune from being accountable for misdeeds.

―――――――――

AL-MA'QAL, BASRA *(KINGDOM* OF IRAQ)

Al-Ma'qal/Maquil, or Margeel, where my three siblings and I were born, was *(in the utopian times of the 1950s, up to July 14, 1958)* a small part of the greater Basra metropolis; aside from 'Old Basra', al-Ashar is the other and much larger part of Basra, being the seat of the municipal government. The importance of the comparatively tiny al-Ma'qal then lay in being the headquarters of the Iraqi Ports Directorate, a large two-storied building topped by a blue dome in its middle; also, Basra's airport happened to be in that town, as well. The Ports had English-staff management between the two 'Great Wars' and for a few years more after the second. The British brought with them what they had been used to in Britain; there even was a laundry facility, a lone building that had large varicolored windows. In al-Ma'qal, we had English-style soda drinks (Siphone, quite resembling present-day 'Jones' soda drinks) that weren't available anywhere else in the country, and also sometimes we even had the luxury of watching movies on the Mobile Cinema's screen, a free service provided by the British Institute for the Middle East.

The Ports commendably had the **Ports Club**, comprising indoor and outdoor cinemas, a large dance hall (yes, some Iraqis, commonly Christian, had the freedom to enjoy Western dancing then), a sparkling clean swimming pool and a large courtyard hosting a tombola game every Thursday evening during summer. In short, the British brought with them a semblance of English culture and every-day normalcy to that small town. At the time (1950s), they had the **'Levy/Levies' Army** supplementing their own forces in Iraq; I remember seeing a few of those soldiers in al-Ma'qal wearing slouch-hats (upturned sharply on their left side), some with blue plumes and others with red ones, standing guard. A small part of the town was even called 'Chinekem: for **China Camp'**, named so after the Ghurkhas who were fighting with the British Army.

There were four 'principal' parallel east-west trending roads in that small town then, known as Ethel (a drought-tolerant, desert-grown evergreen with rather narrow, flexible and uniformly-shaped grayish-green needle-like leaves), Mina'a (port), Dhubbatt (officers) and Mahatta (railway station); I lived (with my parents) on both the first and last of those roads, up to age nineteen. Many houses in al-Ma'qal were built as English-style duplexes by the British between WWI and WWII, and each unit had a small garden often kept by gardeners hired by the Ports; very few houses had typically Western-style double-pitched roofs, rather than flat.

The British properly managed all aspects of life in that town, as would be expected, keeping it tidy and well maintained. Care of the town continued for several years after the British turned the management of the Directorate over to the Iraqis (in the early 1950s). I do not remember a cut in electricity then (at least up to 1958, when the country started to plunge into turmoil and darkness of anarchy after a coup d'etat in the capital, Baghdad). Nowadays, almost sixty years after the coup, severe shortages in electricity supply, not to mention a host of other aspects of life, including, among others, medical facilities, sewage and garbage collection, are universal problems plaguing cities all over that country. *Those changes of status faithfully reflect the* **stellar '*progress*'** *achieved in that country in the last sixty years. Such rarely envied 'progress' was subsequently further enhanced by incredibly abysmal* **civil mismanagement** *of that country on behalf of the occupying American forces following a militarily successful invasion in 2003 (The Occupation, below).*

THIS IS …

Between 1955 and 1958, my brother, Owen, and I found an outlet to the Christian West through foreign radio broadcasts on the radio's short waves; in addition to brief international newscasts that we could trust from the VOA and BBC, we also enjoyed American music/songs and classical music programs. During those years, there were three distinguished radio presenters, who will lovingly reside in my mind as long as I live.

The most memorable of those personalities was one whom we looked forward to hear on the Voice of America's 'Special English' program; that presenter had fifteen minutes of jazz in the morning (8:45am Basra time), which he started

with: *"Mieeeusic USA; this is Willis Conover".* My brother
and I still remember that rich, confident voice vividly; God
bless his soul. It was not just music; for some of us in Iraq
those treasured broadcasts were AMERICA personified. That
program, and its presenter were outstanding gems of the
1950s era; also, it was because of that program I became
familiar with such great African-American figures as **Duke
Ellington, Louie Armstrong** and **Ella Jane Fitzgerald**. It
is rather intriguing and disappointing that our present world
lacks prominence of African-American names like those, be
it in music or other facets of life. Also, I very well remember
another VOA newscaster: **Kay Gallant**. And from the BBC,
my brother and I still recall **Victor Silvester** and his Ballroom
Orchestra's dance music program. Those personalities and
programs invoke solemn unshakeable nostalgic memories
that are deeply embedded in our psyche; memories, which
are not destined to fade away at any time.

Back there in Basra, we used to enjoy those programs
with open windows and as loud as we wished. By stark
contrast on July 20, 1969 (post-1958 era), both of us sat
huddled in front of a small portable short-wave radio in
Baghdad listening to the Voice of America broadcasting the
historical event of the first human moon landing. Our radio's
sound was barely audible then just in case the regime's secret
police might hear (that much freedom we had then)!

THE KING'S VISIT / THE LAST
OF IRAQI 'MOHICANS'
(A salute to James Fenimore Cooper)

While still at that high school, around 1957, I heard
that the king (Faisal II) was paying the city a rare visit, and
that the tour's route came very close to our high school. So,
I decided to skip class and go; it was only a two-minute
walk. The king arrived on time, as scheduled, and there were
hundreds of people waiting to greet him as his car approached
with a small entourage. *[By comparison, it was rumored
that an Iraqi dictator, many years later, used to travel in
processions of fifty black Mercedes sedans, so no one could
tell in which one he was, just in case some conspirators
targeted him!]* When the king's car passed by on the road,
I couldn't even discern its color because of the multitude of
people swarming around it; I could, however, hear people
excitedly talking about carrying the car with its occupants!
Not too long after that visit, that king (protected by the Iraqi
Constitution as being *'unaccountable and safeguarded'*, as
his position/status was only honorary) was murdered during
a coup d'etat in Baghdad (July 14, 1958). The leader of that
operation had been singularly treated by the prime minister
at the time (Nuri al-Saeed) as **his own son** (Redefining the
Term 'Trust'! under General, below)! The same 'courageous'
army, who are now losing town after town by running away
from the enemy and leaving vast amounts of American-
supplied weaponry behind, **murdered the king's four sister
princesses**, as well! **Such is valor!**

The very next day following the coup, all or most of the higher-ranking Christian employees of the Iraqi Ports Directorate (accused by some in the new regime as being supporters of the monarchy) were fired, thereby our then-thriving Christian community in al-Ma'qal was decimated. My father, who had only one year left to retirement, was fortunate in being granted that status.

Thousands of the same Iraqis, who were exulted by the demise of the monarchy, witnessed one coup after another for the next ten years. One day (1963), as I left home heading to the American Library in Baghdad, I heard a jet fighter over my head going 'tuk-tuk, tuk-tuk;' I then, naively, thought there was something wrong with the airplane's engine and that its pilot had had a problem. I took a taxi to my destination; surprisingly, the roads were semi-deserted and, halfway there, a women stopped us and anxiously asked the driver if there was something wrong at the Ministry of Defense! I then realized what had happened and asked the driver to take me back home; that 'tuk-tuk, tuk-tuk' had nothing to do with the plane's engine, but actually was related to machine-gun fire directed at the Ministry of Defense itself, which was situated only about a kilometer away from where we lived! That jet-fighter attack actually signaled the start of the next coup by the same army, one that was directed against the ruler who five years earlier had deposed the monarchy; after several hours of a fierce battle, the coup leader was killed by his collaborator in the previous coup.

On a subsequent occasion (while visiting my cousins in Basra), I remember sitting on a bench having my shoes shined, when I saw unusual troops movements in the 'Mutasarriffia' (the Basra local government building), then heard on the radio that there had been a coup d'ctat in Baghdad and that a nation-wide curfew was imposed. It was my last day of the visit, and I was duly preparing to travel back to Baghdad on the same evening. The curfew meant that there was no travel that day; leaving my cousins was always an unhappy occasion for me; that coup was the only one I was happy to hear about!

THUS ENDED IRAQ AS A DECENTLY VIABLE COUNTRY

OF ANCESTRAL HERITAGE AND LEGACY

HERITAGE

The Ancient Lands of Mesopotamia

At this juncture, where a glimpse of recent Iraqi history has been related, I intend to delve into a brief analysis regarding my ancestry, a topic that is crucially central to my very existence. I spent much time and effort trying to find out what I could about our ancestral lineage, and have concluded that likely our ancestors were closely related to peoples dominating northwestern Iraq/northern-northeastern Syria and eastern southernmost Turkey; they were possibly, and quite likely, Arameans and/or ancient indigenous peoples inhabiting **Mesopotamia**. The latter term denotes **'between two rivers'** (map below, lower right); that region is also known as "Beth Nahrin" (and/or Beth Naharaim). The expression "Beth" 'occurs frequently as the appellation for a house, or dwelling-place, in such compounds as the words that immediately follow." *(In: M.G. Easton M.A., D.D., Illustrated Bible Dictionary, Third Edition, published by Thomas Nelson, 1897. Public Domain, copy freely).* The Aramaic word "Beth" is closely related to the Arabic 'beit', with both meaning 'house'. Similarly, the term "Nahrin" is analogous to 'nehrein', both indicating 'two rivers'; here, they refer to 'Dijleh' and 'Furat' rivers, commonly known in English as Tigris and Euphrates, respectively.

Mesopotamia, alternatively, is also depicted historically as "Aram Nahrin", or "Aram Naharaim", indicating 'Aram of two rivers'. **Aram**, by itself, refers to a region which is mentioned in the Bible and located in present-day central Syria, including where the city of Aleppo (known as 'Halab' in Arabic), one of the oldest cities in the world, now stands. Aram stretched from the Lebanon mountains eastward across the Euphrates into the Khabur River valley (formed at the confluence of those two rivers) in eastern-northeastern Syria / northwestern Mesopotamia (present-day Iraq) on the western border of Assyria *[https://en.wikipedia. org/wiki/Aram_(biblical_region)]*.

The Ancient Peoples of Mesopotamia

Mesopotamia / Aram Nahrin, covering all of Iraq and adjacent parts of Syria, was historically inhabited, over several thousands of years, even preceding the introduction of primeval writing, by several indigenous peoples:

a) Non-Semitic **Sumerians** started to be permanently settled in Mesopotamia, spreading in its southern region about seven thousand years ago (between around 5500 and 4000 years BC), and more densely thereafter *(https://en.wikipedia.org/wiki/Sumer).*

b) Semitic **Akkadians** (3rd and the 2nd millennia BC), extending briefly (during the reign of Sargon of Akkad, in the time interval between 2334 and 2279

BC) all the way into Syria *(https://en.wikipedia.org/wiki/Akkadian_Empire).*

c) East-Semitic **Assyrians** (dwelling in central to northeastern Iraq: 25th century BC to about 600 BCE *(https://en.wikipedia.org/wiki/Assyria).*

d) Semitic **Babylonians/Chaldeans** inhabiting central-southern Mesopotamia in the interval 19th century BC until the mid-6th century BC (then overpowered by the Persian Empire). Founders of Babylonia/Chaldea, in essence being Semitic Amorites, probably emerged from western Mesopotamia (modern-day Syria); those peoples, who spoke **northwestern Semitic Aramaic / Canaanite languages** (including Hebrew, Phoenician and Edomite, among several other languages and dialects from the eastern coast of the Mediterranean), were followed by Kassites at around 1500 BC. *(https://en.wikipedia.org/wiki/Babylonia).*

Aramean Migration

The ancient history of Mesopotamia is long and extensively diverse, with a treasure of astounding data now being available on Wikipedia and the internet in general. This history at present amounts to a whole 'science', something that was unimaginable during my early schooling days. However, delving into the available information leaves no doubt that Mesopotamia, an uninterrupted entity, also known as "The Fertile Crescent", has for thousands of years been occupied by peoples who were of non-Arab ethnicity, peoples who were indigenous, but also heavily augmented by natives from the northwestern part of Mesopotamia known as the "Levant" (upper part of the map, above). Large groups of Semitic Arameans from that region migrated to Babylonia in southern Mesopotamia during the tenth and eleventh centuries, BC. Additionally, other Aramean populations (mostly nomadic tribes) in Syria/Jordan and contiguous Mesopotamian areas to the west were later forcibly extradited by Assyrians to Chaldea (also in the south); Babylonia/Chaldea and Assyria previously constituted southern and east-central –to– northeastern Iraq, respectively (upper part of map).

Over hundreds of years, those migrants and displaced peoples intermixed thoroughly, during frequent wars, but also through the conduct of commerce, with indigenous Mesopotamians, especially those residing in Babylonia/ Chaldea. Human 'movements/relocations' were to a large degree facilitated, *actually made feasible*, by the presence of the Euphrates River, where both water and food were available. *Arabs, by stark contrast, were absent from Mesopotamia.* They were, instead, heavily concentrated 1300 – 2000 kilometers away to the south of Mesopotamia and completely isolated from the life-sustaining fertile lands between the Euphrates and Tigris rivers by an extensive **inaccessible desert** (lower-left figure) that in part is called the "Empty Quarter" (where no humans, or other forms of life, existed). Understandably, there was hardly any Arab population augmentation to Mesopotamia from that region during most of the ancient history outlined above.

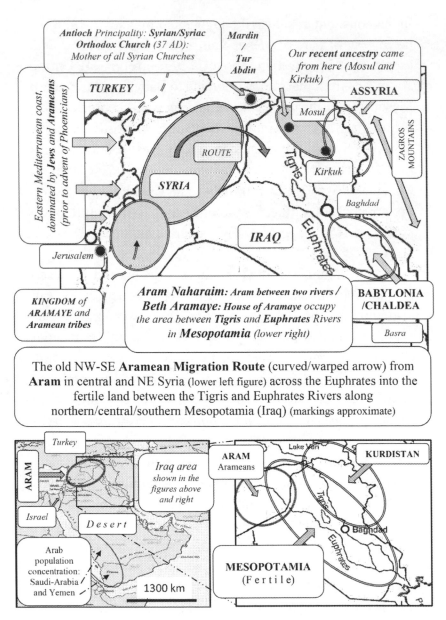

The old NW-SE **Aramean Migration Route** (curved/warped arrow) from **Aram** in central and NE Syria (lower left figure) across the Euphrates into the fertile land between the Tigris and Euphrates Rivers along northern/central/southern Mesopotamia (Iraq) (markings approximate)

Destruction of the Aramean Identity

In their long history of inhabiting Mesopotamia, Arameans (in their hundreds of thousands) never had a strong and long-lasting kingdom of their own, but were subjugated by other peoples and absorbed within other, well established, kingdoms like Babylonia and Assyria; and with time several others, as well. In Mesopotamia, they initially underwent amalgamation with the indigenous people and consequently their own western Syriac Aramaic language, or dialect, fused in those of the new locales. As time went by, they did not only lose their language, but their own *identity* was *blurred, and eventually vanished.* Most, if not all, of the resultant amalgamated Mesopotamian identity was later swiftly demolished during the advent of Arab hordes (basically under-educated horse-riding and sabre-wielding nomadic Bedouins) from the Arabian Peninsula, bringing in an intolerant culture during the seventh century. Present-day manifestations of such adverse cultural exercises abound, and have lately been repeatedly demonstrated in Syria and Iraq, where Christians and Yezidis have been forced to adopt a different religion, pay 'jizyah' and stay, abandon their homes and leave the land altogether, or be killed forthwith. The third principal populace of ancient Mesopotamia, namely the Assyrians, by contrast, living in a geographically/topographically protected northeastern part of present-day Iraq, have survived forced Arabization and kept the essence of their ancient language, culture and religion; they still are thriving in that country.

In this regard, I refer to the following citation: ["Another point of concern is that our people and spiritual leaders are forced to deny any form of discrimination or persecution. This is a well-known tactic which some countries avail themselves of in order to cover or deny any problems of minorities within their boundaries... Other spiritual leaders are oppressed to deny our rich heritage for example by identifying our people as "Arab Christians", which of course **we are not**! Neither are we Turkish Christians nor are we Kurdish Christians, but we are the **indigenous Arameans of Aram-Naharaim** who have been present for thousands of years in this part of the world.] *(Reference: Syriac Universal Alliance/ Indigenous 2004: Arameans of Iraq. [http://www. aramnahrin.org/English/Statment_indigenous_2004.ht] [COMMISSION ON HUMAN RIGHTS/Sub-Commission on the Promotion and Protection of Human Rights, Fifty-fifth session Working Group on Minorities, Ninth session 12-16 May 2003]*

Although the social identities of Arameans and Mesopotamians have been destroyed, **they are still physically there** (in Iraq). Identification of those original indigenous peoples on individual basis is difficult, if ever possible. This difficulty, however, does not negate their logical and actual presence as people, and this is the best that can be hoped for, for the time being (until more research and satisfactory evidence, if ever possible, can be gleaned). Inference is all that is available now, and that is good enough for the time being, as long as I am concerned.

Present-Day Iraqi Christians

There is a strong interrelationship between Aramean/ Mesopotamian decedents, their lands and Christianity, and this connection is well depicted in the following quotes. ["In the ancient times the cradle of the Aramean forefathers was called Aramnahrin (or: Aram-Nahrin) in Aramaic. In Hebrew it was called Aram-Naharaim which we encounter in the Old Testament. When the Old Testament was translated into Greek, the term Aram-Naharaim was translated into Mesopotamia, which many become familiarized with through reading many educational and historical texts. Roughly speaking, this area is situated in present south-eastern Turkey/northern Syria. The northern area of Aram-Naharaim was called Paddan-Aram, meaning the land of Aram where Biblical figures like Abraham and Jacob lived and walked. A section of Paddan-Aram is now called Tur Abdin in the Aramaic (Syriac) language, which means "the mountains of the servants of the Lord", due to the overwhelming presence of monasteries and churches.]

[According to the Aramean historical traditions, the area of Paddan-Aram – in particular 'Tur Abdin' – is the proto-land of the Aramean nation. From this proto- or indigenous land, in the course of time, the Arameans started to expand all over the near east. Because of overwhelming presence of Arameans in the southern part of Aram-Nahrin, in the era of early Christianity, it was called Beth-Aramaye, meaning (in Aramaic) "the house of Arameans"] *[(http://www.aramnahrin.org/English/ChristiansOfIraq.htm)* Found under: Testimonies of the scholars of the Syrian Church of Antioch on the synonymy: Aramean/Syrian]

Christianity in Iraq started quite early in history, as is implied by the following quote: "The Christians of Iraq are considered to be one of the oldest continuous Christian communities in the world. The vast majority are indigenous Eastern Aramaic-speaking ethnic Assyrians, descendants of the ancient Mesopotamians". (*https://en.wikipedia.org/wiki/Christianity_in_Iraq*). According to the same reference, Christianity was brought to Assyria and Babylonia in the first century AD. Actually, Iraq's Eastern Aramaic-speaking Assyrian communities are believed to be among the oldest Christian in the world.

Some of the Aramean descendants in Mesopotamia reverted to calling themselves **'Kildanyeen'** around the sixteenth century (my family and I belong to this group); alternatively, other Arameans started (in the 19th century) to use the term 'Assyrians' to define their ancestral *ethnic origin*. My father, whose family originated from Kirkuk (upper part of map below) could understand mass in a language related to Neo-Aramaic dialects evolving from ancient Syriac language(s) in our church (al-kaniisa al-keldaneeya). The latter is an **Eastern Syriac Church** (established in the middle-eastern part of Iraq), whereas my mother's side (from Mosul) followed the **Western Syriac Church** (originating in Syria);

both churches are branches of the Mother Catholic Church. My father in-law, in turn, came from Mardin (Tur Abdin, southeast Turkey, adjoining the Syrian border close to the Iraq/Syria/Turkey border triangle). In brief, our grandparents came from northern Iraq, not too far away from the Turkish/northeastern Syrian borders.

At this junction, it is imperative to make a short **comment on the above passages**. To those who believe that Arabic-speaking Iraqi Christians are ethnic Arabs, implicitly originating from the Arabian Peninsula (Saudi Arabia and Yemen), I present this simple question. *Have you ever compared the facial features (some with blue eyes, including my sister, cousin and aunt), skin tone (as white as bleached cotton) and demeanour (loving) of those Christians with Saudis / Yemenis? Are you kidding!* Also, logically, where did all of those Arameans and Mesopotamians go? They did not just disappear in thin-air; people, conversely, are naturally prone to **multiply** peacefully and lovingly through a well-known naturally instinctive animalistic process that is considered as being an accepted pillar of marriage. **I do firmly believe in our Aramean ancestry and heritage**.

THE KURDS

In continuation with the account above, I personally felt that I was out of place (actually a hybrid) in the southern

Iraqi environment where I lived since I could remember; *I felt that people around me were radically different.* One day, around age seven, a fellow student from the primary school where I went, a kid whom I knew to be an Assyrian Christian, asked me who my king was, to which I replied, and in a matter-of-fact way (as far as I thought was correct): "**King George the Sixth** (of England!)". He told me that his king was **Ashurbanipal**! [668 BC – c. 627 BC: the last strong Assyrian king (*https://en.wikipedia.org/wiki/Ashurbanipal*) of the Neo-Assyrian Empire (*https://en.wikipedia.org/wiki/ Neo-Assyrian_Empire*)]

Even at that young age, I tenaciously abstained from participating in singing nationalist themes, which were sung at the primary school every morning. I also found traditional Arabic dress, commonly worn then in the south by rural people, as alien and outlandish as that of a primitive tribe; I just did not belong there. On the other hand, with time I perceived a sense of ethnic kinship towards the Mosulliis (inhabitants of Mosul in the north, where my grandparents on my mother's side came from). The latter (Mosulliis) are in several ways related to Syrians to the west, especially in their local spoken dialect and kinship, which is suggestive of common lineage between those two peoples and probable migratory relocation (my family and I speak the Mosulli dialect at home). Also, with time, I developed strong empathy towards the Kurds.

The Kurds have (for millennia) lived in the mountainous terrain of northeastern Iraq, southeastern Turkey and northwestern Iran, with a sliver-like extension into northern Syria, all present within a region known as **Kurdistan**. After the culmination of World War I, negotiations between triumphant European powers (with the exception of Russia) and the defeated Ottoman Empire (present-day Turkey) concluded a treaty (Treaty of Sèvres, 1920). The latter in part *proposed* the creation of an autonomous homeland for the Kurds, a territorial entity for about twenty to twenty-five million Kurds in the areas where they were concentrated (a suggestion that was later rejected by the Turks and **allowed to elapse** by the West). *The above treaty was replaced (1923) with another (Treaty of Lausanne), which divided the Kurdish areas between those four countries where they existed, thereby denying them a unified entity of their own (talk about the fairness of the West!).* Both a Kurdish uprising in Turkey in 1925 and a burgeoning Kurdish Mahabad Republic in northwestern Iran (1946) were swiftly and firmly crushed in both countries.

Mustafa Barzani, a legendary leader of the Kurdish Democratic Party, revolted against the Iraqi government in 1961, demanding the creation of an independent Kurdistan in the northeastern part of Iraq, which had been dominantly inhabited by Kurds for thousands of years. Starting with that revolt, fighting between the Kurds and Iraqi governments continued for several years, until 1970, when a peace agreement was signed between the Iraqi government and the

Kurds of northern Iraq, granting the latter a degree of self-rule. However, during the latter stages of the Iraq – Iran war (1980 - 1988) and for several subsequent months, hundreds of thousands of Iraqi Kurds were slaughtered and uprooted from their historical homeland.

Coalition forces, led by the US, eventually (in 1991) established a no-fly zone in the northern part of Iraq (*https://en.wikipedia.org/wiki/No-fly_zone*) aimed at protecting the Kurds (Halleluiah!). At present, **Iraqi Kurds** control an autonomous region in Northern Iraq *(https://en.wikipedia.org/wiki/Iraqi_Kurdistan)*. It is populated by an estimated **5 – 7.5 million** Kurds and spreading over much/most of Kurdistan in Iraq; the estimated population of the country of Liechtenstein, by contrast, is around 37,500! It is only fair that the Kurds have their own independent country.

[This text is briefly historical, not intended to be presented as a research topic.]

THE PLIGHT OF YEZIDI WOMEN

My sister's kidnap incident (The Saving of My Sister, above) sadly reminds me of the reprehensible treatment of **thousands** of **Yezidi females** (Iraqi women and teenagers of northern Iraq in Sinjar; https://en.wikipedia.org/wiki/Persecution_of_Yazidis_by_ISIL). They were kidnapped, raped and **sold in the slave market** ('lovingly' known by some as Souq al-Nekhasa in Arabic), and for two years since have been living in the grip of fear and in shameful disgrace. Occurrences like these taking place during the enlightened modern times of the 21st century and under the very noses and impassive stares of the 'Christian' Western World and the 'United Nations!' And what are those 'institutions' doing, in all their might? Do they still have eyes and ears, or are they busy following the female slaves' prices? Shame!)

Herbert Morrison's cry of anguish: **"Oh, the humanity!"** as he and the rest of the world witnessed the *Hindenburg* disaster on Thursday May 6, 1937 (Wikipedia, *https://en.wikipedia.org/wiki/Hindenburg_disaster*) still resonates. Where are those 'supreme' powers who do not miss a chance to boast of their 'human rights record?' Here I have to refer to Shakespeare's: **'To be, or not to be'** (in *"Hamlet"*). Either they are **'be'** (guardians of that noble principle of championing human rights) by taking drastic measures to **free** those **Twenty-first century sex slaves** and liberate them from the sordid realities of life they have inexorably been forced to experience, or else stop the hypocrisy! Little wonder that these Yezidis' plight keeps reminding me of **Victor Hugo's** *"Les Misérables!"* Could any decent woman be more miserable?

As this manuscript is being finalized, it was the spirited and trustworthy Kurdish Peshmerga (together with their Yezidi-brethren volunteers, eager to free whomsoever they could rescue of those women and avenge their lost honour) who in the middle part of November, 2015, reclaimed Sinjar/Jebel Sinjar. And with what? All they had was their courageous hearts, dedication and stone-age weapons (compared with those of their adversaries). It is not only worth noting, but firmly emphasizing, the fact that those Kurdish heroes have been begging the Christian West for heavy weaponry and equipment that are on par with those of humanity's enemies, with no response.

With time, following the withdrawal of the American forces, Iraq saw the demise of humanitarian values. Many of the Iraqi Christians had to leave their country of origin due to 'incompatibility' with rapidly developing lawlessness and adverse sentiment, amounting to blatant unambiguous animosity towards the descendants of Arameans, Chaldeans and Assyrians, the **original inhabitants** of the land *(such is the Middle East, now. How much is the West really helping those who should, at least on religious grounds, be considered as brothers and sisters?)* In one instance, on 31 October 2010, a group of terrorists (totalling six) burst into the Syrian Catholic **Our Lady of Salvation church** in Karradah neighborhood in Baghdad during a Sunday-evening mass, locked the doors and took about one-hundred Christian worshippers inside hostage. After failed negotiations, following refusal of the government to release jailed militants, its forces stormed the church; at least 52 people were killed. An estimated 56 to 62 of those Christians (many of them women, being the more steady church-goers) were wounded; considering these figures, practically all worshippers were either killed or wounded. One Iraqi official later commented that the operation was ***'successfully performed'!*** Maybe he meant to say that only two or three, out of a hundred, escaped unharmed (shameless hypocrisy comes in different forms).

Many attacks on Christians in Iraq were carried out since the US-led invasion of 2003 had taken place. Also, many churches have been damaged by bombs in various parts of the country where Christians lived, especially around the city of Mosul (a bastion of Iraqi Christians for almost two thousand years, but at this moment devoid of them) in the north and the capital Baghdad, but also Basra in the south. [Christianity was present among the indigenous Assyrian people in Mosul as early as the 2nd century. It became an episcopal seat of the Nestorian faith in the 6th century: (*https://en.wikipedia.org/wiki/Mosul*)]. Over one million Christians from several ancient denominations, mainly Assyrian Nestorians, Chaldeans and Syriacs, have lived in Iraq (formerly part of Mesopotamia). [When is the 'Ostrich West' going to learn that oil and water never mix?!]

———————————

THE OCCUPATION

There is quite a controversy regarding the American 'intervention' in Iraq, with a wide segment of 'rejectionist' voices emanating from the Western world itself, strangely enough including the United States. Their objection centers on the premise that the Iraqi government at the time had no weapons of 'mass destruction', as was alleged (although the Iraqi army had in previous years used such weapons on the Kurdish population). So far as that particular accusation is concerned, intensive investigations by the occupying forces failed to find acceptable, substantially convincing evidence to show to the rest of the world, in support of such an accusation. I, personally, agree with the rejectionists as far as that 'stated reason' is concerned. However, I do not understand why those rejectionists do not, instead, and rightly so, take the massacre of 180,000 Kurds in northern Iraq as the **right reason** for ridding that country of a nightmarish regime. Weren't the destruction of thousands of Kurdish settlements, mass deportations, firing squads and chemical warfare *(https:// en.wikipedia.org/wiki/Al-Anfal_Campaign)* during the al-Anfal Campaign (1986 - 89) important enough?!

While the job of destroying the incumbent Baghdad regime was efficiently handled by the Americans, in military terms, their governance of that country, starting soon after the 'fall' of Baghdad, was abysmal, as evidenced by the broad daylight plunder of the Iraqi museum by Iraqi thugs in the presence of American soldiers. **The civil governance of that country should have been left, in its entirety, to the British from day one.** The latter had performed that undertaking successfully and wisely for many years before, had the required experience and understood the mentality of Iraqis and their social structure well. They were even instrumental in advancing political and economic reforms before. The British were best suited for that task, and if such a course had been pursued at the time, Iraq would have been in a much different state than it is now; also, a geopolitical disaster and terrible human tragedy in several countries in the Middle East region could have been avoided.

PART TWO: HOME-COUNTRY STORIES/ ADULTHOOD (1958 - 1964)

REPTILIAN

A couple of times, I thought of changing the heading, above, but chose not to, since somehow I found some familiar ring to it. Then, all of a sudden, the word **'Pygmalion', George Bernard Shaw's play**, came to my mind, not that there is any connection in reality, context or literary significance between the latter and my present story! I only kept it for the sake of apparent rhyming.

The year was 1958, that is when I passed the Iraq Governmental *Baccalaureate* examination at the end of May. I was one of six who did so, out of twenty-six in our class. At the time, even with only an average of 70%, this result amounted to a feat. Those students who failed one or two subjects were, as was usual, given a chance to retake exams in relevant subjects in the coming September; those failing in more subjects had to repeat the year, that is all subjects. The results came out in June of that year and, with a mediocre average like mine, I was not accepted in either of the coveted College of Medicine, or that of Engineering. A miserable coup d'etat that summer brought with it new ruling faces to power. The top-authorities behind that coup wanted to have the people's support in any way possible, and one of their first decisions, coming in the form of a decree, was related to that *baccalaureate* exam. That decree mandated that all of those high school students who did not succeed in May/June were allowed to repeat exams of all relevant failed subjects in September, irrespective of how many they had failed.

For about two weeks before the September examination, *all exam questions related to all subjects were leaked* and thereby made available to every student through a coup-related miracle and assuredly not one from Heaven. All repeating students successfully finished the *baccalaureate*, but this time with some grades amounting close to 100%. Many of those who failed the legal exam at the end of May were now eligible to be accepted by the best colleges in the country, most importantly those two identified above! That year (1958) was at the time known as the Year of the 'Zehif', or 'Crawl,' that is *crawling* out of high school. As such, these graduates were called crawlers/zewahif, the latter being a term that signified **'reptiles'**. By comparison, my exam results netted me **76% in the English language** and puny **53% in the Arabic language**; right after the coup, and because of that 'imbalanced' result, I had disturbing thoughts of people accusing me of being a foreign agent!

About a month or two after that memorable scholarly event (October/November, 1958), friends of our family gave us a visit. As it happened, they had a son of about my age. After several minutes of silence, that guy, who was a little shy, turned towards me and, in a voice that was more akin to that of a girl, asked me slowly: "Are you one of those reptiles?" I quickly answered: "**Oh, no**! I am a *Homo sapiens!*" I still remember his: "Huuuuh?"

[In retrospect, I was fortunate that I couldn't enter either one of those two faculties, since that would certainly have changed my life, and very likely I would have been stuck in Iraq, God forbid. Now, all that I have in common with that country, after the reprehensible murder of the king and his sisters, is my ancestry (all the way back to three or four thousand years ago).]

OUR TRIP TO BASRA

One day in summer, my sister, her husband Nebeel and his younger brother, Na'il, (two of the heroic personalities presented above under 'my beloved cousin and the trench') visited us in Baghdad, driving all the way from Basra. The husband *(first cousin marriages there were, and still are, not only accepted, but socially favored and sometimes mandated)*, had then a used black car (an English Vauxhall). It worked fine, but a couple of its tires were worn out, and there was no spare tire; my cousin couldn't afford to have them changed at the time.

After staying with us several days, it was time for them to go back to Basra; since I had strong brotherly friendship with both cousins, I asked my father for permission to go with them. *[I was then twenty-one years old; children in Iraq had profound reverence for their parents. In that regard, I still remember visiting a friend (Tuareg) at his home one summer afternoon; I was promptly introduced into their reception room. My friend's father, a dignified ex-police chief, came in and said that his son was taking a shower and that he would be with me shortly. Then, for a while, I had the honor of the senior's company. Within a few minutes, Tuareg entered the room and headed directly towards his father, who was sitting on a couch, bent and kissed his hand! Tuareg was then twenty-eight.]*

Back to the story. Considering the dire condition of the car's tires, we had but one alternative and that was to drive to Basra (a 300 mile-trip) during the night, since the desert-like terrain we had to cross was relatively cool then. The vehicle, notwithstanding its condition, was overloaded and thereby comparatively more difficult to navigate than the average car. Based on an arrangement between the two brothers, the older (Nebeel) started driving at around eight o'clock in the evening, heading south. He drove for three hours, after which he retired to the back seat to sleep, and his younger brother took over; I sat next to the latter.

We drove along the desert road connecting the two cities; the night was moonless and totally dark, except for the car's light. The darkness, in a way, was fortunate, since it gave me a chance of a lifetime to marvel at the unmatched **magnificence of the sky**, which was fully studded with shimmering billions of stars; it was a sight to behold, an untold wealth of diamonds created to adorn the Oriental Heart! I spent hours marvelling at the universe and examining details of separate segments of the sky, as though navigating through them!

My younger cousin, Na'il, as tough as they come, drove carefully at a constant moderate speed, just in case we had a flat tire; tires came with an inner tube then and, in the case of puncture, released the pressurized air in an instant, rendering the car uncontrollable. We chatted for a long while about many subjects, including one that has always stayed on my mind; my cousin talked about having a problem with the carburetor of the car once and how he was able to fix it in time. Then, as time passed by, we ran out of topics and our chat became intermittent, then stopped altogether. The couple were asleep in the backseat, so the car became drearily quiet. I almost never was able to sleep in a moving vehicle, especially when sitting upright, even though I was very tired, so I kept awake. My cousin wasn't any less tired than I was, especially driving the car. Then around four o'clock in the morning, the time when people usually become sleepiest, he told me that story about the carburetor again, to which I responded with a short reply; I already had heard it. At that stage, my younger cousin's weariness and absolute concentration on driving eventually caused him to acquire a 'mental block' depriving him from reaching tales stored in other corners of his memory's vault, and he certainly could find many more stories to tell. That story was repeated every ten minutes, thereafter, as he was trying his best to stay awake.

One tale that I would like to relate is about his ferocious appetite. At an age of sixteen or seventeen, he sometimes went to a shish-kebab restaurant in al-Ashar accompanied by a friend of the same age. They were both tall, strong and healthy, and could easily devour sixteen-pound steaks each, or finish a whole lamb (cooked as 'quozi' that is) between them. Instead of ordering ten or twenty lamb shish-kebabs, each, at that restaurant, however, they could afford only one. That restaurant normally served dishes of olive oil mixed with balsamic vinegar, the Italian way, as clients waited for their barbequed kebab to arrive. So, in the meantime, each of them would order five or six loaves of bread, which they systematically dipped in that blend and ate it. The meal would then be culminated with half a loaf-sandwich, in which they stuffed the kebab. Every time they went through that simply-configured ritual, they would leave the restaurant patting their tummies and saying: "That was good, wasn't it!" In order to give an idea of the size of those loaves, one third of a loaf was enough for my breakfast, and that took me ten minutes to chew. Likewise, *or in this case un-likewise*, my younger cousin, who didn't like breakfast but ate it only because his mother pushed him to do so, ate only one loaf (poor guy) in two munches, or essentially by mouth stuffing and cramming!

At last, we arrived safe and sound at their home in Basra, and that was just before sunrise. Inside, we had a little rest, then the cousins' mother prepared a hearty breakfast. Just before 9:00 am, the younger cousin told his brother that he was taking the car to a car shop to have it checked and left ten minutes later; the sun was already four hours up in the sky and heating the air quite rapidly. He drove only a few yards, then we heard a huge bang, like a bomb; one of the tires had blown up. **How lucky we were! The tire decided to hold out until the morning;** thank you so much tire for being so considerate!

ON MICROSCOPES

After spending one year (1958 - 1959) studying the English language at Baghdad's College of Arts, I entered the Geology Department at the College of Sciences. In the first year, I quickly found a friend, Jawadet, who was quiet, polite and docile; we matched well, even in size, and were always together. The second year's curriculum included, among others, the subject of 'mineralogy'. We had then a professor from the sub-continent, who never combed his hair and always said politely: "Good morning, peleese", while scratching his head. Being, in a way, a true scientist, he made a good job of teaching us a fascinating subject. As a consequence, I acquired enough solid scientific ground and personal affection for that subject to make a life-long career of it.

During one of the earlier lectures on this subject, Jawadet and I sat in the middle of the front row; that professor was intensely involved in describing the microscope's parts and how they worked. Because of his heavy accent, both Jawadet and I had a problem understanding a particular part of what he was saying about light. At the base of the petrographic microscopes we had, there was a light source; light passed through a 'polarizer' before entering a rock thin-section slide. So far, so good; that sequence was understandable. However, there was difficulty understanding what happened to it when it passed through the polarizer. Following an illustrative drawing on the blackboard, with his back turned towards us, the professor said that as it did so, the light was propagated, becoming **'vavy-like',** and kept repeating those words for emphasis; that particular characteristic embodied our comprehension difficulty.

Jawadet, imagining I was the Iraqi Shakespeare of the English language, certainly without any due credible basis (except for spending a year studying the language), turned and quietly asked me what the meaning of 'vavy' was. I hadn't then the slightest idea; no clue at all. As he repeatedly and enthusiastically pronounced that word for emphasis, its scientific importance gradually became more and more weighty. We definitely had to find out what it meant; the sooner, the better. Then, all of a sudden, it hit me; he was saying **wavy-like**, that is having wave-like properties. I nudged Jawadet and excitedly told him so, and we both burst laughing, quietly, that is. The professor heard that commotion and turned towards its source; he was mild mannered, but at that moment appeared upset and, I thought, he was going to give us a piece of his mind. As he turned, some movement at the open classroom door caught his attention; that movement happened to be associated with the timely passage of the most beautiful female-student on campus. As he faced us, he asked: **"Vy are you laughing?"** The passage of the beautiful one instantly gave me what I thought was an escape route; I pointed at the open door and said nothing. At that, he mumbled something like: "hum, hum", and, while vigorously scratching his head, turned back to the blackboard; the beautiful one **saved the day**!

Both of us passed the first year; I passed the second, but he failed (it was almost impossible for him to study, since he and his family had only one room to live in). Early in my third year, I developed an anxiety problem (pertaining to the prevailing political oppression and fear) and decided to skip the year; it wasn't serious, by any means, but at the time I decided to have a break and visit my cousins in Basra. Next year, Jawadet and I had the chance to continue our friendship. As to his personality, the following unforgettable story is well worth telling. During that year, both of us were once sitting together in the backseat of a Land Rover during a field-trip. It was a hot day in May and Jawadet had been fasting the whole day. At sunset, he had a sip of water and then opened a small blue can of Australian Kraft cheese. After stuffing a piece of bread with a generous portion of that delicious cheese, **he handed it to me before he put anything in his mouth!** On the fourth year, I passed, while he failed again. I met him only a few times thereafter.

THE ALLEGED DEMISE OF MARTYR SHEKHNOOB!

Following the coup, Iraq in the early 1960s became under military dictatorship. *[A few years earlier, that country (then peaceful) had the misfortune of witnessing a bloody military coup-de-tat against a stable and relatively West-leaning regime, with most of the national oil revenue going towards developmental projects and also paying salaries to a majority of the working force. These days, the oil income, amounting to several tens of billion dollars, a year, is being **methodically and efficiently plundered** through illicit, or semi-open, wide-spread corruption: plunder, commissions, bribes, etc.]* Anyway, since the early days of the coup, that military take-over received the full support of a small opportunistic, but well organized, Communist Party. In the ensuing political vacuum, the party grew fairly quickly, prompting its leadership to continuously requesting a prominent position within the government, in terms of ministerial portfolios. That request was invariably met with refusal from an unmoved 'triumphant' coup leader, who kept everything under his firm personal control.

With time, friendly requests turned into angry demands, and eventually led to rather small demonstrations in different parts of the capital, Baghdad. As those tactics failed to bear fruit, the Party decided to raise the ante. One day, it organized a demonstration and headed towards the Ministry of Defense, where the coup leader had been dwelling protected by his troop. The demonstrators were carrying a coffin over their heads. They claimed that government forces had killed a fellow party member, called "Shekhnoob" (a weirdly outlandish name) whose body they had in the coffin.

As the demonstration halted in front of the Ministry of Defense, it became rather boisterous and angry. An order was then issued to the Ministry's guards to shoot over the heads of the demonstrators. *As Kalashnikov-gun fire started, the demonstrators **unceremoniously dropped the coffin** on the road and started to run as fast as they could; one would think that they had just filled up with high-octane gas-fuel. As soon as the coffin hit the ground hard, its top came off, and to the utter amazement of curious bystanders, the body of the presumably dead Shekhnoob jumped out of it and **ran faster than anyone else; this one had 'turbo' force behind him, and he shot forward like a 'Tasmanian Devil'!***

FOR GOD'S SAKE, I AM ONLY A THIEF!

Around that time another event took place in Baghdad. That same dictator was a 'victim' of an assassination plot, himself; he was actually shot in the arm while his car was being driven in the town's central street (al-Rasheed Street) and spent several days at the military hospital. Members of a small, then unpopular, Ba'athist Party took credit for that attack, and ironically one of the attackers later became *president* of the country (such was/is life in some places).

Soon after that incident, there was this guy who attempted to rob one of the stores in the town's commercial centre. His action, however, was soon detected by the store's owner, who promptly chased him out of the store. As soon as he got on the street, the owner began to shout: "A Ba'athist, here is a Ba'athist, get him!" Several shoppers in the area heard that cry and saw the store's owner running after the culprit; they quickly joined that holy chase, all excitedly shouting: "A Ba'athist; a Ba'athist, catch him!"

The poor would-be robber tried to take refuge in one of the office-buildings along that street; he found an open door, entered the building and ran up a staircase but, alas, he only found locked doors on both sides of a corridor. Soon, he realized that the chasers were right behind him; sensing that he was about to be apprehended and likely killed, he suddenly turned around and screamed: **"In God's name, leave me alone; I am a thief, not a Ba'athist".**

THE ARTISTS

During the second year of my geology education, our class was invited to have a session at the college's art section (the faculty's artist studio), in order to learn how to draw facsimiles of rocks. That section was rather small in room size, but huge in the presence of a prominent Iraqi artist, **Hafidh al-Durubi**. The session, taking only a couple of hours, left its mark on the rest of my life; at that artist's studio, I met the artist himself and acquired valuable new friends. That circle of friends, in addition to the artist himself, forming a group with familial bond, met there on a regular basis.

The artist, without preaching us on art, had, by his mere presence, an enduring positive influence on developing my love for art, jump-starting me towards a life-long course of deep interest in it. He also was a fluent talker; one of his stories that I cannot forget went like this: He studied art in Paris and, having a likable personality, made several friends. There was, in particular, a French gentleman who liked al-Durubi, always welcoming him when they met as 'monsieur Hafian'. Hafidh didn't like that word, since in Arabic it meant **'barefoot'**; so, every time he heard that name, he had to correct it for him. With time, al-Durubi finished his studies and went back home to Iraq.

A few years later, al-Durubi had occasion to visit Paris and, lo and behold, who should he meet there but that same French friend, who, with outstretched arms goes: **"Oh, monsieur Hafian!"** (Again?)! This story reminds me of British actor **Martin Alan "Marty" Feldman**, who, in one of his appearances is cast as a priest taking photographs in a busy shopping area. A gentleman leaving a department store is photographed, after which he amiably thanks the priest. For the next five to ten minutes that gentleman, who was photogenic, is devotedly chased by the priest over walkways, in shops and even on buses; it was hilarious!

There (at the artist's studio), I also met a young artist, someone who had lost his left eyesight due to an accident. In early 1958, he was crossing a road when a governmental car hit him; the left side of his face took the brunt of the fall. There was little hope for him in Baghdad, and the government (still within the monarchical system) started procedures to send him to France, in order to have a corrective eye surgery, as was required; a few months later, that government was toppled and his prospective operation went down the drain. He often painted beautiful women, who were invariably one-eyed! That artist loved classical music and was one of the most sensitive people I ever knew, next to myself, of course.

Around the mid-1980s, I found extra time that I spent on paintings, using oil on canvas; it was a delightful and rewarding experience. With time I have had several preferences in the realm of art; aside from **Michelangelo**, who, with his magnificent sculptures and paintings, was/is an establishment by himself, I had several artist favorites; three of those include: 'realist' **Diego Velázquez** and 'impressionists' **Claude Monet** and **John Singer Sargent**.

The Captain, by the Author (oil on canvas; 30x39 inches)

THE IRAQI 'JACKAL'
(Not Related to the Other One Caught in Europe)!

In the same town (Baghdad), a fledgling Ba'athist Party started to organize and prepare for covert political takeover; the secret police, however, were on top of what was happening and watched the Ba'athist Party activists closely. Garanfer, a zealous Ba'athist, was one such member; he was a crafty young university student who had eyes that were closely set together, thus somehow reminding one of a jackal in the wilderness [not Carlos the Jackal, a Venezuelan outlaw who is currently serving a life sentence in France for the 1975 murder of three French people].

One day, a secret policeman (plain-clothes man), who was assigned to monitor political activities in the College of Sciences, where Garanfer was a student, knew that he was in the building and waited for him in ambush behind a wall outside the premises of the college, where the frontal gate of that faculty was! *[All security forces were then banned by the government to enter any schools or colleges.]* Close to mid-day, Garanfer, unaware of impending state-sponsored traps, innocently saunters towards the gate on his way home. As soon as he steps out of the college premises, the secret policeman grabs him firmly by the arm and orders him to walk towards a waiting taxi (most taxi drivers, then, were paid by the Secret Police). Garanfer could do nothing but comply obediently.

The secret policeman, an abnormally mild guy (almost pleasant in his own way, sometimes), *who was in a fairly relaxed mood that day*, opens the door for him and asks him to get in. Garanfer politely says: "After you, Sir; you are older!" The secret policeman gives him a mild nudge accompanied by a short laugh and says: "You think so, and give you a chance to turn around and run back to the college; **get in right now**". Garanfer 'innocently' says: "**Yes, Sir, but**

Wallahi (in God's name) **that thought never ever entered my mind, cross my heart**", gets in first, as ordered, and moves towards the other end of the seat. The secret policeman gets in and turns right to close the door on his side. As soon as he turns his head away from Garanfer, and within a split-second, the latter swiftly opens the other door and runs away, never to be caught again!

JURASSIC CABBAGES

During the years I spent at the College of Sciences, I had once reason to go to the head offices of the University of Baghdad which supervised all colleges in that city. Those offices occupied a high-rise building in the rural parts of the southernmost extension of Baghdad. It was built within a sharp meander of the Tigris River, an exceptionally fertile area, which has over hundreds and thousands of years been enriched with silt and clay. Being a city dweller all my life, I wasn't prepared for what I saw next. As the bus I was taking entered that fertile area, we entered a farm where cabbages had been planted; those cabbages were at a fully grown stage and close to being cultivated.

The cabbage heads, on average between twenty and twenty-four inches in diameter each, were globular, with some being somewhat flattened at top. Those heads were characterized by a dark, smooth bluish-green surface; their leaves were tightly layered and somewhat flattish, rather than crinkled. The outer leaves of each plant, averaging thirty inches across, rested flat on the ground; those older leaves were green, some with brown edges. Individual plants spanned around fifty inches across and had been planted with enough space to separate them. It was a spectacle to behold and never be forgotten.

THE LIGHTED ROTHMANS CIGARETTE

As outlined above, I had acquired, through the artist's studio, the close friendship of a few students at that faculty who were always by my side when I needed them. One such a friend, Muneer, was a husky and strong guy, a specimen befitting a **Homer**'s hero, a God-given attribute that sometimes gave him cause to show himself as a mirror reflection of masculine conceit, not to lessen any of his gentlemanly traits.

That gentleman sometimes bullied another student, a well-mannered, wiry and very tall guy. Whenever they crossed paths, the former would go to the latter directly and imperially say: **"Meseer, give me a cigarette"**. The latter always accommodated the bully and, with an obliging smile, he would give him one of his favourite Rothmans cigarettes, an imported English brand that was both expensive and seldom found there; after being lighted, he would inhale smoke deeply and turns to leave without saying another word (but where is the thank you, Sir)! It must be said here that the bully friend was in many ways a gentleman, irrespective of what he once said about my beard, which was: "One needs a bicycle to move from one hair to another on Haney's face (the 'Bugger!')". I kept quiet, since he was too strong for me to argue with.

Finally, Meseer got fed up. He inserted a popping-bang cap mechanism in one of his Rothmans cigarettes and waited for the next order. One day, the bully sauntered into the college-students hall/cafeteria, and as his wont, asked Meseer for a cigarette; the latter opened a pack, got one out and gave it to him. After dutifully lighting it for him, the bully left.

What happened later, I learned from Meseer, himself. Within a few minutes, the bully rushed back to the hall and confronted him. In a raised, but humorous, voice, he said: "What have you done?" In an innocent voice, Meseer said: "Why, what did I do?"

The bully replied: "After I had the cigarette, I went directly to the bathroom. There, I found my Physics professor starting to urinate. So, I said hello and faced a urinal beside him; and with my left hand holding the cigarette and hanging beside me close to him, I started to urinate. *All of sudden, in the tomb-like quiet of the bathroom, there was a bang. The professor jumped backwards a couple of steps and dreadfully looked at his groin. Then, he turned towards me and said: 'My God; I thought it exploded!'"*

ADDENDUM TO THE LIGHTED ROTHMANS CIGARETTE

During those college days, Muneer, his brother and father were visited by the latter's brother. All four gentlemen were huge in size [equalling four Porthos(es)] and loved their food. So, every time they had such a visit, 'quozi' (whole lamb baked slowly for 18 hours) was served, together with 'umber' rice topped by roasted almonds and raisins; that was, and likely still is, the 'ultimate' feast in Iraq. Such dinners lasted a whole hour; as a consequence all of the rice would be consumed and the 'quozi' devoured (except for the bones, that is). [The best part of that 'quozi' is actually the thick lump of fat ('lie'ya') surrounding the tail (it compares well in flavour with the fatty parts of bacon, but is quite soft and melts in the mouth, an unrivalled 'yum' 'yum')]. To make a long story short, the elders then smoked, and all four drank glassfuls of cold buttermilk, followed by several 'istikans' (small glasses shaped in an inverse way to that of a barrel) of sweetened black tea. And as a consequence to those feasts, those four 'grub warriors' were rendered immobile for at least another hour.

Later in life, around the end of the 1990s, I met someone by pure chance while working in Benghazi (Libya). He was my laboratory teacher when I was in the fourth-year at the College of Sciences. That acquaintance told me that Muneer, who was a Ba'athist (but during early adulthood had, for some time, openly supported the rival Syrian branch of that party, not the Iraqi), rose in prominence (after changing sides) on the government job ladder, becoming a manager of a governmental institute. Then, that acquaintance said all of a sudden Muneer disappeared, leaving no trace, whatsoever. No one knew where he was or what had transpired, or even dared to ask about him; such happenings weren't of any abnormal proportions there at that time. Being a person who couldn't curb his tongue, he might have said something untoward against the country's leader, and was 'duly dealt with' (the way they usually put it).

PERTAINING TO EVOLUTION

During those college years, I was fortunate to have a few, but excellent, friends; our friendship continued in earnest, until I left the country. On one exceptionally hot summer afternoon, all of us were sitting and chatting at Muneer's home. Everyone had then removed their shoes and socks to cool off.

Then, I noticed one of them staring at my feet; he then burst laughing and said: "Look at Haney's feet; his toes are rounded!" I didn't get upset, but had this quick reply for him: "In our biology classes, we were taught the Theory of Evolution; **Charles Darwin** says that humans came from apes. I am not arguing for it, or against it, but based on that theory, and by looking at your feet and mine, and comparing them with those of monkeys, I can easily see interesting differences. The ends of your toes are set in a straight line, exactly like that of monkeys, while mine, having lost the straight line arrangement, are rounded. From this analogy, I conclude that I am ahead of you in terms of evolution, which means that you are closer to monkeys than I am!" He gave no reply, but was content to show a faded smile. [Serves him right; making fun of my feet! Here, I must offer apologies to all who have straight toes! Nothing personal is intended; cross my heart.]

Many years later, I was visiting friends, an ideal oriental family of husband, wife and a daughter. As I was leaving at the door, there was some mention of feet, which reminded me of the story, above; so, I related it to them and showed them my foot. When I ended my story, the daughter, who was then a university student, smiled and said: "**What; are you calling me a monkey**?" We all laughed. That event took place **before** she graduated as lawyer; not that she would sue me, but just in case something unpleasant happens.

PART TWO: HOME-COUNTRY STORIES/ADULTHOOD

(1964 - 1968)

ZAVEN

Shortly after graduation, I left Baghdad in order to have an extended visit with my cousins Nebeel and Na'il in Basra, in celebration of my finishing the university studies and obtaining a BSc degree in geology; that was in the summer of 1965. I enjoyed my stay there only for a few weeks before receiving a telegram from my brother in Baghdad advising me that the College of Engineering there needed a geologist to work in the laboratory and that he had consequently submitted my resume; the faculty had asked me to have an interview. I travelled back the same day, taking the train.

At the interview, there was another guy, a young Iraqi-Armenian man with thick black eyebrows and heavy moustache, as well, but applying for another job. We were both hired on the spot and thereafter became the best of friends and brothers. Early during our friendship, this new friend (Zaven) told me that his father had died when he was thirteen (just like my own father some fifty years earlier), and he had to work at a place which was very damp, causing him to develop rheumatism in the heart. I didn't then place much significance to the latter part of his story, since he appeared as strong as steel and showed a personality befitting that metal. We shared the same office and were together all the time during the work day; also, we often met in the afternoons, mostly going to the cinema, then the most enjoyable pastime there. Westerns (cowboy movies) were a favorite, although we also liked those of the suspense genre. Movies then were dominantly American, in part black-and-whites from the fifties and early sixties; neither of those incessant swears, base animalistic sex, nor excessive senseless and barbaric violence (as what is dominating much of Hollywood's productions in these enlightened 21st century times) were encountered then.

That friend was a **jewel among gentlemen**; and they say that the **'good' go first**! Ten years after we met, he died while taking a swim in the Tigris River. He then had his seven year-old nephew with him. After swimming for a while, he had a cigarette on the beach, after which he told his nephew that he was having one 'last' dip before going back home. Soon after getting into the water, he had a heart attack; his anxious nephew started to approach him to help, but he yelled at him asking him to stay on the beach. Even when he was dying, he protected that kid! People came quickly to help, but could do nothing, since he had experienced a massive heart attack. I often remember him and, sometimes, when I do need his valuable friendship, I wish he was still around to the degree that I despondently say to myself: **"He had no right to die!"**

Zaven died on an afternoon in July, 1975, ten years after we first met, almost to the day; without knowing what had transpired I called the secretary of the department he was working at and asked to talk to him. In answer to my request, the secretary, who knew both of us for several years had this to say, with the least indication of either sensibility, sensitivity or emotion: "He died". Failing to absorb what she had said, I incredulously asked what she had meant, only to get exactly the same answer. A day later, his sister managed to find where I lived in order to tell me what had happened. I told her then that I had painted a portrait of him that was still at the University of Engineering, but that I could never enter his office again, in order to retrieve it; I left that to her. The last time both of us were in the same room was at a church, and he was resting in a coffin; now, he must be somewhere in Heaven waiting for me, if I am ever allowed in there.

THE VAN RIDE

I was around twenty-seven (mid 1960s), when I visited my cousins again in Basra. Na'il had just started a job delivering store items for a supplier; he did so using a red van that the supplier provided him with. One day he asked me and two more other cousins to accompany him as he delivered a few boxes to a town (Zubair) twenty minutes from where we were in al-Ashar. That van had no chairs, except two, one for the driver and another for a passenger. There were no side windows, except next to those two chairs; it didn't even have roof lining, or any such a product on the sides, either. Everything about that van was as rudimentary as could be; I don't even remember if it had more than one gauge on its dashboard. Except for those chairs, the van was just a 'hollow' shell of metal; as such, it was as light as a 'feather', that is among vehicles of its 'genus'.

We drove to that village, and everyone was happy to be together on a car trip and out of town! The last mile, or so, was difficult to drive, since it was an old narrow stretch full of pot-holes (the same as mentioned above: In the high school classroom). My cousin drove well, and we arrived there safe and sound. The merchandise was duly delivered, after which we prepared to go back to al-Ashar. At that point in time, our other cousin asked Na'il if he could drive; he was a learner, but there were only a few cars on the road. Na'il, influenced by deep-rooted social customs, reluctantly agreed since the van wasn't his own.

The inexperienced driver took control of the van and started driving; he was elated! We soon reached that same bad road stretch, and at that juncture he was speeding. As we reached the pot-holes, the vehicle started to jump uncontrollably this way and that way like a zig-zagging bug and overturned, landing on its passenger side. During that time, all four of us were tumbling within the enclosure of the van. Soon after it stopped, we realized that everyone was intact and starting to move freely, except for my youngest cousin who was immobile, lying sideways and showing one leg only! We were stunned, but the guy wasn't crying and displayed no stressful signs; he just looked at us. I wondered then if he was experiencing 'delayed' reaction, but couldn't see any blood.

His other leg was actually outside and under the van; as the van jumped and tumbled, the slide door had apparently opened, allowing free access to the outside! Luckily, that leg had found enough space within the irregularly surfaced road to lodge into comfortably and find peace and safety. He wasn't physically hurt, and within a few minutes several drivers of other cars passing by stopped, quickly lifted the van and got him out, all in one piece exactly as he was before the accident; our youngest cousin's demeanor didn't reflect any detriment to his psyche, either. The van suffered mild damage, but that was enough for the owner to fire my driver-cousin.

In few years my high-school friend Newadir (In the High School Classroom) found an engineering job in Kuwait, bordering Iraq from the south. Elated with the job and the good salary, he bought a new car, a Russian Moskvitch, of all car varieties available then and there! It did not even have seat belts! On his first trip back to his parent's home in Basra, he had to drive through the same pot hole-marred stretch of that road; he lost control and his car tumbled several times.

WHY NOT TO LIGHT A CIGARETTE

There is another story worth telling from fifty years ago, one that took place around the episode described above. I was then around twenty-seven years old, visiting my married sister and cousins Nebeel and Nail in Basra. At that time, there was a cute adolescent girl, whom I liked and was hoping to have as a wife, if I could acquire all necessary approvals. Her family knew me well, since Na'il had earlier introduced me to them, and the two of us visited them occasionally. I was very polite in their presence and tried my best to be as presentable as possible, as would be expected from a young bachelor aspiring to marry into the family.

I was residing with my cousin's family, when we received a visit from the young lady's father. When he entered, I asked him politely to sit down on a comfortable couch and presented a cigarette to him, which he graciously accepted. Then I opened a box of one of those 'infamous' Iraqi-made 'Three Stars' matches, the only type available in the country, anyway, and got one out. Those matches were characteristically hard to ignite; so, upon striking one, I was a little too hard, in order to light it in the first try and impress him. I was glad to see a flame bursting out, but it appears that my unceremonious treatment of the match was too harsh, and it broke into two. The farther end of the match, carrying the blessed flame, flew downward in an erratic manner as though trying to escape the sudden onslaught of blistering heat and landed somewhere; I couldn't find it, nor could the visiting gentleman. Then, **I found it**; it had rested in the gentleman's pants cuff. I hurriedly put it out and apologized profusely. But, alas, I could then surmise that the apology didn't in any way make any favourable impression on him and sadly realized: "**No wife**! At least not that one, in particular."

There is another relevant story regarding those celebrated matches. There was a group of workers who had short breaks after working a couple of hours at a time. One of them was an Iraqi-Armenian who felt he didn't belong with the rest or, rather, was unwelcome; so, he stayed aloof. During breaks, he would lean against a wall and bend his knees, then put a cigarette in his mouth and get his box of 'Three Stars' matches. One of the workers noticed that the Armenian guy often struck a match, and after it failed to ignite, threw it away and watched it as he got another one. Out of curiosity, he approached him one day and asked him why he did that. The Armenian guy replied, in somewhat broken Arabic: "You know this Iraqi match is *'dog, son of a dog'* (a typical soft Iraqi swear); it doesn't work, but sometimes it lights up **after** I throw it away and I want to see that when it happens!"

Although not related, this latter story somehow reminds me of something else; I love watching football/

soccer, even with goals being infrequent and far in between, with some games even ending with a disappointing zero – zero score. Sometimes, after earnestly watching soccer on TV for an extended period of time, with no goals, I decide to go to the kitchen in order, say, to make me coffee; as soon as I leave the room, I hear a loud 'Yeah', indicating that a goal has just been scored, **and I missed it**! How come such instances happen so often?

Do occurrences like this lie in the heart of what is called "luck", which in this case may be qualified as 'bad?' **Philosopher Daniel Dennett** believes that "luck is *mere* luck". In my mind, there is logic in that; however, what is debatable is 'why does good luck stick with certain people and bad luck with others?' An example: when I was in Iraq, I heard that there was a police sergeant who had won the lottery's first prize twice and the second prize five times, in addition to a 'horde' of small prizes. Conversely, I recall Muneer's sister, a beautiful young lady, who got married to one of our faculty 'artist studio' friends. She was on a visit to England (the mother of medicine) when she contracted 'meningitis' and died; a few years earlier, her oldest brother, an ingenious doctor, had acquired a PhD in brain surgery from England; at that time he was back in Iraq (a freaky episode).

There certainly are phenomena that have not been convincingly explained. Several cultures in the East believe in what is commonly known as the 'evil eye', with some stories being hard to digest; however, it is relevant here to relate the following story. I was once with an acquaintance who drove a new plush Chrysler on Yonge Street in Toronto. As a small Lada (Russian Fiat, a car as far detached from luxury as one can possibly imagine) overtook us, he went: "Wow, what a beautiful car", a remark which I found astonishing for obvious reasons; only three seconds later, that car got involved in an accident! Was that just a coincidence? I didn't make any comment then, in order to avoid embarrassing him.

TWO ON A BUS

It was summer time (over 45°Celcius) in Baghdad; Newadir ('A simple matter of misinterpretation' and 'Anee hatta tiethee iethoof!' reiterated above) and I were on a bus (one of those red ones: **AEC Routemaster**, which are a principal feature of London; they are/were a major feature of the Iraqi capital itself, as well. In addition to the driver, there were only two more men sitting on separate seats close to the front door of the bus.

As the bus stopped at the terminal (in the town's center), both passengers rose to get off quickly. As it happened, both of them arrived at the front door's opening at exactly the same time and **got stuck** there! The bus driver had just risen from his seat to get off, too, when this unusual exercise of human endeavour took place right in front of him. It was a very hot day, and any issue, no matter how trivial, could cause people's temper to flare up. When he saw that, he yelled: **"There are only two people here, and they have to get their asses stuck in the door; God-damn the government"**. *Eh! I disliked the government then, but what, in all fairness, had it to do with two asses stuck in a bus door in the middle of summer? [So disparate with* **William Shakespeare's** *'A Midsummer Night's Dream'!] Also, a remark like that said in a common place in a police state!* I quickly looked around to make sure that there were no plain-clothed Secret Police around and moved away quickly; we could all have got in trouble then.

Those buses, especially the double-deckers, were a marvel at the time, in terms of accommodating passengers, appearance, rigidity and stability. As a testament to the latter characteristic, I remember this event: Where we lived in al-Sarrafyia (Baghdad) there was a small roundabout in front of what had before (in the 1940s) served as the king's residence (a large house, not palace). The roundabout was a little larger than the two segments of the two-lane two-way road it connected. I was strolling towards that roundabout one late afternoon, when I saw a double-decker speeding towards me. So far, so good; it will certainly slow down before reaching it. With that comforting logical thought in mind, I kept going forward without any hesitation, need for extra adrenalin, or even having to exhibit uncalled-for heroic bravery. I was almost at the contact between that roundabout and the road, when the onrushing, attacking bus reached it; *it did not slow down!* As it turned right to enter the roundabout, the two-decker tilted sharply towards my side; I froze and watched the bus in horror, waiting for it to crush me into smithereens. Both the bus and I survived to talk about it (on my side that is).

MORE OF FISH

Between 1965 and 1969, I made several visits on Friday weekends to my aunt's home in Baghdad, where I had lunch with her and her husband, and stayed until late afternoon. In those days, animal fat was used ubiquitously in cooking; it was sourced as by-product from sheep's fat, and came as a smooth, homogeneous straw-yellow mass that was kept in stainless steel containers. Nowadays, we know better than to touch that stuff; however, I cannot forget the fragrance and taste of Iraqi rice ('umber/unber') that was cooked in that fat.

One day, during one of those visits, there was another visitor, a friend of my aunt's husband. They played dominoes, a game that was very noisy, as they used to slam the dominoes on the table in rapid successions. Generating such sounds, akin to crackling artificial thunder while playing was part of the enjoyment Iraqis got from playing that game; in retrospect, it probably personified defiance.

That day, my relatives ordered a barbequed fish (a mezgoof cooked along the Tigris River). The fish was large and its meat soft and tender, smoked and delicious. There also was rice, boiled freshly harvested long black-eye beans and pickled mangoes (a treat that came in small wooden barrels from India) on the table. The visitor, being a huge person who loved everything on the table, spent quite some time devouring the food; he ate half of the fish and was all the time *munching on whole pickled mangoes and uttering: 'Oh, oh; they are hot, they are so good!'* I ate a little, a habit I have faithfully maintained over the years. My aunt's husband, a tall and wiry guy, as his wont, ate even less; he had two tablespoonfulls of that 'yum-yum' rice, a small piece of fish and about five or six long beans; the latter he opened and ate their content of beans only; that was enough for him! As usual with Iraqi dinners, strong tea was served right after the meal!

ZEHDI

Between 1961 and 1976, I lived with my parents in a rented house in a quiet area called al-Sarrafyia in Baghdad. The house had rather narrow wrap-around yard containing several trees of 'narinj', a kind of citrus that looks like oranges, but is acutely sour. That yard also had four tall Zehdi (also known as Zahidi) palm trees; they bore heavy crops of Zehdi dates every year. We ate some of those dates, in part stuffed with walnut or hazelnut. Most of it, however, went into a 'ttishitt', (a flat rounded brass container, about a yard in diameter and half a foot deep), where the dates were heated, in order to extract their sugar-rich juices as concentrate; the latter is deep purplish-red, thick, viscous and very sweet. That date juice, called 'silan' and known to some as dates honey, is now even being produced in Israel and sold on the international market in jars; silan, if properly preserved, lasts a long time.

Back in Iraq, we loved eating a mixture of silan and 'tahini', a thick oily paste made from ground toasted hulled sesame seeds; some people like these two ingredients partly mixed, whereby the deep purplish-red silan is inter-layered with sharply defined streaks of tan tahini, a mix that gives heterogeneous flavour; some like those two ingredients well mixed. Both ingredients were available in Benghazi, and Kays, myself and another friend had a few opportunities to enjoy that combination after supper, instead of having the sweets that were prepared in the guest-house's kitchen.

PART TWO: HOME-COUNTRY STORIES/ADULTHOOD

(1968 - 1976)

I left my job at the College of Engineering in 1968, moving (through transfer) to a research institute situated about forty kilometres outside Baghdad; I worked in the latter until 1976. Our professional group included seven geologists, who worked together in harmony. Busses transported the employees every working day, arriving there at 8:00am, and leaving at 3:00 pm; we had half an hour lunch break. Now and then, we had extended field trips.

For the larger part of that stretch of time, we had a burly, energetic head of department; that ever-smiling gentleman was one of the craftiest characters I ever met in my life; he could talk his way out of any difficulty and persuade anyone with anything, a perfect salesman. I still remember one of his remarks; he once said: "I can talk to a group of fifty people for two hours, at the end of which they leave happy and content without understanding a word of what I said!" While writing this manuscript, I had completely forgotten about that guy, until now, when I am proofreading it. Hearing repeated empty generalities while listening to some of the electoral speeches (2015) relevant to the 2016 presidential elections actually was what reminded me of that personality.

GUN IN TENT

During one such field trip to the Western Desert of Iraq, all geologists were congregated in one large tent holding the field beds. We had just arrived from home and were, after a long trip, exhausted. A fellow geologist and I sat side by side on one of those beds, while everyone was chatting. All of a sudden, the geologist sitting next to me flourished a semi-automatic hand-gun from his inner jacket pocket and started flaunting it. The coordinator of the trip, another fellow geologist, asked him if the gun was loaded, to which he said it was.

At that point the coordinator asked him to remove all bullets from the gun, as a precautionary safety measure. He complied by removing the cartridge case from the gun and at the same time contending: "All right, you are the boss; it is now empty". The coordinator, who was sitting opposite to where we were, advised him that the gun wasn't completely empty, that there was still a bullet in the barrel of the gun. The young gentleman disagreed and started to make a childish show, turning the gun this direction and that way, as though it was a toy. Sensing immediate danger, the coordinator, who was to a degree knowledgeable about guns coming from the countryside, screamed: "Point it on the ground, point it on the floor; there is still one in the chamber!" The guy replied with a simple: "No, there isn't", brought the gun down between his leg and mine and squeezed the trigger! BANG! I instinctively looked at my leg; it was intact, and his was too! *Lesson: Guns are not toys, and for those who own them in their millions, I say imagine yourself at the other end of that gun before considering using it!*

On a different occasion, I was sitting in a shuttle taxi; next to me sat a policeman holding a Kalashnikov on his knees; no problem there since he was supposed to be well trained on it, except that the nozzle was pointed towards me, and almost touching my stomach. I quickly became nervous, turned towards the policeman and gently and politely asked him if the gun was loaded. He looked at how the gun was positioned and, thankfully, understood what I really meant. He apologetically said: "I am your brother", a commonly used friendly statement, and instantly moved the nozzle away from me. At the next turn in the road, the gun slid back to where it was before, only this time a little closer to its unintended target! At the time I thought if I went any further in my grievance, I might, after an eruption of anger, get shot deliberately without having a decent chance of running away, since the car was moving. I carefully weighed that against how much longer we still had to stay in the taxi until we reached the end of the line and decided that it was safer to take a chance; I survived the potential 'debacle'.

ALADDIN BLUE-FLAME HEATER

With time, our group was augmented with recently-graduated young geologists. During the earlier part of the 1970s, the whole group of geologists went on another exploration expedition in the Western Desert of Iraq. We stayed in tents, with each tent containing two field beds. Since it was winter, an Aladdin blue-flame kerosene heater was allocated to each tent. My tent-mate, a rather eccentric guy from the countryside, was small and slim; but he brimmed with vigor, something he proved quite convincingly with his performance in the field.

After an exhausting first day's work, everyone had supper and went to bed early. Next morning, I woke up and opened my eyes, only to see this guy sitting on the edge of his bed and holding his lowered head between both hands, **a true picture of male wretchedness**. Having typical Middle Eastern compassion, I was duly concerned and asked him if something was wrong. To this question he miserably answered: **"I could not lift it"**. I pondered this 'riddle' for a while, taking into account that all we had in the tent was two beds and a gasoline heater, and then asked: "What was it that you couldn't lift?" He said: "The heater; I am used to lifting it every morning as soon as I wake up". I did not see the significance of lifting a heater and kept silent. After a minute or two he jumped towards the Aladdin heater and lifted it with one hand, in a way suggesting weighing; he then knelt and checked its gasoline storage compartment. All of a sudden, he became ecstatic and yelled: ***"But, of course; it is full to the brim with gasoline; that's why I could not do it!"*** At that point, I was completely at a loss for words, but somehow managed to blurt: "But, you just lifted it with only one hand!" He looked at me curiously, and then pointing at his groin, he replied: ***"Not with my hand, but with this".*** I was shocked into utter silence (5 kilograms worth of heater and kerosene)!

After breakfast, I left the camp to embark on our routine work with another geologist. Once we were alone, I told my partner what had taken place in the tent that morning. He laughed and said: "During high school, this guy was in the Ministry of Education's Students Internal Residence (dormitory), where out-of-towner students lived. Every morning, he used to go from his bedroom to the common washroom in his underwear carrying the exceptionally heavy calculus book on his sex member. There, he would wash his face and carry it back the same way to his room in front of other students".

He reminisced for a while and then continued: "This guy was terribly shy of women and avoided them like they were poisonous snakes. In this regard, one of his friends tried several times to persuade him to get together with hookers, a request that was always met with unwavering refusal. One day, however, this young geologist was tricked into entering a house with his womanizer friend, who instantly had all doors locked. There, he was pushed into the embrace of a beautiful hooker who made an easy work of arousing his most primitive instinct. Finally, he agreed to go with her into a bedroom and closed the door behind him. Two minutes later, the hooker started screaming in agony: **'Don't sit up; lie on me, lie on me'**. The host had to physically intervene, irrespective of the awkwardness of the situation at hand, in order to 'save her life'!"

ARE YOU GOING TO, OR SHOULD I DO IT?

During one of those trips, I and two other co-worker geologist friends from that research institute, Hadeed and Rahdi (*both gentlemanly, trustworthy and dependable*), who happened to be cousins, were on a two-month field trip in the desert, being members of a truly zealous exploration group. The workdays were long, hot and tiring, but in the late afternoons the temperature dropped down considerably, with that part of the late afternoon/evening becoming quite enjoyable.

On one such late afternoon, all three of us had a small square table set up outside our tent, three chairs and a chess set. Always bickering and mocking each other about their chess-playing talents, the two cousins settled on having a game; I sat watching. They faced each other, but with *lowered heads*, as both were deeply immersed in contemplation and pleading silently for inspiration and staunch support from the Heavens, above. Everything was peaceful and quiet, *until* one of them dropped a chess piece on the ground, on the opposite side to where I was sitting. Of course, one of them was expected to retrieve it.

For several long seconds both of them looked at it, but neither moved, each waiting for the other to pick it up *(too much effort involved)*. Giving up, and within a split-second making the same decisive decision, both of them reached for it simultaneously. As they bent down, and being so close to each other on either side of that small table, their heads went **BANG** (as in two saucepans going for it in a mountain-goat manner display of force)! I erupted in loud uncontrolled laughter, but, as I did so, I saw one of the cousins, who had picture-perfect Mongolian features with black slanting mustache, giving me a devilish malevolent look. *I knew what it meant, jumped from my seat and ran as fast as I could;* **he couldn't catch me; that is why I am still around to tell this story!** To both gentlemen, if you happen to read this, I very much value your past **noble brotherly friendship, and please accept a solemn salute!** ("The only way to have a friend is to be one." — **Ralph Waldo Emerson**)

OF GERMAN OPERA

While working with the same outfit in the field, we had extra time during the late afternoon and evening; it was fortunate in the sense that it gave us an opportunity to develop sociable comradery. We had frequent walks in the friendlier parts of the desert in the waning sun's heat; later, during the evening and especially after supper, we often looked for a chess game.

During one such peaceful chess encounter one evening, two employees faced each other. One of the 'combatants' had a **full glass of 'arak'**, a high alcohol-content drink (Alcohol by volume: 40 – 63%; proof: 80 – 126) in front of him (no water or ice added). Everyone around him was sipping at that comforting non-medicinal elixir, except him. One of the onlookers then asked him repeatedly why he was not drinking, but that guy was deeply absorbed in thoughts, which were strictly restricted to 'chess' and chess only; what Arak! **At that time, nothing distracted his attention, perhaps not even a naked young South American woman standing in front of him**, not in the next tent! After about twenty minutes of nagging, however, he came to the inexorable conclusion that if he didn't silence that 'irritating meddlesome person' once and for all, he was going to lose that game. Then after making a move which he was happy with, he leaned back in his chair, gave a satisfied sigh, held that 'arak' glass and went: "Gulp, gulp … gulp", swallowing its whole content, then leaned to the front and rejoined the game without saying a single word.

Having a predilection for the game myself, I was absorbed in following it, almost oblivious to what was going on in the rest of that large tent, where some people were sitting on beds chatting and drinking arak; the German-educated Rahdi was present as a member of that 'congregation'. After ingesting a sizeable volume of that 'blessed' wonderfully soothing potion, he got more and more jovial and vociferous.

Then, all of a sudden he decided to sing an aria from one of **Wilhelm Richard Wagner's German operas**, which drew my attention instantaneously! Impressed, I turned around and looked towards him, only to see that his thin bony face was turned upwards facing the top of the tent; I could barely discern two horizontal slits below eyebrows and two small nostrils on either side of a sharp, upward-raised nose. Under that nose, there was a huge vertically located gaping oval hole, where his mouth was supposed to be and, for a split second, I wondered what had happened to it. Then, as he sang, he exhaled all the breath he had previously taken in his lungs, which was about half an hour ago, or that was how long his voice seemed to sound uninterruptedly; the gap then suddenly closed, only to show that all of his facial features had retrieved their natural, previously existing configuration. That hardly natural facial gap inexorably reminded me of the expressionist Artist **Edvard Munch's** *'Der Schrei der Natur (The Scream of Nature)'*, and thought it was a pity that that

artist didn't have this exceptionally inspiring 'expression' of
that pose to paint then!

BETWEEN MAN AND WOLF

My field geologist partner and I were on an exploration
assignment following a pre-determined survey-line in the
Western Desert; we were taking geophysical measurements
every ten meters as we progressed. The land wasn't sand-
covered, as imagination may paint for some, but actually
resembled the more tolerant and friendly parts of the American
'badlands'; it was treeless but fairly flat and easy to cross. I
remember that we had covered half of the assigned length
of that track in the middle of the day, when all of a sudden
we spotted a wolf at a distance of about a hundred meters
in front of us. We stood where we were without being much
concerned, since there were two of us and both carrying field
hammers. There was no way the wolf could overwhelm us;
we didn't even know if it **wanted to eat us**, or was scheming
to **unlawfully seize the sandwiches** we carried, or even
perhaps **make friends with us**, although I very much doubt
the last alternative and have to discard it whole-heartedly and
unreservedly.

The wolf stood watching us carefully and assessing
(as we, ourselves, did in preparation for defense) the feasibility
of a triumphant 'blitzkrieg' attack on us. This is where it gets

interesting. The wolf wasn't actually along our line of travel, but stood motionless at a narrow angle to our left; suddenly, it ran, not towards us, but across where we were heading and stood to our right to make more judicious combative observations. It duplicated that maneuver twice more and then suddenly left us alone realizing that its plan only had a little chance of success.

That wild wolf's thinking and manoeuver, in terms of **'watch carefully and assess intelligently'**, stayed with me all my life. I always remember that incident when driving where visibility is hampered by obstacles, often in the form of large vehicles, particularly those which are parked close to turns. In such locations I slow down to a trickle, *look this way and look that way* before progressing any further until visibility is clear, **a trait I try to teach my children and grandchildren, the latter especially when they cross roads.**

MIGHTY JOHANUS

Johanus was an Iraqi Assyrian driller I saw a couple of times, but had heard quite a few things about in the late nineteen-eighties while working in Baghdad. He was of medium height and burly appearance. Johanus exhibited a thick mustache and a shaven face that was bluish-gray reflecting tree-trunk-thick facial hair; he had an appearance exuding strength, and in that regard, I remember a couple of stories about that driller. Once he was working on an oil-well drilling rig, when his drill-bit got jammed in the well. He tried all he knew to free it, but nothing succeeded in turning that bit. A witness said that after failing to do so, Johanus fumed with anger; he then moved to that part of the bit still sticking out and wiped it very well with a cloth. Then, he had a good grip on it. After some human exertion, the bit turned; what his oil-well drilling rig equipment could not do, his muscles could!

The other story about him relates to his being in the field once, when he became aware of an encroaching bear. He instinctively grabbed a rifle near him, but it was too late, the bear was only just a few steps away. The narrator continued: "What happened after that was a tug of war, with each of them holding firmly to one end of the rifle. After a prolonged inconclusive bout, Johanus came to the disconcerting conclusion that there was a chance he might lose, be overpowered by that monster and be subject to his sharp teeth. He then rightly decided it was less aggravating to cease his contention with the bear, and to let go and enter a nearby tent." The bear, who had no idea how the gun worked, threw it for being 'worthless' to him and went away mumbling about noisy human sticks.

THAT DAMNED RUSSIAN RADIO!

At about that point in time (circa 1969), Hadeed was still single; so he had extra time on his hands after work. He was very much interested in the Middle East's turbulent politics, as everyone else in that region did. The best way, by far, to get news of the Middle East then (no satellite dishes or internet) was to derive it from foreign short wave stations, where the BBC and others could be reached. However, with the radios available, only those stations with very strong signals could be heard; even then, one had to chase those channels perpetually, because of signal fading. One day in summer, Hadeed came to work and jubilantly announced that he had just bought a Russian short-wave radio, which he showed us. Such radios were our only real connection with the rest of the world; that radio in particular, I understood, had the capability of magnifying short-wave signals to a degree that the hearer would think that the news station was only next door, not any farther! One could also then get so many news stations, even those broadcasting from Timbuktu, or the moon, for that matter! The reception was so clear and loud; that was real entertainment! That radio was phenomenal; and it was so heavy (about 5 kilograms per radio, that is) attesting to sophistication.

Hadeed later happily told us that after it cooled off every evening, he hurried upstairs to his bed, which as a matter of fact was placed on the roof, a normal practice there during summer. He said he would then raise the pillows and lie down on his back. He was thus able to easily monitor the dials on his radio, which he always placed on his abdomen. Also, that way he could pick every single word spoken, and as clearly as possible! So far, so good!

A few weeks later, he started to complain of abdominal pain that didn't go away; his mind, and ours, wondered towards the possibility of a horrible disease! Everyone was sympathetic and advised him to see a doctor right away, before the problem got any worse. For a while, he was understandably scared to do so and resisted our entreaties, but in the end he yielded and saw a specialist. The next day, he came to work laughing and jubilantly saying that the specialist ordered an X-ray exam, which he did right away. When the specialist examined the image, he told him that the **'abdominal pain' was related to a flattened stomach, and said that he had no idea what had resulted in such hideous abnormal deformation!'** (We learn something every day)!

THOSE CELEBRATED SANDWICHES

As was pointed out above, the research institute where we worked was situated forty kilometers outside of Baghdad; it took us as many minutes to get there by a specially contracted procession of red Mercedes vans. When we reached the compound, which was situated in a sparsely wooded area, we had to enter through a narrow door (not the gate) and sign our names in front of plain-cloth policemen before heading towards our respective offices. Our building was closest to the gate; its doors were always open, and the windows had no screens to keep insects (and other undesirables, like lizards) out.

Once, it was that part of the workday that we always waited for, called lunch time. I started to open my desk's drawer to get my sandwich, when I heard something scurrying inside; right away, I realized it was a rat, and my instinctive reaction was to rapidly close the drawer and jump from my chair in order to protect myself from a hideous rodent monster!

Good old Rahdi, who was sitting in the room, together with other employees, asked what the matter was; then, in an answer to his next question, I told him that it was a **chicken sandwich**. As I talked to him, he proceeded towards my desk, opened the drawer and took my paper-packed sandwich out. The tip of the sandwich, together with some paper wrapping, had been munched by the rat. He calmly went back to his seat, removed the wrap and cut off about *half a millimetre* where the rat had chewed, then started devouring it!

At another time, our geologist group was congregated in the same room, in order to perform that same holy ritual. I had a Middle Eastern bread loaf (with two pointed ends and a fat middle) stuffed with chicken; that sandwich was made in a hurry, and most of the latter was concentrated in the middle of the bread bun. I wasn't very hungry and ate only two-thirds of it before throwing the remnants in the garbage can. Rahdi cried: "What are you doing?" to which I explained that there was no more chicken left in the bun. He responded: "Oh, yes, there is!" and then jumped and crossed the room to where I was sitting. He dug his hand in the can and got the sandwich remnant out, **opened it, showed me a piece of chicken and said: "I saw it from over there!"** One of the first lessons that a geologist learns is "observation"; but that is not the point!

WHAT?! THEY STOLE MY CAR!

One day (around 1974) the same two cousins, Hadeed and Rahdi, decided to go to a certain state-of-the-art movie-theatre (Cinema al-Nasir) showing one of those glorious old American movies, which now we are lucky to still be able to watch on **TCM channel**. *[Those great irreplaceable actors and actresses! All the way back to 1910].* The movie at that cinema was scheduled to start at 7:00 pm, a regular evening show time. The Mongol-looking guy (Hadeed) drove his new **white Volkswagen Beetle**, arriving at the movie-theatre at around 6:00pm. They had a whole hour to spend, and it was a pleasant, mild and bright late afternoon in spring. After a short discussion, they agreed to go to a certain restaurant close by, where they could get delicious **shish-kebab**. That restaurant was located in a rather narrow side-street on the other side of a major city-road, opposite to where the movie-theatre was situated; that road also happened to be the one that vans took us *(the above-mentioned company's employees)* to work outside the city every working day in the morning, and brought us back in the early afternoon. So far, so good; the two cousins drove there, parked the car at some distance beyond the restaurant and walked back to it.

Half an hour later, they slowly emerged from that restaurant, fully content (stomach-wise and in mind) and, with toothpicks in their mouths, talked about that scrumptious shish-kebab. While resuming their chat, they turned left and sauntered towards the movie-theatre. Hadeed's car was parked on the other side of the restaurant's entrance, opposite to where they were heading, thus they did not come across it while walking towards the movie-theatre.

They got there in a few minutes and entered. Two hours later, they came out happy with what they had watched, stopped a taxi and went home! The car-owner was the last to get off at his house. He walked, actually bounced elastically up and down like a spring at every step, to the yard's gate and, as he was in the process of opening it, he experienced the shock of his life; his car was not there! Running into the house, he got to the phone and dialed his cousin, who was with him all that afternoon. In a horrified voice, he goes: **"Rahdi, the car is gone! It has been stolen!"** Rahdi goes: **"What?! Did you call the police?" "No; I'll call them right away."**

For the next two days, there was no call from the police regarding the 'lost' car. On the third day, however, the company van was driving us back from work and, as it got by that same movie-theatre, Hadeed suddenly shouted: **"Rahdi, we left the car by the restaurant! Remember?"** They stopped the bus right away, got off and ran towards the road where the restaurant was, and 'lo and behold', they found the car still parked there. When they told us this story the next day, we were amazed; for three days, no one had stolen it, in a town where hundreds of cars got stolen every week! The owner of the car smiled and said: "No problem; the car is a **white Volkswagen!**" Then, we understood everything; only the secret/security police used those cars; no one dared go near them! *Hadeed was inadvertently allowed to own one.*

IT IS ONLY A MATTER OF PROTEIN!

Two friends entered a restaurant, oddly called the "Restaurant's Restaurant", after one of them passionately persuaded the other, who identified such restaurants as being "dirty places", to join him over a 'hamidh-hilu'/sweet-sour dish (dried prunes, raisins, apricots, etc., cooked as dark soupy sauce, usually eaten with rice). After a reasonable wait, their meals were brought in.

Just before starting, the guy who issued the invitation took his fork and started poking the sauce. The guest asked him what he was doing, to which he responded: *"I am looking for something"*. Then, his fork came out with a big, fat **fruit-worm**, after which he told his friend that it was an *excellent source of protein* and ate it. Then he explained that such worms were commonly found in the dried-fruit mix.

The guest sat there stunned, but started to eat his dish although with hesitation and some trepidation, fearing that another worm might appear in his own dish. Halfway through their meal, they heard commotion nearby within the restaurant and saw people leaving the restaurant rather in a hurry. After asking what was going on, they were told that a **fat rat was roaming around and 'choosing' what to eat**; hmmm!

THE BEER DRINKERS

One hot afternoon (late 1960s), two of my friends (Tuareg and Tabah) and I went to a pub before going to a nearby state of the art movie theater (al-Khayam Cinema). On arrival, I ordered, as was my habit, a glass of red wine, which lasted me a couple of hours. The other two, both tall and wiry, found it convenient to order two one-liter bottles of cold beer, each. After downing the contents of one within the first minute of arrival, they took it 'easy' handling the second; that took a *whole* ten minutes, during which they ordered the third. We sat there chatting about two hours, during which

I went to the bathroom three or four times, whereas, with four liters of beer, they unfailingly found it unnecessary to do so, not even once! I found that somehow intriguing, since both of them had lean abdomens, and asked them **if they had redirected the beer to their legs**, after it got to their stomachs!

When they had had enough of that stuff for a day, wc left the bar to watch a movie. After that we headed back to the area where we lived; one of them (Tabah) drove a Škoda as far as I remember (a small car that wasn't the most stable of all cars driven on the road; no Siree, Bob)! At some point, we reached a medium-sized roundabout by the College of Sciences where we had originally met. As we reached it, the driver pressed harder on the accelerator. Tuareg started to protest, indicating disapproval of that manoeuver and advising him that he should slow down, instead, when driving on roundabouts; that advice was sharply rejected, and the initiator of that argument was told he was indisputably wrong and to please shut up! (You tell me how to drive after only four liters of beer!)

I experienced wary anticipation and apprehension when we were on that roundabout, but took a deep breath of relief as we passed it. A week later, I met Tuareg; he had bruises on his face. After the customary cordial inquiry about health (a must there), I asked him how he got those bruises. *He said that he was with Tabah (the driver of the Škoda) when the latter sped at that same roundabout and his small car overturned and tumbled several times like a ball!*

OF FRIGHTFUL DREAMS

At about twenty-five, I was unmarried yet and still living in the Middle East. During the 'warmer' months, temperatures went up to 55°Celsius (and even higher, but only 'occasionally' that is); most people then waited for sunset before flocking out on the streets. My friends and I sometimes went to the 'river-side' cafes (Abu-al Nu'as), where we drank tea and played dominos and backgammon.

On one such occasion, Tabah brought with him an acquaintance whom I hadn't seen before. As they were having a game of dominos, Tabah casually asked the guest how he was 'coping' with his dreams, a question I found out of place. The guest's answer was: "Oh, the same as before". Tabah turned to me and told me that the guest *'often' had* ***nightmares***.

The guest continued absentmindedly, while still playing backgammon: "A few nights ago, I had one of those, and the **nightmare was so real** that, in the process, I kept checking my surroundings, in order to confirm that I was *actually awake, not dreaming*".

"I **dreamed** that I suddenly woke up from sleep and saw the silvery moon light streaking in through the window. The illumination inside the room was intense enough for me to clearly discern my desk with a couple of books on it, and that it was somewhat turned askew, the same way I left it before going to bed. My gaze wandered around the room, at the walls and the rest of the furniture, while breathing normally in a relaxed manner. There was an eerie quiet that lasted a few minutes, **then** my ears picked up a strange sound from downstairs. I was shocked, since I was aware that there was no one else in the house.

Other sounds followed, growing a little louder, as though someone was moving around, indicating an uninvited intruder. The thought scared me, but when I heard the wooden stairs leading to the upper level slowly creaking, I froze with fear. My thinking process became sluggish and my body numb, but I had enough wit around me to turn my head towards the door to assure myself that it was bolted, but found out it wasn't safely locked with the door latch. At that moment, the creaking became louder and **then** I discerned my room's doorknob slowly turning and the door opening. **All of a sudden, I heard a loud hysterical scream and opened my eyes! Sigmund Freud** once called dreams as the "**royal road** to the unconscious"; not that one, I bet!

Some adverse consequences of outlandish sleep-related situations, such as nightmarish dreams and sudden dreadfully emotional/psychological shocks that are experienced simultaneously with waking up, are not to be trifled with; take this fictitious story for example. A schemer planned to *obliterate the obstructive presence of his wealthy old uncle* from this world, in order to inherit his wealth. He extensively analyzed the viability of different methods of human elimination, all of which he realized had the disadvantages of his *illegal input* being discovered, thereby leading to his own dear person being thrown in prison, or even having to endure a worse fate. However, his conspiring mind at last concocted an ingenious and diabolical method of implementation of what he firmly believed to be a fool-proof scheme.

This schemer knew that his uncle was indescribably terrified of sloths, in the same way that some people consider clowns with faces hidden behind layers of paint-paste frightening. But, what is so scary about sloths to some people? Could it be their mesmerizing eyes, or what some people may consider wicked half-smiles, or is it their agonizingly slow and creepy movement? Anyway, everybody is afraid of something; I, for example, am afraid of scorpions, and my **huge and dauntless dog** is always startled by **tree-leaf rustling!** (There you are, sloths, scorpions, leaves, etc.).

And now I remember writing about something; yes, yes, I go back to the story (my mind is always in the habit of actively shifting here and there). This conniver capitalized on the fact that his uncle had had a weak heart for many years; all he had to do then was putting the two of them (the uncle and sloth) together, ideally when neither of them knew of the other's presence. This devious 'gentleman' developed a plan that was both simple and as far detached from implicating him personally as possible.

He soon embarked on a trip to Latin America and bought one of the oldest and ugliest sloths he could find there; one that was huge and had *long, coarse and shabby/ frizzy hair* that grew outward towards its head, in contrast to other fellow four-legged animals. Its sub-spherical head showed *ribbon-like white 'eyebrows' overlying bulging, frontally-located and widely-spaced black eyes separated by a flat and wide nasal-bridge.* That sloth had *well-defined upper eyelids, which were sharply slanted downward and inward towards the nose, thereby hiding a significant part of each eyes in such a way that gave them the appearance of a **vicious uncompromising frown**, only to rise suddenly against either side of its nasal-bridge.* Its eyes, characterized by an *'eternally' dull, transfixing and intrusive glaring stare*, appeared indeed **treacherous, conniving and intimidating**.

The sloth's head sat on a short neck, stemming from very narrow shoulders, at the end of which dangled long arms; the latter, seemingly originating from the neck itself, culminated in long and curved 'claws' ending with pointed tips. As a whole, the arms and claws gave the uncomfortable impression of being capable of **reaching anything, anywhere**, though not at any time (that is not at will!).

During a night that was lit by a full moon, our scheming gentleman waited for his uncle to go into deep sleep, which he could ascertain by hearing the latter's unceasing and loud, though irregular, snoring. Then he went on top of the roof right above his uncle's large bedroom-window, which as a matter of habit, the uncle kept with the curtains fully drawn to the sides, so as to be able to enjoy the sunshine and his estate's garden when he woke up every morning. He tied one of the sloth's legs with a rope and dangled his whole body down the window; then, with a stick's end, he tapped the window's glass several times. Soon, he heard a scream emanating from that room, a scream that was both fiendishly terrible and shriek-like, but short, in terms of seconds. At that, he withdrew quickly to his own room, then left it to join others who were investigating the source and cause of that maniacal scream. The doctor, who was quickly summoned, **declared the uncle dead of a hugely massive heart attack!**

---

46 - HIGH AND WIDE

Still in the same city of Baghdad, a couple of years later, I entered a shoe store looking for a pair of Italian make. The store was small, as it was situated in the middle of the most expensive business area in the city (Rasheed Street), and its door was rather narrow. As I got inside the store, I noticed that the place wasn't well lit; the electricity was cut off, which was a normal occurrence there. However, there was ample illumination through the door attributed to reflections from the brightly sun-lit outside.

I pointed out to the store's owner the shoes I liked to try and said: "**Size 39**, please (7 in North America)", a rather smallish size within a European shoe-size system, in which sizes 40 – 42 fitted most men, and size 43 fitted large men. I sat down on a brown, leather-clad bench, and soon the store owner brought the shoes and knelt down to help me try them on. As my foot went into one of them, all of a sudden almost total darkness prevailed inside the store, and a hoarse voice bellowed: "**46 - HIGH AND WIDE?**" We both turned towards the door's opening, which now was dark, except for a narrow sliver of light defining the silhouette of a huge man. The store's owner quickly replied: "I am sorry, Sir; I don't have that size". *[Not only size 46, but it had to be high and wide! That is twice as large as my foot; is there, I ask you ladies and gentlemen, any equitable fairness in this world?!]*

EARTHQUAKE DETECTION

One summer afternoon, around 1969, I was lying down on my back in my bedroom upstairs and listening to the BBC international news on the shortwave; I always rested like that after finishing a day's work and having had a fat satisfying lunch.

All of a sudden, I felt vibration in my chest; I opened my eyes, fearing it was the beginning of a heart attack. At that moment in time, I saw the tip of my radio's antennae, which was fully extended in order to be able to receive short-wave radio signals, sway like a pendulum. The first thought that came to my mind then was that at that specific time there was no actual physical connection between my heart muscle and the radio's metallic antennae, and that the former's soft human tissue couldn't possibly, in any way, move the latter. This thought was consequently followed by another which, at the moment, was gratifying: "I did not have a heart problem!" It didn't take me long, thereafter, to realize that: a) I had just experienced an **earthquake**, and b) that there was no prior USGS warning of that well-known natural phenomenon (as if)! What intrigued me, however, *was where the earthquake center had originated*; Baghdad rests on many feet of soil, and is far away from the mountains (the closest being two hundred kilometers to the east). Wherever its origin in the mountain-belt to the east and northeast of that city, that earthquake must have been quite strong in magnitude, enough to be felt where I was (so distant) and sitting on a soft cushiony soil.

THE 'FLYING' MERCEDES

Kuwaiti tourists used to flood Basra (Iraq) in the 1950s through the 1970s. Basrawees, then, viewed those particular neighbours to the south unfavorably, since the latter, who were rich compared with the locals, often *looked down upon the Iraqis*; they went to Basra in their huge American-built cars and often spent money freely.

Once, in the early 1970s, one such visitor went all the way north to Baghdad in his new convertible Mercedes. After staying there a few days, it was time for him to go back to Basra and then Kuwait. He started his journey south in mid-morning of a windy day. Witnesses say that his car was going at well over 150 kilometer/hour on the wide and well-built road. Then, they say, probably because of the blowing wind, he decided to close the car's convertible roof (A no, no at high speeds)! Sadly, and apparently without giving due thought to a *seemingly simple operation*, he started the relevant mechanism *without slowing down*! **Mid-way up, the forward moving roof acted as a sail, and the car half flew in the air, as it tumbled!** (Too late to go back to square one with regard to driving lessons).

PART THREE: IN THE UNITED KINGDOM (1976 - 1979)

Between 1970 and 1976, my wife, children and I had a stable lodging where my parents lived in Baghdad, supported by a routine job; however, there is an end to all stages of life and start of new ones. In the time period of 1976 – 1988, my family had to reside at fourteen addresses in Bristol (UK), Windsor (Ontario), Saskatoon (Saskatchewan) and Calgary (Alberta).

POST-GRADUATE STUDIES IN ENGLAND

I left Iraq with my family in June 1976, heading to Bristol (England) in pursuit of higher education; our three kids were then two to five years old. Bristol, a maritime city, lying on the northeastern side of Bristol Channel, has been inhabited since the Stone Age; pre-historic **Stonehenge** is only 60 km to its southeast. The city was then quiet and peaceful, likely still is, and we were lucky to start our stay in the United Kingdom in the picturesque town of Alveston (about 15 km away from the center of Bristol).

I spent most of my time in Bristol on my studies, which were initially intended to lead towards an MSc degree in geology; those studies were, however, upgraded later, based on my supervisor's advice, so that they could lead to the PhD, instead. Going to the university took about half an hour by bus; the last 200 yards of the route was a 'route stage' by itself, as it went along a steep hill, where busses could barely ascend. I remember climbing that road on foot, in order to save some money, and then going up a less steep road to the Geology Department. That part of Bristol is a lovely area, and the dearest place to my heart there was a small bookstore selling used hardcover classics; I am proud to still show those books, among others, on my bookcase at home.

My studies required taking trips to the field, in Devon, which is a spectacular countryside. On my first introductory trip with my supervisor and another English student/assistant, the former decided to have a lunch break at a pub. I remember entering an inn, the entrance of which was two and a half feet deep. The building definitely looked old from the outside, in terms of facade. Inside, the pub [brief for public place, described in the writings of **Samuel Pepys** as the heart of England] was ameliorated, immaculately fitted with old furniture and very well lit. The bar itself was a picture-perfect display of variously-shaped bottles and shiny glasses, a reflection of which appeared on a large mirror behind the display. The walls were painted and shiny, in places reflecting bulb lights. The ceiling had stout, darkly painted wooden cross-beams that contrasted artfully against a pale-coloured ceiling.

As we sat down, my supervisor turned towards his assistant and said: "Did you notice the sign above the door outside; it said 1568". I was pleasantly shocked; being in a building which was that old and so immaculate! But that is Europe, where people take real pride in their possessions and nothing is wasted! We had beer and started chatting. Then, I heard two ladies talking; I turned to my supervisor and excitedly said: "We have American tourists around!" He gave a short laugh and told me those ladies were indigenous Devon natives, and that the 'American' accent was typically derived from Devonshire in southern England, not the other way round! An eye-opening or, in this case, ear opening revelation.

That same English assistant always drove me to the field and back, by arrangement with the Geological Department of the faculty; he also helped me in my field work. On another field trip, our route took us from Bristol down Exeter, Taunton and Torquay to Torcross on the southernmost part of South Devon. Our explorative effort that day continued into the late afternoon. Earlier, we had moved south along the eastern coast of Torcross, then rounded a promontory of rocks at the base of a cliff. At that time, there was around a twenty-foot-wide patch of flat, though somewhat inclined, beach sand separating the rocks at the cliff's base from the sea, but that sand patch was quite smaller at the promontory's end. We crossed the latter patch and after taking several steps in that same direction, found a large fully treed gorge which we entered, anticipating that rocks are best exposed there. We had about an hour's time of geological work before going back, since my associate was aware that the sea-tide was due to start moving in shortly afterward.

Within an hour, I finished my work and was ready to go back. I turned around looking for my partner, but couldn't find him; so, I waited for a while to give him more time to finish what he was doing. Fifteen minutes later, I called him; there was no answer. I waited some more and called again and again as loud as I could. Then, I heard his reply from somewhere up the escarpment, but couldn't see him because of the dense foliage. I was then anxious about getting stuck in that gorge and reminded him of the tide, after which I heard him say that he was coming down; another ten minutes and he was still up there!

After quite some time, he came down, and we started right away to retrace our steps. However, as soon as we left the gorge, we found that our sandy-beach path was then covered with a yard-high of angry sea water that was splashing here and there; not only our path was completely blocked, we could only see the tip of the promontory of rocks at the cliff's base! I thought then that we had to go back into the gorge and stay on dry land until the morning. The waves went out and came in rather briskly; as they moved out, the base of the promontory rocks, where the beach sand was highest, became exposed. My associate told me that the next time the sea waves retreated, he was going to run for it, which he did successfully; he was able to scale the rock and waited for me on top of it. I hesitated because of my small size, which makes it more difficult for me to reach the top of the rocks. Then, when I sensed his sincere enthusiasm to help, I similarly ran towards those rocks, and he lent me a hand getting on top of them; the rest wasn't that difficult.

Soon we reached the Land Rover he had driven there and drove away. *At that juncture,* **we had enough reason to celebrate; we stopped at a pub where we had fish and chips and chicken and chips!** (I had the latter). So ended a minor field 'adventure'.

THE UNANTICIPATED ENCOUNTER

One day, around the latter half of 1978, I was deeply engaged in writing notes for my thesis, when I heard my name being called. I raised my head only to see someone from the department's management office accompanied by a smiling stranger from the sub-continent, who was of my age. The latter was introduced to me as Bindra, a PhD researcher from Norway, someone who was acquainted with both my supervisor and the head of the department.

After some pleasantries, I was asked if I could help with taking photographs of thin-sections the visitor had brought with him, a request which was met with immediate assent, realizing that the department, or my supervisor in particular, were aware of the high quality of microscope imagery I was capable of; I always enjoyed helping others whenever I could. Photography of those samples definitely required experience and sharp eyesight, since most specimens on the slides were just a few microns-across, and had to be photographed using very high magnifications; he warmly shook my hand in gratitude and left.

Ten years later, I made an application to join the Arabian Gulf Oil Company (AGOCO) in Benghazi, Libya; I was offered a job as a PhD petrographer and supervisor of core analysis (rock porosity and permeability). I had then several years of experience in both while working for two oil-service companies in Calgary, Canada.

[There is an important note I can't but mention here, as it is so relevant! As I typed this paragraph, I saw the word 'petrographer' I had just typed, underlined indicating misspelling. So, I clicked on it and got three alternatives; one was petrography (science) and the longest word ended with 'er'; so, in my mind I thought that was what I wanted: petrography and 'er'. I have read a lot of text on the

computer, using triple-lens eyeglasses and often am satisfied with reading texts that I do not discern sharply. In this case, I am glad I gave it deeper scrutiny than usual. The word ending with 'er' underlying petrography, the alternative I was to going to automatically click to get what I thought was 'petrographer', wasn't not in any way related to that geological discipline; that word actually was 'pornographer', and that wasn't what I had previously applied for (honestly)! Well, even if I had actually made such a mistake, I must admit that there is quite a lot in common between the two terms, in typography, that is, and I may be forgiven!]

And now back to the story. I packed and travelled to Benghazi, only to find that acquaintance from Bristol (Bindra) welcoming me with a big smile. He was working then as advisor to the Exploration Department's General Manager. Being given the task of going through the applicants' resumes, he had picked mine and showing it to his superior, said that he believed we had met before at the University of Bristol. That previous unscheduled meeting in Bristol probably was one of the factors deciding my next sixteen years!

PART FOUR: RESIDING IN CANADA (POST-1979 TO 2004)

THE WANDERING

My family and I stayed in Bristol three years before emigrating from England to Canada. During those few years we lived in four rented houses, which was upsetting for all of us; we lived in the last address for ten days only, having been forced to leave a previous one at the end of a contract. When the day of leaving the latter arrived, we sat in the kitchen waiting for the taxi to come and take us to our next destination; I personally was demoralized, because I had hoped to receive our immigration papers before we left that address. **Then, I heard a heavy thump at the front door.** I ran there and found out that that sound was related to the mail being dropped through a slot in the door; and there it was, a fat envelope containing our immigration papers! Half an hour later, the taxi arrived! We could have easily lost those papers, and our future could have been different; **immigrating to**

Canada has been the single most important achievement of my life.

Within ten days of the documents arrival, we took the train to London and stayed with my brother Owen for a few days. As it is usual with people of the Middle East, we were treated like a royal family; my brother had already bought us tickets to travel to Canada on Air Canada.

We left England before finishing my post-graduate studies at the University of Bristol, and when I arrived in Canada, my PhD thesis was only half-written. For the next two years, my time was spent between looking for a job and finishing writing the thesis. After arriving in Windsor, Ontario, we stayed a month with my wife's sister and her family, after which we moved four times in that little town in fifteen months. Later on, we stayed in one house for two and a half years in Saskatoon, where I had successive jobs ($32,000/ year) with two mining companies; that was in the early years of the 1980s and the beginning of economic disaster. I had then bought a house with 'floating' interest rate at 13.5%, based on the realtor's advice; in few months, the rate shot up to 21.25%; stupendous!

We left that house with a realtor to have it rented out on our behalf, or sold, and moved to Calgary for a job with a small salary ($20,000 a year). In 1982, I went back to England to 'defend' my PhD work. On that memorable day of the defense, the examining professor, my supervisor and I met at lunchtime. My supervisor suggested having lunch before the fateful discussion. At the restaurant, we ordered the dishes we liked; the two of them ordered beer. When asked what to drink, I said with a sly smile: "Not for me, thank you; I want to remain sober; you two please go ahead and drink to your hearts content, and I am willing to pay for that!" Everyone laughed; they stuck to one pint, each. After the defense, the examiner told me the thesis was accepted, but I had to cut it by one third, which proved to be more difficult than writing it (in the absence of our present-day computers)! On hearing that it had been accepted, I saw all my life's happenings flash before my eyes (in my mind that is) in the matter of one or two seconds. Finally, I was awarded that degree in 1983.

By 1988, we had to live in another four houses in Calgary. In total, we moved twelve times in twelve years! We stayed in the last one in this group for nine years, during which I was employed by the Arabian Gulf Oil Company (AGOCO) in Benghazi, Libya. Thereafter, we settled where we are now and found some peace, thank God!

A CHANCE ENCOUNTER WITH AN ANGEL

While working in Saskatoon, we lived in a rather small, but new and very well built house in a new development area for two and a half years (1981 - 83). When we took that house, the yards were pristine and ready for landscaping.

There was nothing separating it from our neighbours in the back but a 6 foot-high cedar fence. Those neighbours had two children who were just a little younger than ours (then 6 - 9), but whom I had not seen before. One day they said 'hello' and, after a short friendly chat, asked us if it was all right with us if they left a couple of the fence's planks attached with one nail, each, only at the top, so their children could come into our yard and play with ours, a request we were only too happy to grant. However, we did not have the pleasure of such visits, and had no idea how those kids looked like.

One day, a few months later, I decided to cover the base of our two-door Malibu 1975 with a heavy plastic sheet ahead of the snow invasion, and in preparation for our three young children's messy boots. I had just removed a metallic trim from the floor where the driver's door closed, and was down on my knees on the garage cement slab. I was totally engrossed in fitting a piece of plastic sheet on the floor, right under the pedals, when I could hardly feel something soft, fluffy and light leaning against my right side, and at the same time heard a barely audible bird-like voice slowly and in the softest of tones asking: "What are you doooing?" I turned around only to see a kid who was one and a half foot-high dressed in white; she had a pink face, blue eyes and short curly blonde hair; could anything be more suggestive of an angel! I couldn't help myself but laugh and explain, at the same time wondering how she ended up there; then I remembered our neighbours and took her there.

While staying at the same house, my wife was taking a stroll one late afternoon with our next-door Quebecois neighbour, who had her three year-old son with her. That kid was walking like a small duck several steps ahead of the two, *when all of a sudden he bent and looked at something on the walkway, which he delicately and lovingly picked up for further, more intelligent observation and scientific examination, all to be performed as best as the occasion called for. At that point, his mother, realizing a potential for a humanly undesirable action, called his name anxiously, said something that sounded like "Tu'shba!" and jumped towards him. As soon as he discerned the maternal attack from behind, whatever he had in his hand went quickly upward towards his mouth, where it was professionally deposited and readily swallowed.* Noticing the apparent concern on the mother's face, we asked her what had just happened; she said: "**He swallowed a spider**". (Uncooked? Hmm!)

MOVING TO CALGARY

Soon after the mining company I worked with in Saskatoon announced it was closing down, my wife and I discussed what had to be done next, and decided to move to Calgary, home of the oil industry, notwithstanding the "doom and gloom" disposition pervading that industry at the time. I soon found an inconsequential job, as petrographer, with a Calgary-based service company. We then had a moving company transport our furniture to that city while my family and I were driven there by a friend in our own car.

Prior to moving to Calgary, I stayed for about a month with an acquaintance, but was able to visit my family back in Saskatoon every weekend with a friend. The trip took ten hours, one way, but was well worth it; we travelled at night, and on one such a trip (returning to Calgary), we were lucky to watch an unscheduled 'firework' display of the 'Northern lights' *(Aurora Borealis)*. Once during my early stay in Calgary, the latter friend asked me if I liked to have supper in Banff after we finished work in the afternoon. I agreed, but had to ask what dishes they served. He laughed and told me that Banff was a town, not restaurant. Then, after more inquiry, he told me it was 120 kilometer west of Calgary; I quickly persuaded him to stay where we were.

PART FIVE: OVERSEAS (AT THE GUEST-HOUSE)

THE SINGING NEW RECRUIT

The oil company (AGOCO) I worked for in Libya started hiring expatriates (geologists, geophysicists and petroleum engineers) in the late 1980s. When I arrived in Benghazi in late June of 1988, my first impression was that all shops were closed and shuttered. It was early in the afternoon when I arrived at the old guest-house, where I met two 'elderly' (as myself) Arabic-speaking expats from North America, Kays and Thabik; they had arrived there three months earlier. By the time we had our supper, the building was still well lit by our eternal patron, the Sun. My acquaintance with Kays developed and matured quickly to a lifelong, unselfish brotherly friendship; we shared comparable family situations and values, and respected each other's privacy. My next impression of the city was that, when night came, all buildings in the area, including ours, were swept in darkness, with one exception; there was only one room lit by what is commonly known as an 'electrical bulb'. That room was occupied by the *people who served the Expats as kitchen 'staff', a small group from just south of the Sahara in Africa.* After enquiring, I learned that there were no such bulbs around on the market, and that there was nothing else, either! These temporary quarters had small rooms, each accommodating two expats (not conveniently private) and one general bathroom that was not, by any measure, clean, or private, since it couldn't be fully closed. The food, made of 50% fat, was horrible and dangerous to eat on a protracted-period basis.

Since there was no light, everyone went to bed early; I ended up with one of the two expats mentioned above, Kays. We reclined on our respective beds and started chatting, mostly about our new and strange environment, including unforeseen difficulties regarding bewildering living conditions and overwhelming boredom in the afternoons and evenings, and also during 'empty' weekends, with no TV. My new friend, then, told me an interesting 'story' with regard to such boredom.

He said that for some time he and Thabik were bedroom partners. One night, after exhausting subjects as food for conversation, he said that both of them reclined comfortably on their beds in silence. Kays was deep in anxious thought about his family overseas, while the other used microphones to listen to "Umm Kulthum", an internationally famous Egyptian female singer, with songs that lasted an hour, each (including several long repetitions). He said that the latter, while listening, was going "khriesh, khriesh" scratching his hairy chest; everything else was as quiet as a tomb! Then, all of a sudden, as Kays started to doze off, he heard the other fellow scream: **"Ayieeyah"**. With that unanticipated shriek, Kays jumped to his bedroom partner, thinking he had had a *heart attack*. He quickly touched the other's shoulder and anxiously asked what was wrong with him; the latter responded that everything was *just fine*, and that he was only *singing* with Umm Kulthum, and apparently was carried away a little bit!

THE LODGING

Ten days after my arrival in Benghazi, all expats were moved to the new AGOCO's **guest-house**, a recently constructed building. I was pleasantly shocked; by contrast to the temporary/old lodging (above), the new four-storey accommodation was like a five-star hotel; there were two rows of rooms on either side of a corridor on the second, third and fourth floors, enough to accommodate sixty people. The rooms were large and fitted with good quality furniture manufactured in Scandinavia; each room had a bathroom and a small kitchen; we weren't allowed to use the latter, though, but was nice to have, since it gave us an assuring, though deceptive, sense of 'home'. However, for a few years after arrival, there were no telephones or television sets. Both of those commodities arrived at a later date but, even then there were no receivable television channels to watch. Only occasionally, however, when that region had a 'ghibli' (dust storm) were we able to receive one channel (Rai 2) from Italy.

The ground-floor was 'exquisite' for that part of the country; the floor was covered with white Italian marble, streaked with gray; the building was well insulated against dust. There were five rooms on that floor used for the expat's convenience, one of which and for several years contained a billiard table; another served as "bridge" room! The lunchroom/cafeteria was large and contained several eating tables. For the first year after it was opened, we were fortunate to have the professional culinary services of a Portuguese catering/cooking kitchen outfit.

Upon my arrival in the city of Benghazi, there was fresh-water problem. There was no supply of safe purified water to drink; the running water coming out of faucets was not clear and sometimes muddy. A doctor living with us then is reported to have said that that water wasn't even safe to take a shower. On some occasions, the expats would get information regarding the availability of bottled water, prompting some to rush to buy it. Aside from scarcity, water was expensive, three times as much as gasoline; this comparison, however, is only comparative and not truly informative, since gasoline there (93, 95 and 97 octane, unlucky people!) was only ten cents a liter, or thereabout.

Shortly after arrival at the guest-house in 1988, however, AGOCO started to procure fresh-water from wells dug in 'Genfuda', not too far away from the Geological Laboratory and the Mediterranean coast; it wasn't pure, nor sweet, but nevertheless drinkable, at the drinker's own risk of course when it came to bacterial contamination. I opted to fill a two-liter soda bottle at the laboratory on a regular basis and carry it to my room at the guest-house; and that was what I drank for sixteen years. Aside from the high likelihood of contamination in that 'primitive' environs, that water was fairly rich in salt (being retrieved from the proximity of the Mediterranean Sea coast); as such, the spectre of developing bladder stones loomed for those who took it upon themselves to consume that water for prolonged periods of time.

The guest-house was safe to live in, but so was the city as a whole; solitary women walked at night, without fear of any type of harassment. At the time (1988 - 2004), there were extraordinary manifestations of fraternal comradery among the locals. One morning, soon after arrival, I was crossing a large yard in front of the company's offices, another four-storied building, in order to take the company's bus to the Geological Laboratory, when I saw the president of the company strolling leisurely towards the offices. At his side walked an employee I had recognized as being a local technician who took the bus with us to the Geological Laboratory compound (20 km south of the city). The latter had his arm around the president's shoulder while he talked to him amicably. In another instance, I heard from my office two of the laboratory's technicians shouting at each other in the large hall next to the room [that was the first of only two such incidents in many years in that country that I can remember]. Within a minute, their anger grew exponentially and I thought they were going to demolish each other, but soon all was quiet. Ten minutes later, I had to leave my office; I saw both of the 'belligerents' sitting at a small table, drinking tea and chatting like brothers!

For the whole period of my dwelling at AGOCO's guest-house (sixteen years), I heard one swear only coming from the locals; quite a few, however, came from 'Western-educated' expats, with one such 'swear' being directed towards the writer of this 'episode' personally!

GIVE, GIVE!

While working for AGOCO in the time interval 1991 - 2000, I had the luxury of working two months, seven days a week, and taking one month paid vacation with travel tickets. Since the company supplied the tickets, I had to go to the Personnel Department and plead with them to give me the travel route that suited me best. To get to that end, I brought back with me two Rothmans-cigarette cartons every trip and gave them *discreetly* to a chain-smoker employee in charge of making travel arrangements, when I returned to Benghazi.

After returning to Benghazi from one of those vacations, I dutifully brought the cigarettes hidden in a bag and entered the corridor where that guy's office was. There was no one in the corridor, so *I crept forward, slowly and cautiously like a cat*. However, reaching his office's door, I heard voices, so I did not enter realizing that he wasn't alone. But, as I passed by that door, he had already seen me and gathered why I was there. Then I heard a thundering voice, befitting that gentleman's gigantic size, calling me: **"DANEELIZ, come"**. **It wasn't anything as enjoyable as that of a 'tenor', and most certainly not that of a Pavarotti!** I felt obliged to go in, otherwise he would certainly have felt insulted. I had to consider then that he was the guy in charge of those tickets the company provided me with; more importantly, the re-entry visas we expats had to obtain before leaving the country came through his office, as well.

As I entered, I saw three employees sitting around that clerk's desk, and behind that desk, there was a cloud of smoke, through which I could somehow discern his huge head! Then I saw his arm moving all the way forward, almost two meters out, and heard him roar: **"hat, hat"**, meaning **"give, give"**! I was then in a dilemma, either risk his wrath, or be seen by those employees as offering something that could be construed as a 'bribe', a potential reason for dismissal from the company (and in public too!). It took me only a second to make up my mind and try to avoid the more fearful menace, his wrath! I resolutely dug into my bag, got the cigarette packs and, with as much courage as I could muster, handed them over to him in front of witnesses. As I left, perspiring profusely, I said a short prayer asking God that nothing untoward happens; thankfully, my prayer was favourably answered.

During the first three years I spent there (1988 - 1991), however, I had to stay six months at a time, before being allowed to go out on leave. Travel tickets (with confirmed travel dates provided by the company) and visas, together with **our returned passports**, were like presents from heaven! I and some other expats had lots of worries, until we got all approved documents for travel in our own hands; we used to complain to each other about how slow the process was, sometimes taking up to the day of travel, itself! With time, however, I learned this saying: **"Don't worry; at the end everything works out all right!"** Later on, this thought helped me a lot in combatting some difficulties of life.

THE BEACH

The following story happened soon after my arrival at AGOCO's guest-house. That city had a beautiful northwest-facing beach but, due to social and cultural reasons, no girls were to be seen there at any time, with the 'rare' exception of some female nurses from the eastern part of Europe, who happened to be working at AGOCO's Clinic at the time. Anyway, foreign workers/expatriates, having nothing to do, used to flock there every weekend, girls or no girls.

It was one of those weekends, and we (the expats) were in line in the company guest-house's dining room/cafeteria, waiting to be handed our lunch. A Portuguese kitchen server, trying to be nice to one of the expats, asked him in broken English: "Did you go to the bitch (meaning beach) today?" I heard the expat answering sarcastically: **"Oh, no; I had a headache!"**

WHAT HOMESICKNESS DOES TO SOME!

On arrival in Libya, many, if not all, Expats, in particular those who were born in an Arab country, were exposed to a significant **'reverse culture shock'**. One such effect that I cannot forget regarded one of the Portuguese kitchen staff. That server was of medium height, on the burly side, and exhibited a thick black moustache reflecting manhood as solid as a rock. I met that gentleman every morning at the kitchen-serving counter when ordering breakfast; the atmosphere, there and then, in contrast with the overall primitive environment outside the company, was like being in a restaurant in the middle of Europe.

During the first few weeks, when an Expat ordered a fried egg, this kitchen crew, standing at the counter, would only turn his head towards a closed double-sided door separating the cafeteria/eating-lounge from the kitchen itself and in thundering, ear-splitting Portuguese shout to his fellow cook what sounded like: "**UM OVO ESTRALADA**" (one fried egg). Two months later, he would go half way to the doors and say "um ovo estralada", and four months after that he had to crawl, with drooping shoulders and bent back, to the doors, open one feebly and with a voice, barely exceeding a whisper in intensity, slowly utter: "um ovo estralada".

BREAKFAST ORDER

Again, this took place within the same setting above, while working for the same company. I was an early bird, always enjoying a warm cup of tea and a boiled egg in the morning. So, one day I went downstairs into the cafeteria, and found myself to be the second employee to get there. I approached the serving desk, where a British expat was ahead of me already; apparently for having to repeat his order more than once, I heard him say irritably and impatiently, with the bottom of his hand up in the air and being flipped upward and downward: "**Frieyd** both **sieyds!**"

The kitchen server, who knew nothing of the English language except, perhaps, 'hello' and 'good morning', stood there at a loss and in total awkward embarrassment. So, I lightly crept up to him and, in a low voice, told him in Arabic to fry an egg on both sides. *A potentially explosive international crisis was thus averted, thanks to my timely intervention; I should have been a 'foreign minister'!*

BETWEEN CAKE AND CROISSANT

At another instance, there were three of us, including Kays and another expat from the sub-continent, eating breakfast at the guest house's cafeteria; the latter had a slice of delicious cake on a plate in front of him, which he had set aside, apparently keeping it for last, something that I invariably do myself (eat the tastiest last). There were only two more expats sitting at a distance at another table, and all was quiet.

Midway through breakfast, I noticed one of the kitchen's hands carrying a tray full of fresh-baked items. When I saw that, I said: "Now, we can have croissant". The expat jumped from his seat, and with his palms upturned in the air, said: "Crosso! Crosso!" Then he walked gingerly towards the serving kitchen counter. Mental reflections (or notions) appear to come from nowhere and consequent decisions are sometimes taken in a split second, and this is exactly what happened then. Like lightning, Kays' hand shot towards the other guy's cake and did likewise in its return trip, only to stuff it in his mouth, which worked like juggernaut; in two seconds, the cake vanished in thin air.

The expat walked back slowly in frustration without a croissant, since there actually was something else on the tray, only to find his cake was now missing; he looked incredulously, albeit silently, at his empty plate and sat down without saying anything.

THE OKRA DISH

This is another event taking place in the mid-1990s at AGOCO's guest-house in Benghazi. I was in line in the cafeteria waiting to get my lunch. At the kitchen counter, a couple of steps ahead of me, it was an Iraqi's turn, a stocky middle-aged guy, who loved every single word in the culinary dictionary, especially 'okra', a term that ranked amongst the most valuable of gemstones. That day, the guest-house kitchen was serving 'okra' cooked in sauce with mutton/lamb, a dish that the Iraqi firmly believed was holy and exclusively served in heaven, but that sometimes evil menfolk managed to steal and have it served on earth, especially for their own personal gratification!

The kitchen server heaped a large flat plate with rice, something that looked like a small mountain. On top of the rice he piled another mountain of okra and handed it to him. As he was in the process of doing that, *I heard a shocked Brit standing in line behind me, give a short, but emphatic: 'fook!' under his breath.* Anyway, the plate was duly received, but the Iraqi did not budge. Next, the server, apparently expected to do so, picked up a deep plate, heaped it with another mountain of okra and handed it to him. The Brit, now apparently totally dumbfounded, said nothing more!

I knew the Iraqi expat well and joined him at his table, in order to have lunch together. He was then indulging in mixing spoonfuls of okra with rice and having mouthfuls of it, almost oblivious to what was going on around him. After a few moments of wondering, taking into consideration the ample size of the Iraqi, but also the enormous size of his first plate, I said to him, as a friendly advice: 'Do not leave the second okra dish here after you are done; take it to your room and keep it in the fridge for supper'. *He did not raise his head, but stopped his ritual for a fraction of a second, and then continued eating, without saying a word. Right away, I realized that I had made a serious mistake! I should have known better and kept quiet!* **After finishing his first plate, it took him only a few minutes to gobble all the okra on his second plate**. *As we were leaving the lunch room, I found it proper to pat him gently, but firmly, on the back in order to lend brotherly support to his epic endeavor, while at the same time saying the customary and, in some cases, obligatory:* **'Awafi'**, *which in Arabic meant:* **'Bon appétit; eaten with good health'**.

A CASE OF REGRETTABLY
MISTAKEN IDENTIFICATION

This Iraqi friend was a great companion, especially when I was experiencing a bout of home-sickness during travelling back to work, because he never failed to show a warm, comforting, easy-going attitude; nothing really stressed him, except once. This guy, Kays and I were at the central telephone office at Tibesti Hotel, calling our respective families; the Iraqi's turn to talk came first, when the telephone operator informed him that he had dialed his home number in Poland; the connection at that office was indicated by a phone ringing in a booth beside where we were waiting.

As soon as he picked the receiver up, he exploded with loud hardly controlled mirth and cheerfulness; he was then exuding joy and happiness, and talking incessantly. But all of a sudden he stopped, listened to the other side for a while, then continued, but with subdued low-voice that was full of disappointment. That call ended quickly and he left the booth, a picture-perfect display of misery. I got so concerned that he may have just heard bad news from home, which prompted me quickly to ask him if there was anything wrong there, based on the sharp change in his mood and responsive attitude. He replied disconcertedly: *"No, no; everything is all right there. It is just that when I picked the phone, I firmly believed that my daughter was on the other side; it turned out to be my wife.* (A true case of regrettably mistaken identity; all the expectations he had!)

AFTERNOON WALKS

Kays and I were on a quiet mild afternoon walk, a ritual that we had, through several years, gone through many, many times before. While on those walks, we had dabbled in varied subjects, including anecdotes offered by this writer. Jokes, interestingly, do not just jump to memory, unless prompted to do so by other subjects handled during conversation; on such occasions, they appear to spring to life from where they had been discreetly vaulted in the mind. Since there were only a limited number of jokes which I knew, some of those were repeated over and over again, with a few having a better chance of being reiterated several times more than others.

Unfortunately, jokes are fun only when first heard, and their repetition greatly degrades their potential for making people laugh. Since, between the two of us, I was the sole source of jokes, I had also to be the culprit, who knowingly committed the unforgiveable sin of repetition; however, what had to be done, had to be done, and if the occasion *demanded repetition*, so be it. That afternoon saw one of those inescapable experiences, where the hearer had bear the burden of having to listen to the talker; etiquette and friendship demanded such sacrifice, anyway! So, I went on methodically relating a relevant joke. My friend, Kays, listened quietly and politely, without saying anything or even showing any hint on his face, as was his commendable celebrated habit. That certainly was cause for inward gratification on my side, since I thought that he might have forgotten hearing it before. That satisfaction was good and rewarding, but only for about ten seconds, when he slowly, but convincingly, said: *"Haney, I have heard this for the eighth time!"*

On another occasion, actually preceding the above by several years, I ventured into hinting that I was Christian, a subject I had always refrained from touching while being in a Muslim country. I noticed a smile of bemusement cross his mouth. After some hesitation, he asked me if I knew any Latin, since it is used in some churches. I presently said: "Yes." He then asked me enthusiastically to say some words in Latin, to which I quickly replied: *"E Pluribus Unum!"* which I had previously seen on American coins (meaning "One out of many, or one from many" and referring to the historical fact that the United States was formed, on July 2, 1776, as a single cohesive entity from thirteen colonies). Then, he said: "Tell me more". I quickly replied: *"Sure; E Pluribus Unum"*. He did not make any comment; case closed!

On the serious side of conversation subjects, I remember quite well kays' prophetic words: "We are witnessing history in the making", with reference to the monumental historical events marking the dissolution of the Soviet Union, starting on December 26, 1991. Its collapse led irrevocably to enormous geopolitical significances, not the least of which was the end of the decades-long hostility (existing since the end of World War II) between NATO and the Warsaw Pact power blocks. During those exceptionally consequential times, ethnic nationalism flared within individual Soviet republics, prompting calls for independence. The re-emergence of independent East European countries and re-integration of Germany serves as a shining beacon in the dark recesses of a pre-existing oppressive ideology.

The West has hailed the collapse of the Soviet Union as triumph of democracy over totalitarianism, and that it evidences the superiority of the capitalistic economic-political system over socialism. While there is substance in this general assumption, the eventual demise of the USSR had deep-rooted causes, including excessive focus on military build-up during economic stagnation and spiralling cost, both in man and materiel, of a ten-year catastrophic Afghanistan quagmire (December 1979 to February 1989).

UNCONTROLLABLE, BUT DECIDEDLY SHOCKING!

A few years earlier than the event above, and in the same guest-house, my co-worker friend Kays and I, both in our early fifties, had just finished watching a television program in the TV Room, 'called it a night', and started going back to our respective rooms down the corridor. In those days, I became aware that I had elevated cholesterol. For that reason, I had strict instructions from the doctor to drink a cupful of water with Metamucil after every heavy meal. It was supposed to remove the bad fat present in the food before it got absorbed in the body.

This potion, however, always gave me a serious bloating problem, and on that night, in particular, I had more than the usual of intestinal gas, in terms of both volume and pressure. As we walked down the corridor, I felt that my abdomen was like an over-inflated balloon, and had an overwhelming urge to release the pressure. I tried very hard to keep it in for propriety reasons, as it was a shameful thing in the Middle East, at least until I got to my room. *But, all efforts were futile, and all of a sudden there was a loud BOOM, followed by a string of about thirty continuous small 'firrrrts'. As soon as the initial big one was discharged, Kays* **jumped in the air** *(more like catapulted),* **landing two meters ahead of me, right in front of his room's door; before the firrrrts had ended, he was already in his room,** *with the door closed and firmly locked behind him. I knew him for a long time, but never had seen him so agile; just like a startled bird!* I entered my room and laughed so uncontrollably that I had difficulty with getting enough air in my lungs as I breathed! As I was gasping for air, I realized that I had had a serious situation on hand, one that could potentially develop into undesirable fatality; so, I forced myself to stop and deflect my thoughts the best way I could. *Lesson:* **Even a fart can kill! And, it doesn't have to be toxic!**

BUT, WHERE IS YOUR SENSE OF HUMOUR, SIR!

While working for AGOCO and residing at the guest-house, life was routine; in contrast with mind-occupying work hours, the afternoons were rather dull, and time moved at a slow pace; so, a few of us developed the habit of playing bridge a few times a week. So far, so good!

On one such afternoon, four of us sat around the table and started playing. After a few rounds, I looked at my newly-dealt cards and saw a good hand, but someone objected, because of some technicality, and we agreed to discard what we had and have another one dealt. As I threw my cards on the table, I remarked that I had had a good hand. Another hand was duly dealt, and this time I got an even better cards, so I said: "**All right; this hand is even gooder!**" At that point, the gentleman to my right turned towards me and slowly said: "Huuuh? My six-year-old son says that". But, where is your sense of humour, sir! The same esteemed gentleman later gave a presentation at the National Oil Company's bi-annual meeting at AGOCO. He then was giving a description of an oil field, as indicated by his geophysical studies; in an assessment of its size, he then continued: "The **circumcision** of the … the **circumference** of the field's area..." There followed a spurt of subdued laughter from the expats, who caught that unbefitting 'noun' (considering the serious professional environment at that meeting and the group of listeners present) as soon as it unguardedly exited his mouth!

The sunken lounge on the first floor at the guest-house (also where the 'bridge room' was) frequently saw a small group of Brits chatting in the evening; such occurrences gave me the sense of comradery and a degree of normalcy.

Recollections like these certainly bring back nostalgic memories.

BRIDGE GAMES AND TEAS

While working in Benghazi, Kays and I were courteously invited to a Bulgarian couple's home once every week to play bridge; the husband and I played against the wife and Kays. There was a logical explanation for that arrangement. The husband, although tall and strong, had a mild friendly demeanor; he never complained about the endless mistakes I made playing as his partner. The wife, a beautiful lady, was very polite; she wouldn't have verbally rebuked me, if I had played as her partner and made those mostly-silly mistakes. Even if that ever happened, I could have brushed it aside with a funny remark. But, *detecting an angry look on her face!* That would have sent a cold shiver down my spine! With that 'ingeniously concocted strategy' (on my part of course), I could go there, enjoy the company (while losing) and leave with a happy and content heart. No excessive remorse for playing badly and causing my partner to lose; maybe just a tiny little bit of a feeling of guilt! But, then what are good friends for? They should be able to graciously endure some loss now and then, and maybe a little bit more!

While on such visits, we were treated like family; there were roasted peanuts, coffee, tea, coke (as in coca cola) and 'flash'. The last item, a concoction of pure alcohol retrieved from distilling white grape juice, is composed of ethanol distilled three times (to remove any poisonous methanol). The extract, mixed with coke, is a heavenly treat! That is why I always lost! (Certainly not to be believed)!

A request for such a drink prompted a loud exclamation on an airplane once. As she reached my seat, the beautiful hostess asked me if I liked to have a drink, to which question, I said: **"Yes, please; gin and coke"**. In amazement, or rather disbelief, she said: "Gin and ..." I then repeated my request, to which she said: "I have never heard that one before!" All I had to say then, with assured conviction, was: "Try it!" While I am in the process of finalizing this manuscript, I had a chance to watch an advertisement showing coca cola being added to Canadian rye whiskey! I wouldn't do that, though, since I would lose some of the natural rye flavor.

ENGLISH SOLVES A MISUNDERSTANDING IN ARABIC!

Fairly early in our Benghazi friendship (The singing new recruit, above), Kays and I, together with an Iraqi-Canadian drilling engineer (Thabik), were invited to another expat's apartment located within the huge, fenced multi-building AGOCO apartment-compound adjoining its offices building. The gentleman issuing the invitation, a bachelor from Bulgaria, brought a bottle of 'flash' and another of coca cola. The engineer took it upon himself to serve the rest of the group who were present, and under the wondering gaze of everyone; we were all waiting in anticipation of being handed an invigorating replenishment, something that we certainly cherished. He started to pour some in Kay's glass rather slowly and carefully, until there was as much as a normal 'double' portion.

As the colorless and almost tasteless pure alcohol rose to that level in the glass, Kays said politely: "Hajitna", which in pure Arabic, and as we Iraqis understood it, exactly meant **'our need'.** To the engineer and I, as well, that meant he **needed more** of that stuff, which was the opposite of what he had meant; in his own country's dialect, 'hajitna' meant **'I have my need',** or **'that is enough'.** At that, Thabik poured some more, which was followed by another 'hajitna', but this time with a clear tone of uneasiness. When Thabik heard that, and he wasn't one who could boast of endless patience, he turned the bottle upside down, thereby filling half of Kays' glass. Then we heard the latter scream: **"Stop!"** in English. The Iraqi responded with: "No need to get excited; why didn't you say so in the first place?"

DAVID'S TEA

During the first few years at AGOCO, Kays and I, together with David, an English language teacher and a true gentleman, were not on a rotation system; so, we were off on weekend Fridays. On those days, we enjoyed strolling to the nearby market in **Fuehat**, which was about a fifteen minute leisurely-walk away. There were several **fruit and vegetable stores** there, in addition to others catering for other foods. Libyan fruits and vegetables are indigenous, grown within the country (no fertilizers added) and seasonal; similar to those of Iraq, they are exceptionally flavourful and sweet scented. So, it was a pleasure to have them all the time. We walked along both sides of the market road, which was lined with large *Eucalyptus* trees (allegedly planted a long time ago by Italians), and stopped where some houses had *bougainvillea* bearing shades of red, pink, orange and white flowers; we were also attracted to a fragrant Jasmin bush overflowing the fence around one of the house's garden.

On our way back, David often invited us for a cup of tea in his apartment. There, he brewed Twinning's Earl Gray, fortified with black Ceylon tea, then added milk and a little sugar; those were memorable occasions that are close to my heart. All three of us left the company about ten years ago, but never stopped communicating.

BENGHAZI BRITISH CEMETERY

During the first three years (1988 - 91), as well as post 2000, Kays and I were not on the rotation system and unable to coordinate our vacations and travelling dates. On one warm and sunny weekend Friday morning I was, in the absence of Kays, strolling with David off Fuehat shopping area in Benghazi. Our walk eventually took us to a World War II cemetery, where dead British soldiers were buried during the Second War. I didn't know of its existence, although I was well aware of the famed North Africa campaign and the relevant historical importance of Benghazi and al-Alamein in northeastern Libya, where Generals Erwin Rommel and Bernard Montgomery fought that renowned desert war (June 1940 to May 1943).

I was overwhelmed to see how tidy the cemetery was, and the excellent condition of the grave rock markers, all being intact and painted white and clean in a Middle East country. After expressing amazement, David told me that there were people at that location who were paid to take care of it. We moved around reading names of slain soldiers, mostly Christian, but also Jewish, as indicated by the Star of David. I realized then the presence of a shack belonging to a local caretaker in one corner, but also soon noticed a ferocious dog coming towards us from that direction and told David right away. He was reading an epitaph then and did not reply. The dog got closer to us and I warned David again; when I still got no response, I became nervous. At two feet away, the dog barked and got an irritated 'shoo' from David, together with a movement of his arm indicating 'scram'; my friend didn't even bother to look at the dog! I had heard before of how 'cool' and composed the English people were; but that incident was eye-opening. As a result of that obvious but not too harsh unwelcome, instead of the usual shouting and swearing followed by rock throwing, the dog looked dumbfounded at David, turned around and moved away, but all the while wondering 'why doesn't everyone speak in Arabic?'

As I am writing this story, I tried to find the cemetery's location, using Google maps, and found images of it; it was gratifying to see it as tidy as when I first saw it. Then my eye caught another source of information, actually both as images and video, showing the cemetery being desecrated in 2015, or possibly had been in 2012, according to that information!

UNDERSTANDING THOSE BROKEN ACCENTS!

While at that guest-house, I was one day having breakfast with two Canadian expats. I said something about the beauty of 'cathedrals', but had the misfortune of pronouncing it: *"kathedrils"*; in response, one of the gentlemen present at the table politely asked: "Pardon?" After three miserable failed attempts on my part at pronouncing such an inconceivably 'outlandish word the right way', the other gentleman turned towards the first and said: *"kethedrils"*, to which that esteemed gentleman showed indisputably ample comprehension.

On a different note, and at a later time, another expat colleague (Erhan, a petrographer working with me at the Geological Laboratory in Benghazi) told me that the last time he was in the capital's company guest-house, the following took place. He said that soon after arriving from home after vacation, he had asked the front-desk official about the chances of catching a flight to Benghazi that day. That official, whom we knew to be a truly friendly and helpful person (God bless him), said in broken English: "My frrriend, go airport now; if no aeroplane, come back guest-house; afternoon go in *'Ttinattir' (with a heavy Arabic 't' sound)"*. My colleague made that trip the same day.

The word **'Ttinattir'** kept ringing in my head; something in the word sounded 'familiar', but I just couldn't tell how. After a few days, however, and as I was walking leisurely towards the car taking me to the Geological Laboratory, the following two words suddenly hit me like a hammer on my head, screaming: **"Twin Otter"**; but of course, upon my word. At that moment, I had a good reason to remember the cathedral 'encounter'!

BRUSH WITH DEATH

Kays and I were on one of our daily afternoon's leisurely walks in the quiet (then exceptionally peaceful) city of Benghazi; as was our wont, we strolled to the nearby Fuehat shopping area, bought some fruits and headed back to the guest-house, where we resided. The road we took was rather narrow, but could comfortably accommodate one car going in each direction, in the absence of a median. As we strolled, I heard a rather loud and apprehensive female's voice; I turned my head towards the source and saw a woman, apparently calling our attention and waving her arm frantically in the air. Also, I discerned some movement, which turned out to be a two to three year-old boy on the road walking like a duck towards us; kids, whatever their ages, in that town somehow readily recognized expats, whom they liked and unfailingly waved to, saying: "Hello".

The kid, smiling at us, was on the road, about a foot away from the curb we were on; a taxi, moving in our direction, had duly stopped a few feet from him. We stopped and I smiled at him reassuringly, then started to move in his direction, in order to get hold of him. For some reason, the kid changed his mind, turned around and started to walk backward. Then, as he heard my footsteps behind him, he moved faster. I knew that there was no danger from the stationary taxi on my left that had stopped earlier, and on my right there was no car coming from the opposite direction. I was rather concerned, however, with cars passing by the taxi-cab, since their drivers' view would have been blocked by the taxi.

My premonition came true; a car, racing toward us from the left, was only a few yards behind the taxi. At that instant I thought: "The kid is dead"; that was when he suddenly decided to flee and run towards the other side of the road, where his 'mother' was! At that moment he had just cleared the taxi and was on the open road; I had to make the decision of my life and was seriously considering the thought: "Now, we are both dead"! In a split-second I jumped forward and snatched him upwards towards me, just as the onrushing car started to stop with a loud screeching sound just a couple of inches from where we were and veering to its left, but couldn't do so for several yards on my right as it passed by us. By a miracle, both the kid and I survived; I carried him to his shaken mother on the other side of the road. *Moral: A* ***sobering thought: How sometimes death could be hovering furtively so close to us, and we would still be oblivious to it until the last few seconds of our life!***

WHEN USING ENGLISH WAS REWARDING

During one of those afternoon walks, Kays and I had just left AGOCO's compound and turned right into a road; as we passed a large grain-storage building, I noticed that the gate of that compound was ajar and saw three large guard-dogs inside. I didn't pay much attention to them, since they didn't prove troublesome on previous walks; also, I realized at the time that there were people there, as well, and thought they would very likely restrain the dogs in case of trouble.

I was wrong; as we passed the gate and took about ten steps, I heard a dog running behind us. I turned around and saw one of those dogs charging at us. I instinctively stopped, looked at the dog and while pointing to the ground, I shouted: **"Sit"** in English of course as I would have instinctively done here in Calgary. To my surprise, the dog stopped cold in its track and looked at me in a stupid way; it had never heard that word before but appeared to have an idea of what it meant! It wasn't long before it turned and walked back to the compound. Kays and I continued our afternoon stroll and laughed while talking about what had just happened and the difference the English language made in the outcome of the confrontation. Just in case, we took the other side of the road when we went back to the guest-house; that gate was closed then anyway.

DOWNTOWN BENGHAZI

Kays and I often frequented downtown Benghazi, as it was the central shopping area in that city. Part of that area, previously known as the **Italian Quarter** (now Soug al-Hoot, where vicious fighting had taken place during several months of this year, 2015), was still well kept when we visited. That quarter comprised two four-storey blocks of white-washed buildings, each extending uninterruptedly for about four hundred feet; those two buildings were separated by a narrow, tiled road (approximately 15 feet-across). Window sills were then painted straw-yellow, which went in artistic harmony with the dominating white. Quite a few of those dwelling units had their own private balcony, some (in the shady side) being fenced with black wrought iron railings; their presence enhanced the overall look of the entire structure quite substantially. The upper three floors, the front of which rested on concrete pillars, served as living quarters, whereas the ground floor encompassed shops. The pillars, joined by arches, were still partly covered by narrow (3-inch) elongate and vertically placed slabs of cream-colored travertine; those slabs, surviving the harshness of weather and age, and escaping the unrestrained hands of looters, were 'monuments' reminiscent of previous grandeur.

I very well remember that one of the shops, occupying the ground floor, was very well lit and sold higher-end watches; it was the most prominent in that area. One end of those two buildings accommodated a couple of fruit-and-vegetable shops, together with food stores. I remember an instance when, after a walk in that area, Kays and I started our trip back to the guest-house. We stopped at one of those fruit shops examining their display, when about five local kids (around twelve year old), passing by, stopped and looked with admiration at the fruits for several seconds and left. The owner of that shop then hurriedly came out of his store and called them back rather tersely: **"Hey, you; come here"**. That call took me by surprise, since I would have sworn in any court that none of them touched any of what was displayed outside that shop. The kids stopped and, looking quizzically at the owner, came back obediently looking rather puzzled. As they stood beside us, the owner's hand grabbed several of his store's apples and went: **"Here, take this"**, giving one to each of them. That truly heartening gesture is not uncommon in the Middle East!

That particular Italian Quarter market was interconnected with both the **'Gold Market'** and the **'Covered Market'**; although those two markets were inferior to their counterparts in Europe, we very much enjoyed them. The former, displaying a wealth of varied, exquisite Middle Eastern gold ornaments (mostly between eighteen and twenty carat) was situated on a road curiously named (in Arabic) *"The Garbage Road"!* Those stores also sold a wide array of Italian twelve-carat gold jewelry; the latter were delicately crafted and often immaculately ornamented with colorful rather expensive stones, in marked contrast with their Middle Eastern counterparts (mostly comparatively 'heavy' and intricately designed gold necklaces). The doors of those stores were made of metal and reinforced with iron bars. Where closed, each door had two, or three, huge padlocks which were enough reason to deter burglars; their monstrous presence wasn't enticing at all!

The **'Covered Market'** was long (about five-hundred yards), very narrow (ten feet-across) and rather tortuous, with a narrow (half foot-across) and shallow trough in the middle that served as water drainage; it often carried water during the rainy season of winter. That market was always busy with shoppers, and this reminds me of an incident. Kays and I were just leaving the 'Gold Market' and entering the 'Covered Market', which were not lined and separated by a small open area. From a rather short distance (twenty-feet away), I saw two older and one younger women emerging and coming towards us. As they did so, they were occupied with some store display on their right, and weren't looking in front of them; thus, they were not aware of our presence. They stopped right away, in order to examine what attracted their attention. As we approached them and were but just one yard away, the young lady, who had her back towards us all the time, suddenly turned and looked me straight in the eye. Her eyes were mesmerising pale yellow, nothing comparable with the yellow-amber color that is commonly exhibited by ladies originating in the eastern and north-eastern parts of Europe; that strangely haunting look is still firmly embedded in my memory like that of a ghost.

In retrospect, as I am writing this passage, my mind is flooded with nostalgic memories of those occasions when the two of us walked in downtown Benghazi.

THE LURE OF FRENCH FRIES

As pointed out earlier, I had elevated bad/saturated fat for several years; since becoming aware of that 'predicament', I was meticulous in avoiding anything related to such fats: no eggs, no cheese, cakes, etc. That, in reality meant all the tasty foods that make life much more enjoyable! However, I always had strong self-control and an unwavering discipline, only because I was advised, time and time again, that such fats are **experienced killers** of humans, and that I should never trust them, since they are lurking behind everything that is good (or in this case not good) to put in the mouth.

After a normally long trip home from working on a 'rotation system', with hardly any intake of food, since all I was offered to eat was 'fatty', I arrived in Montreal. I was happy going back home, but also hungry, a feeling I had learnt to ignore. But (and there always is a 'but'), where I was sitting in the waiting hall, there was a food shack, which at the time, against all rules of etiquette regarding the sensitivity of those people plagued with having high levels of bad fat (apology for the long break!), was preparing a fresh batch of **'French fries'**. *The latter made its presence noticeable with its 'resistance-subduing' aroma floating and wandering around the waiting-hall, seeking the nostrils of unsuspecting hungry travellers.* **Talk about the lure of the Sirens in Homer's Odyssey.**

What followed then was an eruption of an unholy struggle between the **malevolent 'pro'** and **benevolent 'con'** forces regarding allowing myself to even consider looking at them, let alone having a 'few' bites of that *'dream food'*. After only a short conflict between the two, the former party won a decisive victory, and those potatoes proved to be the most delicious *'French fries'* I ever had in my life! While enjoying a whole pack of potatoes, I had this resolute thought on my mind: "To Hell with that medical advice!" (Present-day medicines have brought such fats down to normal levels! Olé!)

This instance reminds me of an earlier incident. I was working with a branch of a **large, rich oil company** for a while. One day, that branch received a stern 'memo' from the president of the company, himself; the 'memo' advised everyone to *make every effort humanly possible* to cut down on expenses, specifically mentioning office supplies. One morning, while working there, I heard the sound of an electrical pencil-sharpener nearby, a familiar sound in a busy office anyway. Then the sharpener stopped and, unexpectedly, I heard a hoarse but subdued voice go: **"To Hell with the President's memo"**! I turned around and saw another geologist trying frantically to save the life of an extremely short stub of a sharpened pencil, with only its back tip showing, from a resolute embrace inside the sharpener. After several futile efforts, the gentleman went away and came back with not one, but **two**, brand-new pencils!

OF EATING HABITS AND ETIQUETTE

One day (around 2003), a new expat (geologist I believe) arrived from the Far East to work at AGOCO; he was of a markedly different culture than those of both the Middle East and the Western World. At some point in time, though, he might have acquired some information on the customs that were followed in that new and unfamiliar environment, which is certainly a commendable and necessary practice in such cases. Some of that advice may have been related to eating dinner and supper: soup (or salad) first, to be followed by the main dish and dessert, respectively.

Within one or two days after his arrival, I was taking lunch in the cafeteria with Kays. Halfway through that solemn daily ritual, he drew my attention to the new-comer and asked me to prudently look in his direction, which I did. I saw him take a spoonful of soup, followed by another of the main course (mixed rice and vegetable-meat), only to be topped by a bite from a piece of cake, a sequence of events that was repeated.

THE ACCIDENT!

When I arrived in Benghazi to start my new job as geologist, there were very few cars on the road, and those *invariably showed evidence of previous unpleasant encounters with other cars;* there were no new ones around!

That North African country is huge and has thousands of miles of desert roads. Because of the small number of cars available, one could drive on a country road for an hour without meeting another car. One day, however, the following event was narrated by one of the field-based expats. He said: "Yesterday, as we were coming back from the company's field office, guess what I saw? In the middle of the road, in all of those vast empty expanses there were two cars that had demolished each other in an accident!" *[They must have driven in the desert on a moonless night, with no lights on; even then, there would still be enough star-light, as the sky would be jam-packed with them, a magnificent spectacle to behold!]*

Even with the small number of vehicles around, Kays and I barely escaped being crushed, once, by one of those four-wheel vehicles. We had just left the guest-house on our daily afternoon walk, one of few pleasures we had there. We soon arrived at a cross-road junction of 2 two-lane roads, each with a narrow (one foot-wide) median island. At the intersection, we halted for a while, since I never crossed a road without looking both ways for cars, a trait my father had taught me when I was very young. I looked around and saw one car going in our direction on the same road we were taking, and another that was coming towards us from ninety degrees on our left; they were at different distances from the intersection and both cars were driven at moderate speeds.

There were no problems that I could anticipate, thereby started crossing, a move that was directly followed by Kays. The logic behind the decision to cross the road was that it was safe to do so, since those two cars were at different distances from the intersection where we were; the closer to it (the car moving parallel to us) was logically expected to cross first. As we reached the median island, we heard a huge bang, and when I turned to my left I realized that both cars had arrived there at the very same time; neither one gave way to the other. However, the car coming from our left (apparently speeding in order to get there first) crashed into the one moving in our direction; the latter, whose driver could have then been half asleep, veered sharply and I saw it charging towards us. At that moment I vehemently thought that if we were lucky enough to survive, then we would be guests at a hospital having neither experienced doctors, nor medicine. Miraculously, the car stopped barely an inch from us, and we survived with all our limbs intact; it was a close call!

CHEEZA!

When I worked for AGOCO, the company was in the habit of routinely sending some of its local employees abroad, mostly to the United Kingdom, for 'training'. Those trips, taking three to six months each, were designed as a 'public relations' gesture, with management not expecting much, if anything, in terms of real beneficial training from the employees who are sent out on such pursuits; they (the trainees), as would be expected, invariably came back happy and content, and that was crucial.

Once, I was stuck in Tripoli for a day or so, waiting at the company's guest-house for an airplane reservation and a ticket to go back to Benghazi. At that time, the Tripoli guest-house also had the honour of providing lodging to two such 'distinguished guests' who had the privilege of training in England and had just come back from that country after a stay of six months. They were as happy as could be and talked with each other all the time about their exploits there. During some of those dialogues I heard one of them repeat the 'word' "cheeza", expressing amazement at what his companion was saying. The way he uttered that word, together with relevant circumstances, led me to interpret it as 'Jesus', which the guy may have picked up by association with English people.

What intrigued me, though, was why on earth would someone from that country want to invoke the name of 'Jesus', considering its people's devout overwhelming entrenchment in their own religious teachings and age-long traditions! The next day I had an opportunity to make that trip. On the plane to Benghazi I had some time to ponder the harrowing trip I had gone through, and was waiting patiently to reach the guest-house. Then, suddenly, it hit me; the guy must have thought those English people, with whom he was associated, say 'cheeza' (after cheese, that is, as he understood it, rather than Jesus); at that, I wondered: "Was that all he had learned in six months, and wrongly too?!"

JOSHUA'S FEMUR

Joshua, one of AGOCO's recruits, was of gigantic proportions, particularly when viewed by small men like myself. He lived at the end of the twentieth century in Benghazi and was certainly valuable to society, as most people are.

One million years later, the second-year geology students were having a paleontological expedition in the same locale where Joshua at one time had lived; this same area of North Africa also happened to be one of world's well known locations where dinosaurs had lived for an extended period of time a long time ago. After a few days of zealous search for fossils, especially those belonging to the more cherished dinosaurs, and easily identified by huge bones, one of the students repeatedly poked a promising part of an outcrop with his geological hammer. He was positive that he had found something remarkable, and he was right; it was a fossil of 'colossal' dimensions.

He quickly removed the rocks surrounding the fossil, since they were not excessively hard in that outcrop. As he was working feverishly on clearing the protruding part of that fossil, he became more and more convinced and excited; he could easily detect the presence of a huge bone, about a meter long. At the top of his voice, and with overflowing excitement, he called his paleontology teacher: **"Professor, professor, come quickly; I found it, I found a dinosaur bone"!**

The professor, who at the time was in the middle of pointing out some fossils' features to a group of students, threw away what specimens he had in his hand and rushed to where the caller was. After twice surviving hazardous stumbling incidents, he was able to zoom there within a few seconds. As he approached, brimming with excitement, he yelled: *"Where; where is it?"* The student happily obliged, and the professor went down on his knees to thoroughly examine that fossil. After a few minutes of gradually ebbing excitement, he stood up and in a voice full of disappointment said: **"This is not a dinosaur's fossil; it is Joshua's femur bone".** (Partly a true story, at least where it relates to Joshua's size).

PART SIX: TRAVEL

THE 6/49 OF ALL ENCOUNTERS

Before joining the Arabian Gulf Oil Company in Benghazi, in the latter part of June, 1988, I worked five years with an oil-service company in Calgary. During part of that period (two to three years) I shared the burden of work responsibilities with a female geologist associate. One day she informed me of quitting her job at that company and moving with her family to a teaching assignment in Libya. One year after she left, I moved to that same country myself, but to a different city to start my new job, which turned out to be *the most fantastic that can ever be hoped for, in terms of work type, job location and the pleasure of having humble, good-natured local people around.*

During the larger part of the day I worked at the company's **Geological Laboratory**, situated twenty kilometers out of town; living quarters was at the company's guest house in the city. Soon after arriving, I met Kays and Thabik; a deep sense of homesickness drew the three of us together, and within a short time we started to take afternoon walks along a few roads around the company compound. The road adjoining the company was then rather old and very short, but wide enough to accommodate two cars *[that road was shortly later replaced with a state of the art street built by a German construction firm]*.

On one relatively mild afternoon in late August, all three of us decided to take a walk on that old road. As we took a few steps outside the company compound, an over-loaded taxi passed slowly by, then stopped several meters away in front of us. During those days, there were very few old and dilapidated cars in that city, a state of affairs imposed at the time by the Libyan government. So, it was surprising to see a moving vehicle with four wheels, and more amazing still was that it stopped near us. My first thought then was that its occupants may have wanted to ask passers-by for directions; judging from the car's overloading with household items suggested that the occupants were in a process of moving. A passenger stepped out and turned towards us; I instantly recognized him as being the husband of that female Calgary geologist, someone whom I had met before at the service oil-company, where both his wife and I had worked. I approached the car and saw her, with her children, inside. We talked for a short while, after which they left on their way.

I then explained to my companions the circumstances, pointed out the miniscule likelihood of the two of us meeting there, and how incredible that improbability was, considering timing. I had just arrived in that city, and had waited that afternoon in my room for the temperature to go down before asking my companions to join me for a walk. My previous geologist associate, who happened to have just returned from a vacation in Calgary to start another year of teaching in Libya, recognized me walking there, as her car approached us from behind. Also, that incident took place along a short stretch of road that a car took only a few seconds to cover from one end to the other, after which we would have left it and continued on another road! (What are the chances of such an encounter? Intriguing)!

A CHANCE ENCOUNTER ON THE BOAT

Libya was under a United Nations' air-travel embargo during most of the 1990s; because of that overwhelming condition, travelling to and from Libya in part required sea travel to Malta, or overland travel to Tunis or Egypt, in order to be able to reach Europe by airplane. During the period of time I worked there, the most difficult part of my job was actually reaching Benghazi and getting back home on vacation. More often than not, each one-way trip took three nights and four days, sometimes longer. Travelling meant going on ships of 400-traveller capacity, but loaded with double that number, dilapidated local airplanes that dwindled in number close to zero, fair and horrid weather, excessive pushing and shoving, and having to deal with nice and not-so-nice people.

On one such excursion, I was sitting with Kays in the lounge of the ship heading south towards the North African coast; it was a pleasant sunny day and the sea uncommonly calm. There were four passengers sitting on a table next to us. One quick look told me that I didn't know them as fellow co-workers at AGOCO. As I sat chatting with my friend, I heard my name being called; it was one of those four gentlemen. I had no recollection of him, whatsoever. I answered politely, after which he asked me if I remembered him, in response to which, and while wearing a bemused smile, I replied in the negative. After a few seconds of puzzled wonderment, he announced his name. He turned out to be the older son of a gentleman who was headmaster of the 'boys-only' preliminary school which I attended when I was in grades one and two. *[I still vividly remember my first day of attendance, arriving there, accompanied by my father, during a class session; I was asked then to wait outside Grade One classroom until the recess bell rang. After a few minutes of being left alone, I took advantage of being on a walkway/deck which was raised by two feet above the schools inspection/playground; I sat there in my shorts, with dangling legs, wondering what I was going to find next.]* As I remember that headmaster had two or three sons and a young daughter who was a year younger than I was.

My parents and the headmaster's family were friends, and they visited each other. When I passed grade one, their daughter was old enough to start it. The headmaster wanted his daughter to join his school in particular because of convenience, as it adjoined his own house. At the time he wished that she had a trustworthy companion and he wanted me to be that companion! So, during a visit he suggested to my father that I repeat grade one, a wish which my Father accepted out of friendship. This story happened fifty-seven years earlier, and from those olden days this traveller and I never saw each other. I was then only seven years old and, after all these years, he could still recognize me even when I got old! (Outstanding)!

A MEMORABLE SEA TRIP BACK TO OUR JOBS
(The encounter with the Passport-Desk Officer)

As mentioned above, travelling to and from Libya (then under UN-imposed air travel embargo) in most cases entailed a difficult sea travel-trip from/to Malta. In order to make life a little bit easier, I was fortunate most of the time to be able to travel with my close friend Kays, especially that we both shared similar customs and spoke Arabic very well, although often preferred to use English.

The term 'difficult' only depicts the tip of an iceberg; total fatigue and exhaustion, instead, due to the lack of sleep and proper nutrition are more faithfully descriptive. Further to an account related earlier (The Pilot and His Cousin; 2), the following 'story' is narrated here by virtue of its relevance to such endurance. Fifty years subsequent to that story, my cousin's cousin (the humble writer of this manuscript) had to go through the ordeal of non-sleep several times a year while working overseas. Each trip to work or back home took three or four nights and days, through which there was virtually no sleep (I couldn't sleep on airplanes, cars, or ships, and sometimes even on a strange hotel pillow, *unless we were cordially introduced first of course*). I remember one of those trips, when I had to stay awake four nights, except for a total of six hours of intermittent sleep. At the end of that trip, my body became so used to being in the 'awake mode' that I started to assume that **not sleeping was the norm**.

In between those sleepless stretches of time (not necessarily differentiated as being part of night or day), my mind and body would momentarily, unconsciously and swiftly slide, during a fleeting moment, into the abyss of that dark pit known as 'sleep'. One such plunge into oblivion took place one night on a shuttle-ship as a result of utter exhaustion. I was then lying on my back in the upper bunk; my inseparable friend, Kays, who had similar problems with sleeping during those trips, had laid down on the lower. Being a light sleeper by nature, I half woke up when I heard a faint cough seemingly coming from far, far away, then another and another, getting progressively louder; then, after a short pause, I heard a loud and resolute 'Haney' coming from 'downstairs'. Jolted out of that glimpse of blissful respite, I went: "What; what?" only to be answered by a question from the lower bunk: "Are you awake?" I replied: "Yes; I am, now"! Then he went on talking and talking, and I gave short responses. Within ten minutes, his remarks became less and less audible, and then stopped altogether; I said something, and there was no response. I peeped over the side of the bunk, and there he was, sleeping like a baby! I stayed awake for the rest of the night.

After one of those grueling sea trips, we disembarked at Tripoli's sea port and approached the immigration office. Soon our turn came to have our passports 'processed' at the immigration officer's desk. I, being Canadian, felt more at ease than him, since I could freely work in that country. Kays approached the officer first; and since standing in line meant little there, I had to stand close beside him, but a little way to the back, in order to keep my 'turn'. The **passport-desk officer** at that port-of-entry had an inspective look at my friend's passport, then, instead of following an implicitly understood and specially prescribed procedure in the form of stamping a separate visa sheet without a question, that 'unlucky' officer chose to ask Kays something in Arabic. At that, my friend, whom I sensed felt embarrassingly inconvenienced, **mumbled something incomprehensible** under his breath in reply, something that I couldn't possibly relate to any of the recognizable world languages, or dialects, as far as I could tell with my limited store of knowledge. In the few seconds it took me to try to comprehend what he had actually said, the officer asked him the same question again, this time slowly in order to give it a chance to sink in, but got the same **'valuable' information**. At that point, the officer, with fuming but perfectly controlled face, stamped Kays' visa sheet rather unceremoniously and handed his passport to him without raising his head! *My turn was considerably less 'traumatic' to that officer, as he readily got answers to whatever he had to ask.*

On another occasion, I arrived in Malta the same day that my friend Kays had departed on the shuttle boat, making it doubly difficult for me psychologically. I had to take the Libyan boat (Garnata, or her sister ship Toletela) that same day at 'all costs' and try to get in touch with him the next morning before he travelled to Benghazi. I passed through the customs office of Malta's sea port and headed towards the ship I was taking to Libya. I didn't hurry, since I saw that there already was a large crowd ahead of me. A multitude of men were gathered on the wide and fully lowered gate at the stern of a large sea-going passenger shuttle-ship; that gate worked both as gangway/thoroughfare and car entrance into and out of the ship. That entrance was packed like sardines with people. Since passengers kept coming, I had no option but to go for it; if I stayed behind, I wouldn't have had any chance to get a bunk-bed. Getting one of those was imperative, as I could lie down on my back, thereby reducing the effect of sea-sickness. *(In this regard, I remember that on one such trip, the ship heaved several meters up, taking my body with it, then it suddenly sank; I felt then that the bulk of my body came down with the ship, while my stomach was still up there)!*

The middle part of the gangway at the back of that ship was so densely packed with waiting travellers that even an ant couldn't pass through; as I was not large, but certainly not smaller than an ant, I decided to try my luck at its far left-hand side. The only place I could find on the gangway at that end was just enough to accommodate my right foot. My left foot was free-floating in the air; there was nothing underneath it, but dark, visibly unfathomable and ominous sea water, some ten feet below. It was a difficult and immensely hazardous undertaking, but not impossible to manage; **all I had to do** (as if) **was keeping my body's center of gravity** (plus my carry-bag that was held in my left hand) **over the 'inside' of that edge** (simple physics; easier said than done)! As some sort of safeguard against a potential detrimental fall in the water, I had my right hand poised close to the back of a big guy's jacket in front of me, which I was ready to clutch, like a pair of pliers, at any fleeting hint of a side push, leading to an undesirable splash. There were several agonizingly scary moments, but that tactic worked, and I did have a bunk! The ship's cabins held two or four bunks each, the latter including a small washroom.

The bunks had a firm, but heavily used, cushion lacking bed covers; however, there was a heavy blanket; each bunk had a white pillow that had been used for months on end without a pillow cover, thereby turning into grayish-brown, as opposed to originally white. Some of those cabins had uninvited visitors in the form of cockroaches which had the uncontested freedom of moving around the walls and ceiling. In this regard, the presence of notes in the cabins reading: "No cockroaches allowed in this cabin" could have read: "No humans allowed in this cabin", instead. In either case, or even if both notices had been put on the wall, I do not quite believe that either of the two species would have cared, but for different reasons of course. the Expats counted the time they had to wait for that magic trip (back home) by the seconds, while the locals were more than eager to reach Malta, in order to load their gigantic bags with merchandize they later sold for good profit when they went back home. As for the cockroaches, they found enough food in those cabins to satisfy their own 'king'!

To be fair, however, travellers were always treated cordially by the passport officials and crew on those boats, presented with bottles of water and offered well organized free meals in a clean cafeteria. Taking those ships with all the difficulties they presented, however, for me was the ultimate joy, that is when travelling northwards going back home.

Finally, after fourteen hours of a grueling sea trip (in this case southward), we crossed the Mediterranean and arrived at Tripoli sea port. There was the usual stampede of young locals, carrying bags of merchandize, towards the entrance of the customs offices. I was quick enough to be within the middle of a pack, but that meant a process of **'sardine stuffing'**. After four days of travel, I had little energy left; also, my small body (starting with 110lb when I left Calgary) was not, without proper feeding, capable of pushing and shoving (actually not even in its prime condition). As is the case with small people, I had to rely on something other than muscles and weight; in the annals of military doctrines, it is commonly called: *'Doctrine of maneuverability ingenuity'* *leading to 'survivability'.* (Don't search the internet for that; it doesn't exist).

All around me were larger guys (but of course). Great geologists have in the past correctly perceived that in sedimentary rocks, the larger particles (pebbles) leave more voluminous space (pores) between them than smaller ones (sand); (hurrah for geology)! Based on that principle, I had enough space to squeeze in between larger men, but not enough to 'insert' the whole of my body there all the time. In one instance, my body was distributed in three such spaces, **fortunately all interconnected**. My left foot was firmly caught between two gentlemen, thus being immobile, while most of my body was secure in the middle, but most of my right arm was not visible to me. I knew, however, that it was still there because I could tell that it was clinging firmly and resolutely to my carry-bag, although the latter being out of sight, as well! In that somewhat precarious situation, my main concern was to **stay intact**. So, I appropriately decided not to engage in any futile life-saving fight, but rather achieve the same objective of keeping in one piece by just *'flowing'* with the human tide; I had, though, to ascertain that all of my body parts flowed at the same rate and at the same time! At some point, thereafter, I mercifully heard a young gentleman shout: "Let the white-haired old man enter, let him go through the door", an inward personal wish that was mercifully granted, *albeit begrudgingly.*

THE MALTESE CONNECTION
With No Reference to the Movie's Falcon

The tiny island of Malta was, for the ten years (1991 - 2000) covering the United Nations' air travel embargo imposed on Libya, a pivotal linking juncture that was both distressing and blissfully welcome in the Expatriate's struggle to reach their workplace in Libya and getting back home. It served as the last air-connection point towards Libya and the end of western civilization and culture, while being a coveted starting point going back home.

The island is a place where, over the centuries, different cultures have intermingled in a series of processes that were often related to wars and conquest. Those who are acquainted with Italian, Arabic, French and English languages can quickly detect their respective linguistic influences on the native Maltese language; words, such as 'Triq', for example, constituting a common part of road signs, is markedly Arabic (teriq). The name 'Sliema', designating a major population and tourist centre in Malta, is linked to the opening words of the Hail Mary prayer, which in Maltese are "Sliem Għalik Marija", which is close to the Arabic version "alsalamu alieki ya Meriam". The Maltese word 'sliem' stands for peace or serenity, which, in Arabic is 'salam'. In this regard, I once became pleasantly surprised while waiting at a hotel's reception desk. A young employee was in the middle of writing down the personal information I gave her, when a young man, apparently someone she knew, entered and said something to her in a low voice; without raising her head, she sweetly responded: *"Shinoooo?"* This word is typically Iraqi for 'what' (as in gruff American usage, rather than the British version 'I beg your pardon', which usually is uttered politely).

The Tranquil and peaceful tiny island of Malta is ideally located in the Mediterranean Sea, serving as a strategic point between Southern Europe and North Africa. The sun seemingly has an eternal contract with the island, whereby the former guarantees the supply of joyful brightness all year round, long warm summers and mild winters! In some ways, this service may have helped enriching the friendliness of the inhabitants. Places within the island's towns, where I had a chance to visit, were markedly clean; signs of cleanliness of the inhabitants were ubiquitous, in terms of tidy roads and the external appearance of their rather small dwellings, which, typical of older sections of European cities, characteristically line narrow, in part tortuous, roads. Tidiness is also reflected on their wide seaside promenades, especially in Sliema, where a long very popular arcuate stretch of shoreline is lined with hotels, bars, cafes and restaurants facing a two-way road and a deep harbour/bay, along which several rocky beaches were carved in the island's limestone.

That promenade, stretching for a couple of kilometres, is ideal for long peaceful walks. I still remember how well that walkway had been finished with patterned pink and cream-coloured interlocking bricks, and dotted with well-spaced young trees, while several benches, strewn at convenient distances, provided places for the locals and tourists to sit and relax. A metal railing, heavily repainted green, had been erected for safety purposes on the other side of that pleasant walkway, where there is a significant sharp drop in ground level.

From its eastern side, the promontory of Sliema exchanges exceptional views with that of Valletta, to its southeast, across the bay. At the time of my visits, there was a covered shuttle boat/ferry between those two areas, which took only ten minutes to reach the other side. A bus ride between the same two points took about forty minutes on the bus, as the latter had to travel a long stretch of tortuous roads built around deeply cut bays. Notwithstanding the difference in the time each trip took, both were thoroughly enjoyable.

Public-transport buses on the island are outstanding icons reminding one of Cuba's ancient, but now coveted, American cars. At the time when I had an opportunity to be in Malta, I was amazed by the common and, in some ways, magnificent presence of old buses (mostly Leyland, but also Bedford, AEC, DAF, Volvo and even Dodge from the nineteen-fifties, *the good old days*); those buses have been customised, detailed and decorated. On the exterior, their lower half is often painted medium 'cadmium yellow', while the upper half is white; both sections are separated by a wide strip of deep 'cadmium orange'. As travellers enter those buses, they are invariably struck by the wonderfully 'unique' display of religious symbols, mostly in the form of images, adorning the dashboard; those items often are placed in front, but also sometimes above the driver's seat. My impression was that many of the inhabitants, including the younger generation, were deeply religious. In this regard, once I had a chance to go to church there on a Sunday morning, and was surprised to see a comparatively large number of teenagers and adolescents attending mass. Propensity towards religion also is well reflected by the common presence of traditional catholic emblems (including mini-statuettes) on the doors of houses. Houses on the island have often been built with sharply cut yellowish-beige, evenly textured and fine-crystalline limestone blocks, about a foot long and half a foot wide. Quite a few dwellings boast beautifully designed and brightly painted balconies, giving living space a valuable extra extension over the road.

The island of Malta bears evidence of rich historical past covering a wide stretch of time, notably reflected in ancient Neolithic temples, both with planar and arcuate enclosures, and not-so-old cathedrals. Two of the latter: the Roman Catholic St. John's Co-Cathedral in Valletta (Home of the Knights of Malta) and St. Paul's Metropolitan Cathedral in Mdina, are truly illustrious. Both are superbly designed and built, and have been magnificently finished. The whole floor of the former cathedral represents a series of contiguous tombs, each of which is covered with a marble slab that has been uniquely and intricately inlaid and showing a singular colourful art composition. *[https://en.wikipedia. org/wiki/St._John's_Co-Cathedral.]* St. Paul's provides a treasure of marvellous frescoes. *[https://en.wikipedia.org/ wiki/St._Paul's_Cathedral,_Mdina]*

While Sliema has its own glamourous persona, especially at night, Valletta is where tourist shopping takes place. Every time Kays and I were there together, we very much enjoyed strolling through that shopping area, be it summer or winter. Sometimes, when chatting, we still remember one of those walks, in particular; it was very cold with drizzling rain, and so we decided to go back to our hotel. As we started our return trip, we saw a small café and decided to have a hot cup of tea first; as the waiter was going back to get what we ordered, I noticed the presence of bottles of liquor and whisky. After a few words exchanged between Kays and myself, we decided to have whisky, instead, so I quickly called the waiter back and asked him to change the order. A little whisky was a great idea; however, it was rather cold, even inside the café. Then, I had a 'brilliant' idea worthy of Einstein himself, and said to myself 'why not'; I called the waiter once more and asked him to bring both orders 'added' to each other. That verbal exchange was a good cause for merriment, and that episode, as trivial as it may appear, constitutes a part of the nostalgic memories surrounding our overseas jobs.

On another trip, we shared a crisp freshly **'baked in Malta'** loaf of bread on a bus, while praising its flavour and marvelling about how good it smelled. I love European bread, several varieties of which are now fortunately available here in Calgary, including: Pumpernickel rye *bâtard,* Rhineland *bâtard,* Reuben rye, black Russian rye loaf, caraway *bâtard,* Kraft corn *bâtard,* Bohemian pumpernickel, ancient nine-grain *bâtard* and *Jewish* light *rye bread.*

Over the years, Kays and I managed to travel together several times. Sometimes, we had enough extra time to wander about the small departure lounge at Malta airport and enjoy a cup of tea. Since we both had elevated bad fat, we stayed away from all forms of 'yum-yum' sweets; simple, dry bread-sticks that I often brought with me when travelling, alternately, gave us a great deal of contentment, that is after they had been dunked in the tea. Such reflections represent awareness of basic contentment, and I relate those outwardly insignificant happenings only to express my firm understanding and acceptance of the varied facets of happiness. The latter can show itself in many different ways, some manifestations of which are anything but sophisticated; it can be so simple as to be readily equated with just 'being content', if only one could recognize that connection. [I should have been a philosopher, instead of geologist; this last statement is not meant for Plato's eyes!]

My memory now takes me to another story, which was a cause for stupefaction and melancholy. On one homeward trip, I checked in a hotel one afternoon and asked the hotel desk clerk to have me awakened at four o'clock in the morning, since someone was picking me up to take me to the airport at five. I was ready downstairs at quarter to five. It was winter then, with long nights, and outside was still pitch black; the reception room inside the hotel was dimly lit, since it was still too early in the morning. At the desk, there was a young receptionist, whom I approached and explained to him that I was expecting a shuttle car to the airport.

A small part of that room was raised two steps above the rest, and that enclosure had several large tropical plants; since at times I felt more comfortable being with flora than among fauna, I decided to wait there. Ten minutes later, the door opened and a young person darted towards the reception desk; he leaned forward and 'whispered' something. There was a brief response from the receptionist, after which that intruder dashed back towards the door and left; all of that happened like a dream. We have a saying that goes 'I twirled my head this way and that way' with perplexion, then amounting to concern; after all, it was the right time for the shuttle driver to appear, wasn't it? Following a short period of hesitation, I moved towards the desk and asked the receptionist who that person was. My premonition turned out to be true when he said: "Yes, it was the shuttle driver; where were you?" I had nothing to say, but ask for a taxi.

The following story, by contrast, is about "as good luck would have it"! Once, during the afore-mentioned air-travel embargo, I had to go from Benghazi to Tunis by taxi, a trip that took about fourteen hours. Then, I had a comfortable half an hour between arriving at Malta airport and catching my next flight from there to Frankfurt. Everyone was on the airplane in time, prompting me to be happily confident that I had no problem connecting at the small Malta airport. Our plane's flight from Tunis, unfortunately, was delayed 45 minutes; that meant a subsequent postponement in reaching my home for a precious whole day. After a short trip, the plane arrived at Malta airport; I had to clear customs, go downstairs and rebook my next flight. There were four people ahead of me waiting their turn to approach the "arrival" passport desk. Within a few seconds, there was a public announcement: **"last call for flight ... to Frankfurt"**. What? The plane I was taking was still there! It was an 'emergency' situation; so, I quickly approached the custom officer and told him that they had just made the last call for my flight. Without hesitation, he picked the phone up and contacted the departure gate; I made it, and there ends a 'marvellous' story!

HANEY   and   KAYS
(Unwavering Support for Each Other During Difficult Times)

NARROW ESCAPADES

While working for AGOCO I used to have three to four vacation trips back home (four within the rotation system). Going home and coming back I had to take six to eight flights per one round-trip; over sixteen years I ended up on a quite few fights. As I am still alive to prove it, all flights culminated safely; however, some were rather scary, albeit only for a short (but seemingly eternal) time.

At around midnight on one trip I was one of about eight passengers on a chartered flight from southern Europe to Tunis. The weather that night was terrible; very windy, indeed; after a while our small propeller plane started experiencing difficulties keeping straight and maintaining its height; it acted just like a kite, moving up and down and shifting sideways. I truly believed that that was the end; after a typically exhausting trip and going in the 'wrong' direction then, it didn't much matter anyway. A week later that particular plane, or a similar one, crashed in the Mediterranean in turbulent weather killing several people.

On another trip, I made it safely to Tripoli and managed to obtain a ticket on the country's national airline to Benghazi. The plane was one of only two that were still in service then and for political reasons all aircraft service had to be conducted locally (not internationally). Some of the expats, including myself, had a very good impression of the local-airline pilots, as experience derived from flying with them so often had taught us. So, I had no concern about flying on those planes, *except once*. As it happened, I was one of the first to board the plane through a door right at its far back end; I headed directly towards the back end of the plane and sat on the last seat, on my left as I approached. Soon after sitting down I started to become anxious, a feeling I never had before in similar circumstances; this feeling turned quickly into nervousness I had rarely experienced at any time. [Was it a 'sixth' sense? If that was the case and such a sense does exist, then I can understand why women, commonly purported to possess one, always beat men when it comes to social issues!]

Nervousness quickly turned into extreme fear; it was terror incarnate, mixed with utter panic, and I wanted to leave the airplane right away. I prayed to God that I could do so, but, alas, if I had tried it, I likely would have been incarcerated and landed in a jail to be excessively questioned by the police for the *'real' reason* behind the change of heart; with my size and age, something like that could have killed me. I tried to calm myself the best way I could. The rest of the passengers took their places, and after a short while the plane was pulled backward for about fifty yards, where it stopped for a customary last-minute check.

One engine was put on full throttle right behind my back, since the thirty year-old plane we were on had two engines in the back, close to the tail; so far so good! Then it was the other engine's turn, and all hell broke loose; there was very loud banging that made me think the whole of the tail section was coming off. I thought: "Oh, my God; this it!" The engines were instantly turned off and everyone were asked to leave because one of the twin-engines had just broken down! It could simply have failed during takeoff, or when we were up in the air, but it miraculously **'chose'** not to! *Was that gut-feeling perception a 'sixth' sense?*

My daughter and I went to our bank (not our own of course!) here in Calgary two weeks ago (November, 2015); we were waiting in line when a young bank employee, bearing a feminine Spanish-name tag, approached us and asked if we needed help, to which I answered in the affirmative, indicating that I needed a credit card. She happened to be the right person to talk to, since she handled such requests personally at that particular branch. As we talked, I had a probing look at the young lady. She was of medium height and slim, and she had tanned complexion; her hair was long, smooth and pitch-black, reminding me of Latin American Mayan natives.

Before moving to her office, I took the liberty of saying to her: "You are Columbian". She stared at me for what seemed to be an eternity, making me wonder if she understood what I had just said, then replied with a simple: "Yes". At that we went to her office and sat down, and I was asked what kind of credit card I wanted to apply for, which I promptly indicated. Then she started working on her computer, but only for a few seconds. Suddenly she stopped, turned and asked me how I knew that she was Columbian. I cited her facial features, plus her name-tag, as indicators of her being of Spanish descent. During the last ten years, here in Calgary, I have been aware that there was a growing number of Latinos coming to this city (known for better job opportunities and more lucrative salaries), and that quite a few of those Latinos came from Columbia because of security concerns over there. That fact suggested to me the likelihood of her being one; but her hair was definitely a determining factor. I was, however, prudent enough to omit any reference to Native American hair, just in case she didn't appreciate it, favouring, instead, references to Spanish heritage; (case closed.)

Today, my daughter and I went to the same branch once more, in order to obtain a "money order". This time, we were politely asked to approach an older lady-cashier. Her complexion was pure white, something that reminded me of English ladies I had come across while living in England for four years. Notwithstanding her pure Canadian accent (rather than British, which is easy to recognize), she didn't look like a 'typical' Calgarian, but decidedly appeared more akin to English immigrants in this city. It occurred to me then that she had come from the far-east (as in Atlantic Canada; that is almost as far away from Calgary as the real Far East, anyway). I asked her if she came from Nova Scotia, to which she replied: "Yes, yes, but I am not a real Nova Scotian; I only lived there ten years". So far so good; then I had the courage to ask if her ancestry came from northern England or Scotland. She was shocked and started telling us how her grand grandparents had emigrated from northern England to Canada, with some other relatives moving to the Carolinas. My last question was: "Was that by any chance a long, long time ago?" Again she concurred saying: "Oh, yes; that was sometime in the olden times, two to three hundred years ago". And then she went on to tell us a long amusing story.

I remember my father, a long time ago, telling us the following proverb: "A blind man, holding a rifle, shot randomly, and in doing so he accidentally hit a hopping rabbit (one of the most difficult animals to hunt!") Were those thoughts, which I had experienced, just **lucky** random coincidences?! Were they **"fluke"**, as in billiards/snooker! **Or** truly a **'sixth' sense**?! Perhaps only a woman can answer that!

ABORTED TAKEOFF

I remember once taking a flight on a **McDonnell Douglas DC-9** from Vienna. I loved travelling on those planes, because they had the ability to shoot up in the air after only a short run on the tarmac and acquiring rapid acceleration; I found it thrilling, imagining myself being on a jet fighter!

On that particular occasion, the plane hurtled down the tarmac until, I thought, it attained the 'speed of no return' and I said to myself: "This is it; we shall be up in the air in a second". That didn't happen; instead of leaving good Mother Earth, I simultaneously heard sharp brakes screeching and what appeared to be reversed engines concurring with a sensation of rapid deceleration, all accompanied by a mild veering of the plane to the right. My thought then was: "Is there enough of tarmac left, which may accommodate halting the plane before we left it!" What perhaps took the plane twenty seconds to stop was, in retrospect, an age-long experience! Stopping the vehicle at that speed was a marvelous showpiece of control; *hurrah for the captain and his assistants*!

The passengers were told that a malfunction had developed with one of the engines and that we had to turn back. Later, we were told that the engine's repair would take an hour and we didn't have to disembark! With an engine problem, I had hoped that we would be transferred to another plane. *At the end things worked out all right; this is the wisdom I learnt from working in Libya.*

LANDING AT THE AIRPORT! SOMETIMES, IT IS ONLY A MATTER OF ABSURD ILL-TIMED SCHEDULING

Kays and I were heading (circa 1998) from Benghazi towards Tripoli, in order to catch an international flight on our way home to enjoy a well-deserved vacation after a long stretch of 7-day-work weeks. There was a problem with the local Libyan flight carrier (one of only two in service) which was scheduled to leave that morning; so, the company we worked for decided to send us on its own private small turbo-jet airplane. For sure that was good news, as it was an 'executive' plane. As we taxied, we saw the national carrier plane we were supposed to take parked at the sole departure/ arrival gate at the airport.

After a comfortable, quiet and uneventful one-and-half hour of flight, we safely got to our destination, and the capital's airport was only a few hundred feet away. Within a short time, the plane was only ten-feet above ground, as it crossed the fenced airport's perimeter. At that point we heard our pilot scream: **"Shiiit?!"** together with commotion in the cockpit, suggesting he was violently moving, apparently in a frenzied attempt to dodge something.

A few seconds later our plane landed quietly and in a normal way. However, as it left the main tarmac, we found that the same national carrier plane we had seen a couple of hours ago in Benghazi taxiing ahead of us towards another gate. As we disembarked and started walking towards an arrival gate, one of the passengers asked our pilot if he had any problem landing. The pilot explained that: **as soon as our plane got over the capital's airport fence, the national carrier zoomed just above our plane as it was landing!** The pilot explained that the national carrier plane must have left half an hour after we did and, being a faster plane, it usually

covered the distance to the capital in just one hour, exactly
when we got there (on top of each other)!

WE JUST CLIPPED A TREE!

Earlier in my career, and while working for two mining
companies in Saskatoon (1981 - 1983), I had at times to fly on
small planes, as small as four-seaters including the captain;
once, I was fortunate to be on one of those large mechanical
'bugs' called helicopters! As for the former vehicle of travel,
those planes landed on dry ground, ice and lakes! The latter
was the most '*funnest*' of all flights; truly exhilarating!

Taking off and landing were generally uneventful
occasions, with two exceptions. Once, we were scheduled to
fly from Saskatoon to the field-area of interest in northern
Saskatchewan. At the airport that day I was happy to see the
lowest, heaviest and densest fog I had ever seen in my life,
and it was hanging just a few meters above the tarmac! I
thought 'no way they can fly in that and, instead, in the early
afternoon I shall go back home, sweet home!' I was even
willing to bet $100 against $1 on 'no fly'.

After waiting for an hour, our chief geologist talked
to the charter-airline employees, then came back to say that
we were to wait on the premises for another hour, since the
'weather may improve'. Sure enough, after one hour the chief

geologist made another inquiry, after which he came to say: ***"All right …. Everyone on the plane".*** I looked through the window and was shocked; the status of the fog was the same as before, if not *'worser'!* There was hardly three-meter vertical visibility range! As I approached the twin-Otter, I wondered if that particular day was *'the day'!* The airplane taxied and then sped on the tarmac, which was quite visible. The plane then took off and instantly **entered the fog**, but rather quickly emerged to a 'fiercely' sunny cloudless sky! What a disappointment, but at least I didn't make that bet!

On one of the return trips back home, the plane had to carry several drilling pipes; everyone was aware how dangerous such freight was, if it was not hermetically secured; and that was what they did, or thought they did! Just about half an hour before reaching our homeward destination, we heard intermittent noises in the back of the plane; after a quick check, the chief geologist came back to say that one or more pipes had broken loose! That news was worrisome, but the plane's pilot was able to manage the flight, though with some difficulty regarding stability. At last we started to land and were only a few meters above ground, when I heard the chief geologist go: "Oh, my God; we just clipped a tree!" I thought that that was all we needed! That incident, notwithstanding, we landed safely.

Life in the north Canadian field was pleasant in summer, weather-wise, but tough in winter, even for a short length of time; temperatures then hovered at around minus 40 degrees Centigrade. At one time during such a cold spell, each employee (geologists and technicians) had their own tent, and each one of those tents had a kerosene-fueled heater. Those heaters, however, were only able to heat up the upper half of the tent, where the mattress of a 'high' bed was conveniently placed, but then the air was smoke-smelly in that part of the tent; the lower half by contrast was below zero! On a different note, take-off and landing during winter, where the camp was situated next to a frozen lake, took place from/on ice; now and then the icy tarmac had to be cleared from falling snow or wind-blown ice by grader-bulldozers.

In summer, there was sometimes the problem of mosquitos and black flies. The former came in as clouds; if one waved them to the left, the 'rarefied air' resulting from that movement would only 'suck in' the rest of the cloud from the right. Flies there are as huge as WWII B-29 bombers and their 'bite' similarly terrible.

———————————

FINDING HEAVEN ON EARTH

During my travels to and from work in Libya (1988 - 2004), I had to spend many hours flying. At the time when I started to work for AGOCO, there were hardly any TV screens on airplanes, but music on radio was available though it came only as short programs that were continuously repeated. I often was unable to sleep on any moving vehicle, even when lying down on trains. After reading for half an hour, I got tired. So, I spent my time listening to classical music; **Frédéric Chopin** and **Peter Ilyich Tchaikovsky** were my favorites. With time, entertainment facilities on airplanes became more sophisticated rather quickly, and those carriers started to have TV screens, as well.

At the start of that welcome development, however, there were only limited viewing options, and only a couple of movies shown, anyway; so, the importance of radio music lingered for a long time. On one such occasion, there was a two-hour program composed of a mixture of classical music and **opera**, the latter of which I had little, or no, interaction with before. One of the latter's themes caught my attention. So, I waited for the program to restart to listen to it again and again; it was **Giuseppe Verdi's 'Nabucco', The March of the Hebrew Slaves,** or **Chorus of the Hebrew Slaves**/Va pensiero, as I discovered when checking the flight's magazine. The theme and what it was supposed to represent in my mind based on general knowledge of history, although I knew nothing of the Italian language, had a prominent influence on my psyche, in terms of developing a heart-clenching passion for this type of music. *That theme was spiritually inspirational and presented me with a stimulus that got me firmly anchored on the overwhelming and fascinating **magnificence of opera.***

With time, I **fell deep in love** with this unique music, **particularly Italian opera**, and soon found out that it was so varied, and that there were so many composers, performers and repertoires. Also, I realized that I liked some performances of the same opera better than others, in terms of presentation and background-decor, in addition to who the performers were. It should not be shocking news to anyone who is acquainted with opera if I listed certain arias as being so passionately dear to my heart. Those include the immortal composer **Giacomo Puccini's 'La bohème'**/*Si, mi chiamano mimi* (Mirella Freni's, the 'perfect' soprano), **'Gianni Schicchi'**/*O mio babbino caro* (Kiri te Kanawa), **'Tosca'**/*Vissi d'arte'* (Angela Gheorghiu) and **'Madama Butterfly**/*Madame Butterfly'*/*Un bel di vedremo'* (Anna Netrebko). Some of the other operas/arias that I cherish include: **Giuseppe Verdi's La Traviata**/*Libiamo ne' lieti calici*, **Vincenzo Bellini's 'Norma'**/*Casta Diva* (Renée Fleming, America's Queen of Opera), **Gaetano Donizetti's L'elisir d'amore**/*Una Furtiva Lagrima* (Rolando Villazón's) and **Georges Bizet's Carmen**/*L'amour est un oiseau rebelle* and *Habanero* (Elina Garanca, mezzo soprano). And how about **Léo Delibes'** **'Lakmé'** *(Flower duet/Dueto/Sous le dôme épais*: Anna Netrebko and Elina Garanca).

While soprano, mezzo-soprano and even some contralto female voices go directly to my heart and play on its strings freely, I found out that tenor and baritone were more impressive, in terms of forceful male power that can impulsively pluck the strings of hearts and make a mountain tremble with love. Take for example Franco Corelli's singing of *"O soave fanciulla"* and *"Che gelida manina"* (both in **La**

bohème), and his performances in singing *"Recitar ... Vesti la giubba"* (**Il Pagliacci**) and *"E lucevan le stelle"* (**Tosca**).

As a final statement, I tend to believe that **Italian opera** was not created because the Italian language existed; it is the other way round: **the Italian language was created in order to accommodate heavenly opera!** And for those who are emotionally inclined to revel in romantic disposition, try **Puccini's Madama butterfly's** love duet *"Vogliatemi Bene"* (sung by Renata Tebaldi and Carlo Bergonzi).

FALLOUT FROM TRAVEL, A WEALTH OF WESTERN CLASSICAL LITERATURE

Being alone, that is without the family, in Benghazi was in a way a blessing, because I had a lot of extra time in the afternoon and evening on my hand. I had then a golden opportunity to follow one of my cherished interests, reading classical literature. I have been interested in western literature since I was a teenager in Iraq, reading the translated books that my mother bought. I enjoyed reading the works of **Alexandre Dumas'**, of which *'The Three Musketeers'* and the *'Count of Monte Cristo'* are prominent titles, and also **Victor Hugo's** *'Les Misérables'* and *'Notre-Dame de Paris'*. *'The Pardaillan'*, written by another French author, **Michel Zévaco**, is another novel that is unforgettable and which I am actually re-reading; (for those who are interested, the original

French version is irreplaceable, and is even worth learning the language).

While studying in England, I had an opportunity to buy a selection of used classical French and Russian books, all beautifully bound in ornamented hard covers and published by Heron Books (London). I enjoyed reading masterpieces by **Ivan Sergeyevich Turgenev** *(Fathers and Sons)*, **Leo Tolstoy** *(War and Peace)*, **Fyodor Dostoyevsky** *(The Brothers Karamazov)* and masterpieces by **Anton Chekhov** *(short Stories)*.

In Calgary, a whole spectrum of *memorable classical English literature* was open to me at Coles' bookstores, with novels being available in affordable paperbacks; those were also comparatively light enough to carry to Benghazi over four days of travel. English authors are prolific writers and too many to enumerate in this short passage. Of those, I choose to mention: **D. W. Somerset Maugham** (short stories), **Charles Dickens** *(Great Expectations)*, the **Bronte** sisters **Charlotte** *(Jane Eyre)* and **Emily** *(Wuthering Heights)*, **George Eliot** *(The Mill on the Floss* and *Middlemarch)*, **Wilkie Collins** *(Woman in White)* and **R. D. Blackmore** *(Lorna Doone)*.

The Grapes of Wrath by American writer **John Steinbeck** is a jewel in literature. Aside from being an 'extraordinary' piece of literary work (in my humble opinion), it opens the eyes wide on the suffering of poor people, now numbering in hundreds of millions all over the earth. I strongly advise that this novel, among others, be taught at high school level; let the kids perceive the immensity of other people's misery. Such realization should make some of them (at least) understand that life is not all about sex, drugs and boisterous dancing parties. While they spend their time doing that, others among their peers are graduating as doctors and engineers!

And, finally, the cream of the crop authors, as far as I am concerned, are: **Homer/Homerus** *(Iliad* and *Odyssey)* and **Dante Alighieri** *(Inferno).*

I often found efforts to summarise any literary work as demeaning to its originality; however, here I find it necessary to present the shortest of summaries for the benefit of those readers who are not familiar with these grand novels.

The epic of **Iliad** chronicles the last stages of the Trojan War (3000 years ago) between the Achaeans (a confederation of Greek cities) and the Trojans. That conflict started after Paris of Troy took the beautiful Helen away from her Greek husband Menelaus, prompting his brother Agamemnon, king of Sparta, to wage war against Troy.

The final year of that conflict witnessed the tragic demise of the great Trojan warrior **Hector**, Priam's (king of Troy) son, only to be followed by the death of his slayer, the great Greek warrior **Achilles**; the downfall of the latter transpired through an act of vengeance assisted by the god

Apollo. Thereafter, Troy was conquered and destroyed, following a trick involving a huge, hollow wooden horse that the Trojans accepted as a 'gift' from the Achaeans for their bravery. Unbeknown to them, Greek warriors, hiding inside that artful wooden structure, opened the city's gates during the night, thereby allowing the Greek army to enter the city unobtrusively and wreak havoc. **Ajax** (son of King Telamon), who wielded a huge shield made of seven cow-hides with a layer of bronze, and was of great stature and combat intelligent, figures largely in the conflict on the Achaean side.

Besides Zeus, several mythical gods and goddesses, including Athena, Hera and Poseidon (supporting the Achaean forces), and Apollo, Aphrodite and Ares (on the Trojans' side), are intimately involved in those momentous events.

It was the Greek warrior and king of Ithaca, Odysseus, who concocted the cunning wooden horse ploy, which ended the Trojan War. Following the demise and plunder of Troy (northwestern Turkey), Odysseus in the **Odyssey** started a trip back home to his wife. To his misfortune, this warrior, who often was at odds with the gods, angered Zeus' brother Poseidon, the sea god. Consequently, the latter arranged for Odysseus' ships to be blown off-course during a terrible storm in the Aegean Sea, causing him and his soldiers to face several harrowing extraordinary experiences over the next ten years.

During a troubled journey, that storm carried Odysseus and his crew (in eleven ships) to where the cannibalistic Thracian **Kikones** (dwelling in easternmost Greece) reduced their numbers. After escaping, they managed after a long trip westward to reach an island just off the westernmost part of the Libyan coast, where some of his crew were intoxicated, thereby rendered ineffectual, by eating fruit of the lotus flower. Odysseus and his men then sailed during a gloomy night to the land of the **Cyclopes** (living in the caverns of volcanic Mount Aetna in Sicily), where Poseidon's son, the one-eyed Cyclops Polyphemus devoured two of them. Odysseus managed to blind Cyclops after the latter gobbled a large amount of wine made by his Greek soldiers, and flee the Cyclops' cavern. Driven by vicious winds, they reached the land of the giant **Laistrygonians** (northwestern Italy), where most of the crew were killed by massive rocks hurled over their ships by the natives; all ships were destroyed, except for Odysseus'.

Next, fate took Odysseus and the remainder of his crew to the island of Aeaea (off Corsica), home of the beautiful witch-goddess **Circe**, where she drugged a band of Odysseus' men and turned them temporarily into pigs. Thereafter, they journeyed to the abyss of Hades/Realm of the Dead (on the coastal border between Italy and France) to consult the blind prophet **Tiresias** regarding instructions to reach their home. Odysseus and his crew thenceforth barely escaped the lure of the seductive melodious singing of the lovely **Sirens** (living on a rocky island off Italy's southern coast) pleading with them to throw themselves in the Mediterranean Sea. Thereafter, they had to navigate between two prodigious menaces, the six-headed **Scylla** sea-monster and the whirlpool daemon **Charybdis**, guarding opposite sides of the Strait of Messina (between Sicily and the Italian mainland).

Odysseus subsequently managed to reach the island of Ogygia (possibly Djerba, off eastern Tunis), where the beautiful witch goddess **Calypso** retained him as her lover for a long time, until Zeus intervened to secure his release. Next, favorable winds luckily took him and his men to the land of the Phaeacians, where he was generously treated and sent on his way to Ithaca, his home. There, he found several suitors seeking his wife Penelope's hand and his own throne, following his lengthy absence from home. After winning a crossbow contest, disguised as a beggar, he proved his identity and eliminated all of the suitors.

The poet Dante Alighieri's masterpiece, the **Divine Comedy**, includes three books: *Inferno, Purgatorio and Paradiso*. In **Inferno**, Dante was guided by the ancient Roman poet Virgil's ghost along a path that took them through *Hell's nine circles*, where he met all kinds of tormented souls.

The First Circle of Hell, **Pagans** were the least distressed of all residents, while inside the Second Circle, Dante watched as the souls of the **Lustful** swirled about in a terrible storm. In the Third Circle, *interestingly*, the **Gluttonous** *lay in mud and endured a rain of filth and excrement*, while in the Fourth, the **Avaricious** and the **Prodigal** were made to charge at one another with giant boulders. The Fifth Circle contained the river Styx, a swampy, stinking gutter in which the **Wrathful** spent eternity struggling with one another. The Sixth housed the **Heretics**.

In the Seventh Circle of Hell existed those who were **Violent**, spending eternity in a river of boiling blood; this group included those who were violent toward themselves and others, and the blasphemers who were violent toward God. The monster Geryon transported Virgil and Dante across a great abyss to the Eighth Circle of Hell housing Seducers, Flatterers, Simoniacs (sinners who profited by shady dealings connected with clerical privileges) and Astrologists/Psychics.

In the Ninth Circle of Hell were those who betrayed their kin and country. Lastly, Dante followed Virgil into **Judecca**, the Fourth Ring of the Ninth Circle of Hell and the deepest. There, he found those who betrayed their benefactors, including *Judas, the betrayer of Christ*, and both of *Cassius and Brutus, the betrayers of Julius Caesar*; those souls were to spend eternity in complete icy submersion. Eventually, those two poets reached Lethe, the river of forgetfulness, and traveled from there out of Hell and back onto Earth. They emerged from Hell on Easter morning, just before sunrise.

PART SEVEN: AGOCO'S GEOLOGICAL LABORATORY

THE ENGLISH LANGUAGE IS NOT AS EASY AS SOME PEOPLE MAY PRESUME! ALSO, DRIVING!

Our expatriate geologist 'contingent' at AGOCO's Geological Laboratory comprised two petrographers, Erhan and me, together with a geochemist (Haci). Most of the time, going to the laboratory, situated in rural Benghazi in an area known as Genfuda (20 km south of the city) wasn't too taxing for me; I was fortunate to have a car ride with Haci, who drove there every work day in the morning. This guy had earlier studied in the U.S. for two years working towards an MSc degree. He quickly proved to be a gentleman, and I went to visit him often during afternoons at his apartment, in order to chat and enjoy the **excellent tea he brewed every day**.

Notwithstanding his extended stay in an English-speaking country, this blessed soul had difficulty with the language, the easiest of all to embrace! However, whatever he had to say was readily comprehensible. We talked about various subjects, one of which led him once to relate a

234

story relevant to his daughter. He started the narrative by mentioning her name, but soon replaced that with 'he', instead of 'she'. As he continued a fairly long exciting story, there was reason for him to become more and more agitated; with that, there came a torrent of 'he'. Besides a daughter, that gentleman had a son, as well. At one time, I wondered if he had changed the subject to the latter, but then realized that she was still the prime subject of his story.

One morning I went to his apartment around seven-thirty in the morning, in order to start another 'trip' to the Geological Laboratory. When I got there, I saw concern on his face as he said: "There is something wrong with the car; the **engine's voice** is different". On another morning, both of us sat in his manual-geared car, after which he started it. As he did so, the car jumped, almost going over a raised pavement; it had been left in gear when he turned it off the last time he drove it! This was promptly followed by: "You know, if I just remember to leave the car in neutral-gear when I stop after a drive, I would be the best driver in the world".

I could not agree less with that statement, I must say! A few years earlier, this gentleman and Erhan, who also drove a car of his own to the laboratory, agreed that the three of us should take one car only, instead of two, and that the two of them would alternate driving on a weekly basis; after all, both were fellow-countrymen and friends. After only a few weeks, however, that expat decided to opt out of that arrangement and use his own car to the laboratory on the pretext that he wanted to go early, in order to satisfy his hobby (making intricate tiny ornamental objects, using a binocular microscope) before the workday actually started. I asked him in private why he really chose to make that decision, since there was quite a waste of both gas and effort using two cars. He answered that he was terribly afraid of his fellow-countryman's erratic driving, getting so close to other cars in a country where few drivers, if any, were concerned with the rules of the road. He also indicated that he could never talk to his compatriot about that issue, because that would be offensive, according to their society's customs, similar to the rest of the Middle East. At that juncture, and based on several instances, both he and I agreed that God kept a constant eye on Haci and protected him (I still firmly believe in that)! Here, I have to present two relevant instances.

One morning, Haci and I were driving through an extremely busy shopping area before leaving town, heading towards the Geological Laboratory; the road there was reduced to the passage of one car only, since its right side was jammed with shoppers' cars, which were parked at an angle. That morning, he decided to buy fresh-baked bread buns; that bread (possibly an Italian recipe) was God's gift to the Libyan people. It was simply heavenly and, eaten by itself, more delicious than any full meal, I thought! That shopping area was problematic in that it was heavily congested and people drove exceptionally fast. When we got abreast with the store where the bread was sold, he pushed hard on the brakes as he suddenly saw a parking space, then he **turned**

slowly into that space. When he did that, I turned my head to the right, as some drivers would instinctively do, even when someone else was behind the steering wheel. I couldn't then believe my eyes; there was a gray "one-thousand ton" truck (weight exaggerated a little) charging right behind us! Luckily, I had enough wits around me (and breath) to scream asking him to **get into that parking space fast**! As he did so, there was a huge gust of wind, caused by the charging behemoth behind us! We could have been hit with the truck's solid metal, instead of the gust of wind it had generated, an accident that had the potential of having our car's gas tank explode.

On another day (and this is a good 'story' not to be missed), we were heading back to the guest-house after finishing a day's work. The road was empty, except for a huge truck ahead of us. Our car was positioned right in the middle of the road, whereas the truck was going on the right-hand side, as is normal. So, the right side of our car was effectively behind it, whereas its left half (the driver's) was in the clear; as such, no part of the truck was directly in front of our driver, which apparently gave him personally a groundless false impression of both quality driving and security. We were driving at around 70 kilometers an hour, which was marginally faster than that of the truck. In a short time we were closely behind it; that is **I, myself** (the genuine author of this 'great book'), **was behind it**, and progressively approaching! *The truck's back-end, which was heavily reinforced with metal beams,* **loomed huge and intimidating right in front of my** *nose*, *my very own nose.* Any sudden slowing down of that metallic monster would definitely have ended up in *'my side of the car kissing the truck's left side rear-end*; it definitely wasn't a lucrative prospect at all! I was in a dilemma; if I said anything, he would have taken an issue with it, since he would see that as criticism of his driving style. But, then, I thought that was the lesser of two evils, the other being the possibility of losing my life. I quickly built up enough courage to caution him, whatever the mutual-relationship consequences were! His response was a determined push on the brake, accompanied by an *'oh', said in astonishment!* That incident gave me the impression that he, Haci, might have been suffering from **HMAS**, corresponding to "**heavy-metal attraction syndrome**".

Poor driving in that country was some sort of a contagious disease that could have spread in epidemic proportions! When I was on the "rotation system", I had to work during the weekends (Fridays), as well. A local employee was assigned to take me to the laboratory those days and back to the guest-house. One Friday, that driver came to the laboratory in the early afternoon to take me back. Being a weekend, the compound where the Geological Laboratory building was situated was empty, except for a couple of guards inside a room at the gate. We started our return trip on a two-way road inside the compound, then reached a junction where we had to turn left onto a two-lane road, with a barrier-island in the middle. According to internationally-recognized driving rules, we were supposed to go around the barrier to the farther lane. When we reached that barrier, however, my driver got **confused**: should he take that more remote lane (which seemed to be a little too far away), or the nearest (wrong way), since there were no cars around during the weekend. I saw the steering wheel go repeatedly and rapidly clockwise and anti-clockwise; *he just couldn't make up his mind* which lane was better than the other! By that time the driver stopped the car just shy of a light pole in the middle of the median island; by a miracle, we avoided a collision with a poor sedentary metal pole, one that was just standing where it was supposed to!

BETWEEN CUCUMBERS AND ORANGES

While working at AGOCO's Geological Laboratory, all employees enjoyed a relaxed atmosphere in a dream working place. At around 10:30 am, everyone had a fifteen-minute break, which often was 'unwittingly' extended (without any malicious 'dishonest notion' in mind of course) to half-an-hour. The geochemist, Haci, and I developed the daily habit of visiting the third expat (Erhan), who worked in a large office; there, we drank tea and chatted. During one of those visits, I arrived a little late and found that Haci was already sitting not too far from his countryman. As soon as I got in the office, I enquired who had eaten a cucumber. With amazement in his tone of voice, Haci replied: "Wow, I ate one ten minutes ago and in my own office! How did you know?" His office was several meters away on another side of the building. I said: "No problem; I have a doggie's nose," which I believe I do!

Not too long, thereafter, and while still working at the laboratory, I had a good reason to go to the bathroom. As soon as I entered, I saw Erhan standing in front of the sink and washing something; another item, sitting at the back of the sink attracted my attention. It was rather shocking, as I got closer, to see a lower human jaw! All his teeth were fake, and I had no idea. He later explained the demise of his natural teeth; he used to live in a village when young. The water that villagers sourced had an abnormally high concentration of fluorine, which ruined his teeth.

During the Arabic month of Ramadhan, **all locals** fasted. The expats were expected to follow the 'custom' of not eating or drinking in public; that custom had to be strictly observed, especially by those originating from Arab countries. The locals believed my life-long Arab friend, Kays, to be fasting too. He wasn't, but was as careful as a 'hermit' during that month not to show anything to the contrary, especially when taking sips of water in his own office. One Ramadhan coincided with late December, when delicious and heavily **fragrant** Libyan oranges had just come on the market from Tripoli area, where they are grown on a wide scale. One day, he just couldn't fight off the temptation any longer. So he left his office in the middle of work hours and went to the guest-house, just a few steps away. In the privacy of his room he unhurriedly indulged in eating not one, but two oranges!

After carefully washing his hands and rinsing his mouth, he went back to the office building and took the elevator to his fourth-floor office; before its door closed, one of the local geologists stepped in. In Arab countries, it is customary and imperative to say hello to others and ask about their health, and such a 'dialogue' took place then, forcing Kays to reluctantly discharge air samples from his mouth, which was just recently drenched with orange juice. Later, he told me that, as he left the elevator, he was both *bemused and intrigued* by the 'unyielding' and probing look the local had given him, and he *good-humouredly wondered* **why** the latter kept staring at him!

LIFE AT THE LABORATORY

AGOCO's Geological Laboratory compound occupies several acres, not far (a few hundred meters) from the Mediterranean Sea coastline. Its complex comprised four buildings of moderate size, in addition to a huge modern 'core storage' structure. Working at the lab is one of those nostalgic memories that I lovingly cherish; it was the countryside peace and serenity of the place, added to the enjoyment of scientific work unencumbered by any office-related supervisory limitations, which was so tranquil and relaxing. In that environment, over the years, I produced hundreds of petrographic and core-analysis reports. In this regard, sometimes I talked to myself during work; actually, that process was inducive to developing ideas quite well. **Curiosity** (people have it too, **especially the feminine type**, not just cats) drove a few of the local technicians to put their head through the door to see whom I was talking to, since they couldn't see anyone else in the room as they passed by my office's open door. Out of respect, they were content with leaving without a comment, but very likely talked about it in their all day-long periods of spare time. Once, however, one of them, whom I knew very well, asked me if I was talking to myself, and he got this reply: *"I am not talking to myself; I am actually **discussing** a scientific issue"*. As word got around, no one bothered to ask me that again; they thought that I was, in some ways, soft in the head (**I loved working with them!**).

We, the expats, had the freedom there to visit others in the lab for a small chat at any time during the day, often with a cup of tea in hand. We also had half an hour of mid-day sandwich eating; my preferred sandwich was a firm crispy bun stuffed with sliced hot green chillies (seeds removed; the bold aroma it emitted when cut!), together with tomatoes and sometimes a slice of onions. Actually, I waited patiently for that time to enjoy that sandwich; there was, however, one alternative that could challenge the supremacy of that 'heavenly' sandwich; it was the local bread! Whenever my expat friend, Haci, stopped at a store along the way to the laboratory in the morning, I bought a few of those; even when cold, they were more delicious than **any** sandwich, except tuna, of course! *In case anyone wonders about my mental health, I say: 'People are sometimes allowed a degree of eccentricity'.*

FIRE IN THE LAB

At the laboratory, we had equipment to clean small rock samples from the natural oil they may have, prior to taking certain porosity/permeability measurements. Cleaning required the use of a hydrocarbon solvent; in our case, we used toluene, which also is highly inflammable. That solvent was contained in a closed-system cleaning apparatus made of glass flasks and tubes that were interconnected and all connections sealed with a special silicone gel. The cleaning process required heating the toluene in one flask; the resulting toluene vapor travelled through the tubes and condensed, as hot liquid toluene, around the rock samples (placed in a special glass container/flask). The toluene seeped through their pores (tiny openings) and dissolved the contained oil. At the end of a 'cycle', all toluene siphoned back to the original container-flask, where it was reheated for another cycle.

Although the apparatus was assembled within a compartment, which was well ventilated, the enclosure became uncomfortably hot, especially in summer. The heat was enough to degrade the silicone-gel sealing, thus it was mandatory to remove adversely affected seals and have them replaced, a chore I often had to remind the technician in charge of running the cleaning process and rock measurement; such instructions weren't usually heeded promptly.

At one time, I was occupied with preparing an urgent report in my office, when I simultaneously heard glass breaking and a loud 'explosive bang' coming from that particular laboratory; I realized right away what may have happened, but wasn't prepared for the relevant 'spectacle'. I jumped from my seat and got out of my office, only to find the laboratory, which was always very well-lit, in total darkness, and its door's opening wholly engulfed in black smoke. Everything was quiet there, but within a second, the technician emerged and, with the right side of his sweater and part of his pants on fire, ran towards my office. Luckily, the coordinator of the laboratory, who was standing close by, had the presence of mind to trip the technician on the floor and cover him with my lab-coat; his prompt action luckily was enough to smother the fire right away. The coordinator tried to remove the technician's sweater, but it was made of material that had 'melted' and got stuck to his skin. Shortly, the technician could walk, and was taken directly to the hospital, where he recuperated fairly quickly.

As this drama ended, fortunately without more serious consequences, I had to wait over an hour for the smoke to subside before I could reenter that laboratory and have the window opened. The flask containing the toluene was on the ground and shattered; there was no trace of the solvent, which had been instantaneously consumed by flames turning into black smoke. **(Lesson drawn: one has to be alert and careful doing anything and everything! I say: do it right by following instructions to the letter, or don't do it at all; leave it to a 'smarter' guy who does)!**

This incident reminds me of another. During our stay in Baghdad, we didn't have running hot water. My brother, then twenty-eight, was carrying a bucket of hot water from the kitchen to the bathroom, when he spilled it on his leg! Over the next few weeks we had to visit a male nurse several times to look after it and keep it clean until it fully healed.

Once, a young lady coworker complained that she had cut her hand with a knife the day before as she tried to get a slice of watermelon. My response was quick, with purposefully hardly concealed sarcasm: "My friend; there are a few things you have to know about knives. The most important of those is that a knife has two sides; one of them is sharp, and this is where wisdom tells us to be very careful in not letting it touch us. We always have to unceasingly monitor its motion. If you are not careful …" I had to stop there and then, as I gave her a sidelong look to gauge her reaction; she was ready to burst at any moment. (Wicked? Maybe, but that was just a hint of what she had given me over quite some time)!

A MATTER OF DRIVING ADROITNESS!

In general, diligent drivers in the Middle-East, and elsewhere in many countries of the "Third World", have to be very careful while on the road, since some drivers do not adhere to driving rules, because of unwarranted ignorance, reluctance to follow rules, aggressiveness or sheer stupidity. I had, more than once, witnessed for instance an oncoming car with its signal on, and that car turning irrespective of the signal's indication. [Now, we are finding increasing examples of those here in Calgary too, exemplified, but not restricted to, drivers failing to stop, or even reducing speed (!), at stop signs.]

Halfway to the Geological Laboratory, there was a storage area belonging to one of the local construction companies working there. At that location, the main road split sharply at ninety degrees to our right; this sideway road was fairly wide and about 70 feet long ending at a brick-fence with a wide metal gate controlling the entrance to the compound. There were four lamp posts along either side of that road, two at either end and two in between; that is eight in total.

As our bus passed by it every day of the week, I could not help but notice the condition of those posts; seven, out of eight, were damaged. Three of those poles were almost flattened, being apparently smashed by speeding trucks which weren't properly driven; four were 'mildly' twisted and *only one stood erect and showed no ostensible damage;* it looked the same way it had been installed previously. Two of those forcefully twisted poles were situated at the intersection with the main road, and were rather easy to explain; someone came in *too fast* to stop and turn, in order to go into the compound, while another was *in a hurry* leaving the compound, or perhaps he was looking the wrong way! The four that were 'mildly' twisted had apparently been subject to less dramatic detrimental shocks. Time proved that there was some credence to this Sherlock-Holmsian reasoning expressed by the way they drove over there, and here is an eye-opening incident.

All of our Geological Laboratory employees stood one afternoon waiting at the Genfuda compound for the company bus to take us back to Benghazi at the end of a workday. That bus was late for half an hour, causing dismay among the *'waitees'*. Then, we heard the sound of what appeared to be a jet-engine roaring towards us; we couldn't then see anything because of trees planted along part of the one-kilometer long road leading to the compound. Being so abandoned in a desert-like location, that sound was more than welcome to hear. However, as the bus drew closer, I couldn't detect any indication of slowing down, since the sound it produced kept increasing in volume; I knew the regular driver of that bus to having shown erratic driving now and then, and wondered. The bus was only a short distance from the gate, when it started to turn right, in order to get inside the compound, but at that speed, the driver couldn't make it. I stood there like a statue watching the bus careen towards an old wild dog sitting on the ground close by. The bus eventually stopped, but not before bumping hard into the curb near that dog; the latter was able to jump, however, thus saving its life. The front right wheel of the bus became warped as a result of that bump, and we had to wait another hour before another bus arrived.

For a short while, I wondered why the eighth pole at that other compound had escaped all damage; upon scrutiny, I noticed that it had been installed flush against the brick-wall fence, itself, and thus was out-of-the-way! **Hurrah for unfailing marksmanship!**

TO PASS, OR NOT TO PASS!

This is another incident taking place along the same road leading to the Genfuda geological laboratory. We had just left the outskirts of Benghazi on a road that was wide enough to accommodate two cars comfortably. Soon, we had the following situation developing in front of our own eyes. A gray truck was going fast in the same direction as we were. That truck was closely followed by a similar truck, which had just overtaken a small old green car carrying one passenger, in addition to the driver. The second truck raced forward in a determined Herculean effort to overtake and pass the first truck too.

The driver of the small car, apparently feeling personally affronted by being left behind, decided to overtake and **pass both trucks**. The car he drove was only a couple of yards behind those two trucks, which at that time happened to be racing parallel to each other and being about **3feet-apart**. Within a few seconds, that small car, now in the middle of the road, became directly behind both trucks and situated right between them. At that precious point, its driver may have had decided it was the right 'magic moment' to 'do the honourable deed' and pass both trucks simultaneously. So, he floored the accelerator pedal, and his car jumped to life. However, now the car being only inches from those trucks, he suddenly recognized the futility of his action and that there was no way his car could get through that 3-foot gap. What happened next can be construed as reflecting misjudgement in terms of perspective, making the wrong driving decision, or even momentary anger-driven madness. **We saw the small car swerve and smash into the truck on the right!**

A LESSON IN HIDING THINGS

In addition to being an enjoyable drive, more where the road stretches along the seaside, that particular road had a few rustic makeshift shacks, which were built without the city's permit. As such, the government there had to mark each of those with **"immediate removal"** painted in large Arabic letters on one or more of those shacks' walls. The owners of those illegal structures invariably didn't approve of their government's legal action and had those markings masked/

overpainted with a blotch of black paint, leaving the rest of the shack unpainted. Such brush treatments were invariably suggestive of what they hid, in a way that was so obvious to the eye, and could never have deceived those of an official.

One of those shacks, however, stood out distinctively among the rest in being a cause for laughter and ridicule; the owner had those letter markings overpainted exactly as the letters appeared on that shack. Now, the viewer would read them in white, instead of black!

SUNSET IN BENGHAZI

Glorious! This word kept encroaching on my mind whenever I was fortunate enough to be able to marvel at the spectacular singularity of **sunset** scenes in Benghazi; scenes that defied onlookers to divert their gaze away from, even for a moment! The best of those sunsets I encountered was when I, with my friend Kays, walked northwards near Tibesti Hotel along the northeastern side of Benghazi harbour (locally identified as a 'lake') during partly cloudy late afternoons in winter. Such phenomenally impressive scenes actually are not restricted to that city, but appear to characterize subtropical localities along such latitudes as those embracing the Mediterranean region.

It is very difficult to give full credit to the majestic beauty of those sunsets, and as for description, they could provide a wealth of text material, enough to fill many pages. What first strikes the spectator is the perceptibly **ever-changing interplay** of a multitude of diverse wonderful colors, as clouds moved slowly across the sky accompanied by delicate, though determined, dipping of the waning globe of the sun towards the sea, with the latter imparting a **sad smile suggesting a shy and tired farewell**, albeit on a temporary basis. As the sun rays, though still fiery in their own right, pierced the clouds just above the horizon in the late afternoon, they **streaked gently and lovingly as they kissed serene fluffs of lingering cumulus clouds** and dyed them with artistic strokes of bold bright yellow intermingled with brilliantly hot golden orange, a truly captivating spectacle to behold! The sky, when observed through openings in between floating, fluffy cotton-like clouds, showed ultimate beauty reflecting various shades of **emerald** and light **yellowish-green along the horizon** transforming vertically into light blue and, eventually, culminating in **azure and deep blue** overhead towards the zenith. The majestic beauty of the sky's colour-contrast was particularly deeply accentuated and better appreciated where perceived and compared through different openings in the clouds, as one followed its vertical modification.

Within only a few minutes and, under resolute onlookers gaze, those bright colors transformed too rapidly *(or so it seemed, as one is unwittingly lost in absorbing the expanse of that heavenly wonder)* into pinkish and deep reddish hues intermingling with ruby-red glows. During that metamorphosis, the **crests of small rolling tortuous wind-generated waves in the 'lake' became awash, in a shimmering manner, with colours found at the heart of a blazing fire**, thereby presenting an artistically striking contrast with the deep blue of the harbour's sea-water itself. As the sun reposed behind the horizon, the warm twilight colours perished, and all earth, sky and sea melted into inconspicuous and unfathomable obscurity; such an episode somehow irrelevantly, but explicably, reminds me of **Ernest Hemingway's** *A Farewell to Arms.*

At its next emergence, the sun is fresh again and bursting boldly into a riot of vibrant fiery yellow and blinding white ball, which, on rare occasions, is surrounded by a barely perceptible pinkish halo. **Those are everlasting memories of that city!**

PART EIGHT: BACK IN CANADA (POST - 2004)

THOSE DREADFULLY DIFFICULT
WORDS TO PRONOUNCE!

The year of 2004 is one of my life's major milestones; it marked my reaching the age of sixty-five and, thereby, mandatory retirement. I left Benghazi with a sad heart, since with time my job with AGOCO, the city itself and the company of generally mild-mannered people I encountered, were exemplary. I had certainly encountered harsh times and barely surmountable difficulties during travel; but it was well worth an unforgettable experience, and I have no regrets.

Upon my return to Calgary, I was offered a combined job (two responsibilities: as supervisor of sixteen employees and petrographic report-writing) with an oil-service company in this city. After about one year of service at that company, I was fortunate enough to have the honour of helping an Oriental Lady, who with time became an eternally dear and irreplaceable life-long friend, with her English-language course; she had politely asked for my help, being a supervisor with a high university degree and speaking fairly fluent English. Working towards that end, we decided to start with reading the book assigned to the class right after work hours at those offices. She read several lines in a sentence fairly well, until she got to the word 'luggage', which she pronounced *'luggagee'*. Being exceptionally gentle with women and mindful not to perturb their sensitive hearts in any way, as most of them deserve such treatment, I delicately asked her to stop and read the relevant line again, just to make sure that what I thought I had heard was real. I slowly and intelligibly corrected her pronunciation, and asked her to re-read the line; *again, I heard the same sweet, but definitely incorrect, pronunciation.*

After repeating the right pronunciation a few more times, but to no avail, I divided the word into two parts: 'lu' and 'gij', pronounced them separately and asked her to do the same, which she did effortlessly. So, I said: "That is excellent; now, let us put them together and try the word luggage again". The answer was a quick angelic: **"*luggagee*; is that right?"** I said: "No; let us try again"; 'lu''gij', and got a crystal-clear 'lu''gij'. That I followed with: 'luggage', for which I got an *enthusiastic*: **"*luggagee*; right?"** in response. At that point, I said: "That is fine; please continue reading the rest of the paragraph". Then, I thought: *What is the point of having words in the English language that are so demanding! After all, isn't it supposed to be an easy language to learn?! [And the following account is one of her best; I arrive at her home to take her to lunch, but she is not ready, yet.*

*While moving around briskly, she would invariably say: "**one minutes** please". I was in the habit of correcting her English, as asked, but in this and other similar cases I refrained, in order to hear it once again! And so that I wouldn't be accused by the reader of being mean to her, she knew and accepted that innocent conduct after hearing my reasons.]*

During few subsequent weeks, we met (together with several other coworkers) a few times in the company's coffee-room during lunch-time. Similar to other ladies from the Orient, she had difficulty with grasping my name and inadvertently addressed me "Honey", instead of "Haney", a pronunciation, I must confess, I enjoyed quite a bit. One day, she came into my office and approached me hesitantly with a shy smile; she then started apologizing and trying to explain something. I understood that her female co-workers asked why she called me "Honey", instead of "Haney", and whether there was anything special going on between us. She was startled and her answer was: "But that is his name; isn't it?" After some repetition of the two pronunciations and explaining to her the difference between the two, she was embarrassingly shocked by the realization of the incongruity and the unintended implication.

Our extraordinary acquaintance at that workplace had fairytale proportions. That lady, who is virtually made of gold, emigrated from her hometown in the Far East in a simple and direct move. As regards myself, the story is quite different. After finishing high school education in Basra,

I had to move to the capital Baghdad, in order to attend university.

After finishing basic university education, I worked in Baghdad for a few years, went to the United Kingdom for a one-year training and returned to that capital to work a few more years, after which I went back to the U.K. for higher education. Thereafter, I immigrated to Canada, lived in Windsor for a while, moved to Saskatoon and then to Calgary, where I have dwelled for the last thirty years. During that period, I worked overseas for many years (relevant stories included in this volume). At the end of my foreign work contract, I returned to Calgary. I, then, contacted a company in this city and discussed with them the possibility of selling oil-analysis equipment overseas; instead of that, I was asked to work with them as supervisor of the geological section. *That English course was a God-sent path to an everlasting magnanimous and deferential friendship.* The two of us later became partners in our own oil-service company "Reservoir Pore Consultants Ltd." in Calgary, Canada.

I grew up in one of those societies, where "Fate" and "Destiny" are tightly embraced pillars of culture. In this regard, I am one of those who firmly believe that every single aspect of our life, covering everything (shape, personality, education, friendship, health, family, etc.) is written in detail on our 'foreheads', and that all courses of events we experience are preordained in detail and cannot be changed, not even for a second. Fate has been accepted as reality by several ancient cultures (including Greek) and has often been conceived as being divinely inspired by the most potent of powers.

SMUDGED EYEGLASSES

I received this story at the final stage of preparing this manuscript; it came in the form of an e-mail from my sister. My mother, who lived in Copenhagen for several years, visited my married youngest sister in Germany. That trip, by train was long and tiring, but she made it safely and was picked up by both my sister Wiqar and her husband Ghassan, together with their daughter and son-in-law. After they reached my sister's home, they had a good meal and chatted for a long time.

Then, when yawning became contagious, my mother asked to be excused, since she was exhausted. Thus, they parted, each to their respective comfortable bed. My mom was the first to do so. She sat on her bed, put on reading glasses and picked up her prayer book to read some before sleeping; she couldn't read as readily as she usually did and, thinking of dirt smearing the glasses, went to the bathroom, washed them and came back to lie down on the bed. Once again, there was something wrong with the eyeglasses; thinking that she didn't clean them well enough, she went back and washed them again.

This procedure was repeated twice more prompting my sister to ask her mom if there was something wrong. To which she replied that there was *something wrong with her glasses, that she can't read with them anymore and that she was going to have them **replaced as soon as she got back to Denmark***. At that point, my sister happened to glance at those glasses and asked her mom if she could see them, after which inspection, she said: "But these are **my eyeglasses**, not yours!" That was enough reason for everyone to explode laughing.

ANOTHER STOLEN CAR AND PARKING!

This story resembles the one narrated above under "What! They stole my car!" But it is much more recent. The same lady of the sweet 'luggagee' went to visit her daughter, then a university student, in another town. Once, at the end of a workweek, she drove her daughter's car and when she came back, she had it erroneously parked in a parking spot other than the one allotted to her daughter's apartment. The gentleman whose parking lot was thus 'appropriated,' called the police; they in turn had it towed away.

On the following Sunday afternoon, that is two days after that unfortunate, but honest mistake, the lady needed to use the car again. However, when she got to the parking lot, there was no "daughter's car"! She called the police right away and advised them of its disappearance!

OF CEILING FANS

I very well remember that about 60 years ago (I was around 15 at the time) we had black GEC ceiling fans in Basra. The climate being often hot there, sometimes exceeding 50°Celsius during some summer days, hot enough to have an egg fried on a cement slab (in the sun of course), those poor fans had to work about 10 months a year continuously (day and night). As far as I knew, those fans may have been working since *Noah embarked on his Biblical Ark;* if not, then certainly longer than I had been around on this good Earth of ours. I have no recollection of ever seeing an electrician repairing those fans (not precise; I was told that they got *greased* once every few years). Since the house belonged to the Iraqi Ports Directorate, such maintenance procedures were carried out systematically.

Aside from *ancient history*, a few years ago (2009) I bought a new 'modern' ceiling fan here in Calgary. Considering it is normally cool/cold in Alberta most of the year, we have had little use for it. Shortly after it was installed, however, I had a good reason to write to the manufacturing company, outlined below in brief:

"In the summer of 2009, we purchased one of your fans (brand new); it worked intermittently (generally at a rate of once a week). So far this summer (2010), the fan has refused to turn. We can turn its light on and off, but only hear a click when trying to get it to move. I recently went to the store where I bought it from and told them about the problem; they advised me to get in touch with the manufacturer, since the fan had worked properly, perfectly and gallantly for **three whole months**! To my misfortune, as I tried to get the fan's model number, I fell down. *[No broken bones, though: a testimony of **their** good quality!]*" Then I asked them if they would kindly advise us, with the fan, that is. To be fair, the manufacturer promptly replied with an apology, and sent us an electrical part (as replacement) free of charge; now, it works beautifully, as well as those GECs we had had.

OF SOLID BONES

The story above reminds me of others. This morning I got out of bed, hurriedly changed my clothes and went down the stairs to see my grand-daughter before she left to school; I was a few seconds late. Anyway, as I reached the lowest step, our big dog came smiling and wagging his tail, expressing the usual "Hi; how, are you!" attitude. As he welcomed me, he inadvertently (with no malicious intention, whatsoever, I bet) stepped on the half-worn sock sticking out on my left foot, which was still residing on the last step. In ignorance, I then took the next step, which was landing on the floor with my right foot, with the intention of following it by the left which was still contently 'glued' to that step. As I did so, I landed all right, but with the left side of my hip first, on the floor. My daughter came to help, but I told her I was all right (no broken bones).

This incident, in turn, reminded me both of the story above and what followed. Soon after that fall, it was time for my annual physical checkup; our family doctor suggested a 'bone strength' test. Two weeks, thereafter, I went back to his office for the results and was told that I had *soft bones* because of my advanced age, and that I needed *to have medicine for that*. I protested hotly, saying **I didn't need medicine**. Then I laughed and told him that I had fallen several times before on ice-covered roads (as hard as steel), while walking the dog, and had no problem. Then, I told him about the fan incident above, and how, trying to get off a stool after copying a number from that fan while wearing my computer glasses, I had fallen headlong, or head first, with part of my legs still being above the stool. At the time, I fell smack on my hip, after which I walked away with nothing broken; the fall didn't even cause any discomfort (maybe just a tiny little bit). Then, I added that my bones were made of aluminium! He laughed humorously and said: "Well, take the medicine, just in case". Actually, in this regard, I now remember that on separate occasions, two dentists told me that I had had 'good quality' teeth, which in my mind is translated into good quality hip, as well!

A couple of other incidents are worth relating, as well. Being young and active, our doggie loved to run about at a small park nearby, while I watched him going round and round, left and right, and encouraged him to do so by pretending to be trying to get hold of his leash. In one of those crazy manoeuvers, one day, I saw him charging determinedly towards me. Being a large and heavy dog, I saw potential impairment in the form of broken bones forming my slightly-built body. So, having a *Homo sapiens* brain that many people solemnly and indisputably affirm is characterized with absolute superiority over all other creatures (and here I must declare that I am not an advocate of that), decided to shift slightly to my right when he got close to me, thereby avoiding a potentially catastrophic collision. The canine, however, having similar reasoning on his mind, since he deplored the idea of having me sent to the hospital, unfortunately moved in the same way I did, resulting in my body being thrown in the air and landing a meter away. After a scream of agony and incredulity, I stood up intact under the doggie's probing glare; 'hurray' for aluminium, light and strong!

On another occasion, I let the doggie run up and downhill with his long extendable leash chasing him wherever he went; he envisaged that arrangement as an interesting sports game of **"pursue and catch"**, that is he being chased by the leash. He often won. I didn't see any harm in that, but rather enjoyed the display, until … the doggie came charging uphill towards me; in a split-second I realized the possibility of getting caught by that leash and entrapped, as he turned around me to go back downhill; so I shouted, asking him to stop. Either he wouldn't, or couldn't, he kept going taking the same course, as predicted. As he turned around me and started running downhill, the swinging movement of the long leash was momentarily hindered by my body; that was enough to cause the heavy leash's handle to fly around me and firmly **tie me around the arms** where I was. Thus, I was catapulted, like a human cannonball, for a couple of meters downhill. After the customary swears, I got up with no broken bones, or twisted neck, but certainly with damaged ego; luckily, I looked around and didn't see anyone around to laugh at that horrendous spectacle. In his turn, the doggie approached me quickly, presenting profuse apologies.

THE VENGANCE OF THE CANINE

This dog was a few months-old when he discovered that there was a vast difference, in terms of size, between him and our cat suggesting a kind of supremacy, so he started chasing him around. Since the latter had resided with us for several years already, he was 'revered' as the informal and honorary *'head of the house'*. The dog didn't hurt the cat in any way but scared him quite a bit, something that upset all of us. That was reason enough for me at times to get angry. During one such moment I chased him, but he was very young and fast; I caught up with him near the staircase, but not quite close enough to catch and give him a piece of my mind. That inability increased my anger; anyway, a kick then seemed the best result I could get, if that was at all tenable. I was wearing a 'jump suit' which was six inches longer than my legs and at that particular moment was actually running on them, not directly on the polished hard-wood floor.

As my right foot shot up in the air and missed the doggie, my left skidded forward on the floor like stepping on a banana skin. My upward movement was so forceful, that my body flew in the air as swiftly as a soaring ball *(arriba in Spanish)*, and for a fraction of a second (during which forces effecting my upward trajectory equalled that of gravity), it assumed a horizontal posture with my front facing upward; it was like lying down on an air cushion. Unfortunately, what goes up must come down, and this time that consequence was achieved with vengeance; the left side of my back landed squarely on a pointed wooden corner of the stairs.

Finally, my body lay prostrate on the floor with my face touching the floor; the pain was excruciating, giving me abundant reason to produce a terrible scream forthwith. I couldn't even move a finger and stayed there immobile for a few seconds. The scream brought my daughter running downstairs and trying to raise me, while my granddaughter gazed speechless at the body on the floor. I asked my daughter to let me stay there for a few minutes, since my back was hurting so much, I couldn't shift. In few minutes, I could move slowly, but painfully, and was able to stand up, though bent forward. As I did that, my granddaughter asked me if I was all right; then, after a couple of seconds later said: "You know, Haney, when I saw you on the floor and not moving, I thought you were dead!" [Thank you for that blessed thought]. A visit to a walk-in clinic had me assured that there were no broken bones and the doctor asked me if I needed a stronger medicine to quell my pain that was **stronger than Advil**, a suggestion I had to refuse politely, though with barely masked indignation (drug, me!).

As for falling on ice which (in Calgary) we have *'six years of every month'*, such incidents are countless. When asked why sometimes I couldn't perfectly control him, I said: "But haven't you driven on ice; I walk on two legs; **the dog has four-wheel drive!**"

BETWEEN VENUS AND MARS (1)

In the past twenty years, or so, my wife and I started gardening, a practice we both loved and enjoyed very much. We always **helped** each other on designing and building a garden, but this 'cooperation' begs for some explanation.

Help, as most people may understand, comes in different ways. The most common form, and scariest of all, is related to **spending money**, not that it makes me regret it! After all, what is wrong with spending tens of thousands of cents (I beg your pardon, I meant dollars) buying trees and shrubs; she knows I love working on the garden anyway and, with that in mind, I shouldn't complain! As the years passed by, both our front and back yards flourished and displayed wide spectra of changes (towards the better, of course; like they say, the more the merrier!). When we moved to this property, the yards were barren, with the exception of two or three small trees. As it stands now, it (the garden) can be described as an organized jungle that is capable of welcoming any lion, elephant or deer. Over the years, actually, we have had quite a few of the last species, and they are beautiful and so peaceable. We had, though, more than once to **explain to the city officials** *(after a specific neighbour 'complained' that we were 'feeding wild life', including squirrels, coyotes and magpies, in addition to those gentle creatures)* **why, of all neighbours, we were unambiguously chosen by those deer to enjoy that honour!**

Anyway, back to the yards! Their designs changed every year, sometimes drastically, by stern orders coming directly from the Chief Home Engineer herself. That, quite understandably, meant removing parts of the lawn, and planting trees and shrubs, in order to accommodate the necessary changes associated with redesigning. The next summer (and every year there is one of those), we would have the joy of welcoming new arrivals, even after repeated pleas that there wasn't any more room left for additions; but *accommodations had to be made*. Soon, the yards became full of trees and shrubs (I love those perennials), but those plants kept coming, since most of the time they are unfailingly on an eternal 'sale'. Such influxes of new plants generated a dilemma for me, in terms of space.

So, I began a process called 'seeking educated council' from the engineer, herself. Sure enough, there always were **'brilliant suggestions'**, ones that also happened to be subtly mandatory: "Plant those trees and/or shrubs here, there and there", the engineer would say. My answer would logically be: "But, we already have large plants here, there and there". The invariable response to that delicately voiced protestation would then be: "Yes, I thought about that; remove those plants from here, there and there and transplant them somewhere else, like there", and in reply to that reply, I respond with: "But those places are already occupied by..." The dreaded answer, as I soon discovered, was: "I'll **help you** with the transplanting", (indeed!)

After I carefully remove those unlucky plants, and all the while *apologizing and explaining to them* why that painful process had to be performed, the engineer takes them away to be transplanted, or re-transplanted, as the case may be. At the end of an exhausting day, I go to see what happened to the plants I had to remove earlier, and would wish that I had gone inside the house directly, instead; I invariably find their **root ball sitting 'naked' in shallow holes**, with three quarters of their root-ball above the ground! After inquiry as to their condition, I am told that they were given a lot of water, and that was how they should be planted! Replanting them, after a gruelling day, never was an event to look forward to.

I repeatedly remonstrated (gently, that is, without betraying any sign of displeasure), but to no avail. One day, that ritual took place once more, at least in part; I got the instructions as to where the plants I remove had to be left, so that she would take **care of them**. Realizing the inevitability of additional work for me, I had the audacity to pointedly say, as we passed by some junipers she had transplanted earlier: *"You know; the other morning, I was passing by those three junipers that you transplanted and heard them say to me: please do us a favour; re-transplant us; please!"* I heard a grunt of disapproval, followed by scurrying feet, to be followed by three days of "silent treatment", a punitive measure perfected by ladies.

All of those changes, to be fair, have resulted in a garden that is reminiscent of European counterparts, gardens which are densely planted, due to the small areas available there for that purpose, and the persistent everlasting rain. In this regard, and in its present form (most people here calling it too crowded), the yards do not look anything like most North American counterparts.

Of note, our yards contain several **Norwegian** varieties, including *'weeping' spruce* and *larch*, producing forms and shapes designed by Paradise itself; the latter (*weeping larch*) I lovingly call the 'bride' of all trees! In addition to their beautiful shapes and 'feminine' drooping forms, they are truly hardy; so are the arctic *willows* we currently have!

Wide spectra of colour are invariably exhibited throughout those yards: Purplish-brown (Schubert chokecherry trees and sand-cherry shrubs, with leaves becoming fiery brownish-red as they are imperceptibly infiltrated by traces of sun light), while some spruce trees/shrubs' needles, on the other hand, are blue, or bluish-gray; others display various shades of green. A few plants are variably variegated white and green, as in dogwoods (excellent for light-and-dark contrast purposes). With regard to the latter, we have artistically used color contrast, in addition to shape and size variations, to our advantage!

We have concentrated our attention on perennials, including flowering cultivars, since the latter have a naturally wild look to them, in sharp contrast with annuals. We found that certain floral species, like *lilacs* are truly hardy in cold areas like Calgary (hardiness zone 3); flowering *potentillas* and *spireas* are great, in that they grow fairly fast and keep their flowers for a long period, while *bleeding heart* is valuable in shade areas, where few other plants survive. We cannot grow *date palms*; however, there are several apple varieties that thrive in Alberta. Here, we have a 'goodland' apple tree, producing tasty off-white/slightly greenish, sour-sweet apples with a circular reddish patch, where exposed to the sun light; when they ripen during early autumn, one can now and then hear utterances of disagreement, sometimes rising fairly loud, between our area's squirrel and myself.

As for design, we have, over the years, transformed our front and back gardens, into winding tree and flowerbeds only parts of which can be seen at a time, depending on the location of the viewer; such design has been conducive to hints of mystery.

Going back to the Chief Home Engineer, it is imperative and out of fairness here to write that she is an excellent cook, a trait she acquired through personal endeavour in our kitchen, without prior relevant education or instruction. Iraqi dishes are as important to us as Chinese dishes are to the Chinese and Italian dishes to the Italians. Those dishes, which are more desirable than others include: A) Dolmé (grape-vine leaves, bell-peppers, tomatoes, Chinese eggplants and onion scales, all stuffed with a mixture of ground meat, rice, tomato paste/sauce, salt and pepper); this dish is known in several counties of the Middle East, including Turkey, although some use only grape-vine leaves and no meat added (that variety is eaten cold). B) Shish-kebab, barbequed with whole onions and tomatoes (on the side). C) Potato 'chap', composed of 'ground' boiled potatoes stuffed with a mixture of pre-prepared fried ground beef, onions and parsley, with salt, pepper and all-spice. D) Biryani, a mixture of rice, barbequed chicken, potatoes, onions, fried ground beef and carrots. E) Kibbee, composed of a mixture of ground beef and semolina stuffed with beef, and the whole being boiled in water and tomato sauce, together with slices of cucumber. F) And I keep the best for last, and that is beef-curry (with potatoes) presented with Basmati rice.

I, in my own right, am a good cook, as well, but differ from my wife in using *quite a lot of black pepper* and different kinds of curry-masala (with curry dishes), together with a variety of herbs. With the exception of kibbee and dolmé, I believe I have prepared everything else that she had cooked, and succeeded at it, too. I feel pushed here, however, to mention this, not in any way trying to take a well-deserved credit away from her, but (similar to her, of course, I have a sense of ego too) only to relieve some wounded feelings on my side! One day, she was talking with her sister about a variety of subjects ending with cooking and the excellent dishes she makes; then, as an after-thought, she said: "You know, Haney is a good cook too". (Thank you ma'am)! There was a break then, which led me to believe that it was the sister's turn to say something, which I realized, based on my wife's reply, had come in the form of a question. I was then working on my computer close by and saw embarrassment and hesitation on my wife's part, apparently trying hard to remember something in response; then I heard her say: "He makes coffee". I went: "What! All I make is coffee, which only needed hot water?" If I had had a surplus of hair on my head, I would certainly have pulled some of it away!

As for creativity, she has produced several beautifully unique silk-flower arrangements, with designs (photo) indicative of exceptional inspirational imagination. She also does excellent intricate designs by using ornamental material decorating jars and wooden toy-houses.

Flower arrangement (by the Home Engineer)

BETWEEN VENUS AND MARS (2)

The following story is another illustration of how men and women are tuned differently, quite differently, indeed. Yesterday, my daughter came to my office smiling happily with the doggie and said: "**Dad, tomorrow is Rex's birthday**", so I was delighted and sang him: "Happy Birthday to You, partly interrupted with 'to me'!" This morning I prepared my breakfast and, as I moved towards the den (my hideout during the day), I heard my son and his mother talk about 'birthday', and saw him give her hug, or receive one; with a smile, I thought, "how much everyone does love that dog!"

Later on in the morning, I was in the kitchen again for coffee. My wife handed me a plate with two slices of cake and an ice cream and said: "If you are going upstairs, can you take this to our daughter; it is her birthday, today; I bet you forgot!" That was her way of telling me pointedly that again I forgot a birthday! Then, after remembering that I had been told, more than once before, that since no one knew when the doggie's birthday was, including the people who sold him to us, my daughter decided to have his birthday coincide with hers and her twin brother's. *I stroke my forehead hard* and said to myself: "So, that is what my daughter meant to tell me yesterday!" As I climbed the stairs, another thought came to my mind *(causing me to strike the same forehead again, but on a different location)*: "And that is why my twin son hugged his mother; it is his birthday too!" **The ladies reading this story are implored not to laugh**; *this is a serious matter! Why do women beat around the bush; that I cannot understand. Most men, if any, can't, either.*

BETWEEN VENUS AND MARS (3)

A few days ago, my son spoke of an advertisement regarding the sale of older models (though brand new) electronics, including receivers, speakers, etc. at very low prices in a garage sale in our area; a previous owner, who had a stock of such electronics, had recently passed away. My son bought a couple of items, including a Yamaha receiver, at about ten to twenty per cent of their original prices when they came on the market a few years ago. Notwithstanding being older models, they are brand new and definitely represent an excellent bargain for some buyers.

As my son and I were chatting about this transaction, my wife came downstairs and heard some of what was said; she wasn't going to let a golden opportunity like this to pass by without making the fullest 'return' on this occasion to indulge in customary gossipy inquiries. Furthermore, I was (as usual) obliged to accommodate her wishes, without showing the faintest indication of perturbation. So, I explained to her, in as few words as possible, but considering all due convenience and courteousness, what had happened. She then asked: "How come he is selling them so cheap?" My reply was: **"He is not selling them; he is dead, but his family is".** Her retort was: "But, why did he have those new electronics in the first place". Exercising the utmost of self-control on both my thinking and the vocabulary I used, I responded that he might have bought them as part of a business transaction and couldn't sell them. Apparently undaunted and in an effort to extend this gossip enterprise to the limit, her next question was: *"Where did he get them?"* At that I erupted: ***"I honestly don't have the slightest idea; why don't you go and ask him?"*** There was no answer, but she just moved away. (All due respect is paid to the memory of the deceased)

MY BELOVED COUSIN AGAIN (4)

My brother and I, together with our respective families, luckily migrated to Canada, while my sisters and mother ended up in Europe; in both cases, we all are fortunate in enjoying the freedom and reassurances of decent human life offered by the Christian West.

My mother died a few years ago in Denmark; both my sister and niece made frequent pilgrimages to her tomb, and I made it a habit of visiting the cemetery, together with them, every time I travelled there. During one of those events, my sister and niece asked my brother-in-law (husband and father, respectively) to come with us to the cemetery, so that we could continue on our way to visiting relatives, thereafter. On the way to the cemetery, my niece, who was driving, told us that one late evening she made such a visit alone, as she loved her deceased grandma (my mother) when she was alive. She said that at that time, as she was offering a prayer at the tomb, she felt a hand touching her right shoulder. *She had then turned around, but saw no one; after hurriedly finishing her prayer,* **she ran back to her car and sped away.** All of us were shocked, especially her father, who was sitting in the backseat.

As we approached the cemetery, and after having heard this mystic story, my cousin asked his daughter to let him get off outside the place; so, she stopped the car where the cemetery's entrance was after entering a side street. He, however, asked her firmly to take him, instead, back to the 'safety' of the main road, where he could wait for us at a bus-stop at the intersection between the two roads. He had never been to a cemetery before, not even his father's or mother's, since that scared him out of his wits. My niece made a U-turn and did as she was bid.

The cemetery was like a huge, well-kept and fully-treed park, a lovely place to be, **both for the living and the dead!** After being there for about ten minutes, we drove back to the bus-stop to pick him up; *there was my cousin, slouched on a bench with his eyes closed,* **sleeping!** When I called his name, he jumped like being electrified with North American voltage, not European, as people usually survive the former, but not the latter. As he made it halfway to the car, I anxiously said: **"Are you crazy, sleeping so close to the cemetery; aren't you afraid that a 'supernatural hand' might pick you up and put you in a hole in there, without you even realizing it?!"** Then, we all erupted in laughter; it was middle of the day, not at night, so we didn't have to make an escape from the 'scene leading to the Next World!'

MEDICAL PRESCRIPTIONS

Back in the old country, some sixty years ago, living conditions were bearable and people still had enough reason to be polite when they spoke. In deference, they often started with 'My eye' (the most precious of our body parts) when addressing others. A woman went to a family doctor. As she entered his office, she said: "Doctor, my eye..." but was promptly interrupted by him: "Yes, yes, all right"; for him, every minute was money! He quickly scribbled something on a prescription sheet and handed it to her, saying: "Take it to the pharmacist". The very next day, the same woman came back to say: "Doctor, my eye; the medicine you gave me yesterday didn't help; my stomach still hurts".

During another checkup, a doctor wrote a prescription for a man and told him to shake the bottle containing the medicine, which was in liquid form, very well before taking a dose right away. Within an hour, the same guy came back and said: "Doctor, I forgot to shake the bottle before taking the medicine; but I jumped in the air a few times; will that do?"

A TALE OF TWO DOCTORS
(Decidedly Not by Alexandre Dumas)

Here is another story related to the well-being of people, but this one from Canada. During my work with

AGOCO, we had frequent visits at the Geological Laboratory from the 'laboratory coordinator', who was interested in what I was finding (in terms of rock porosity); he often found that exciting. One day he was over-inquisitive and stayed with me the whole day, constantly looking at the rock samples I was examining under the microscope, as they were important from the geological point of view, in terms of porosity and pore connectivity. He was pleasant company; however, I was aware then that his eyes were not clear and always a bit reddish, which concerned me as possibly being due to 'trachoma', a contagious eye ailment.

On my next vacation back home, I explained my concern of possibly having that eye disease to our exceptionally humanitarian family doctor, after which he suggested that I see an eye specialist. Since my stay home was rather short, he quickly arranged for such a checkup, for which I was thankful.

On the day of the appointment, I easily found the eye-specialist's office, which was within a medical center in a mall. Upon my entrance, he quickly and methodically started a checkup. As he progressed, I became aware that what he was doing was **checking my eyesight**! I was intrigued, but at that age knew better to keep quiet; the reference letter from our family doctor must have clearly indicated the purpose of my visit. At the time, I thought that during that dramatic examination process, he, the specialist, must have had that specific examination done, as it was the central issue of my visit. At the end, he didn't mention anything about trachoma, but instead gave me a prescription for lenses, and asked me to go to room #... In my bewilderment, I thought the eye examination would continue in another room provided with some relevant equipment!

As I got to that room, I saw a sign that indicated an "Ears, Nose and Throat (ENT) specialist"; the name of that specialist on the sign, unmistakably indicated that he was the eye specialist's relative, likely a brother. I realized that that analysis was correct after I saw him; both belonged to the same ethnic group, and their features and ages matched fairly well. The receptionist of that office quickly took me to an examination room, where the ENT specialist was waiting. After an exchange of greetings, he had my ears, nose and throat thoroughly examined, as one would expect at a specialist's clinic (no mention of trachoma, of course, since those parts of the body do not, by any stretch of the imagination, get infected with that)! At that point in time I thought: **"Well, business comes in different forms"**!

WHAT IS WRONG WITH SOME PEOPLE?!

Why do some people think they are better than others? In my humble opinion, and I am certainly entitled to have one, I honestly believe that all animals (including *Homo sapiens*) are equal and that all living beings, **be it fauna or**

flora (*a deer/buffalo or a Redwood/Sequoia*), have the same right to life!

So, what makes this guy address me the way he did? I wrote an e-mail to the investment company I have dealt with a short message indicating my intent to **urgently** withdraw a certain amount of money from my own investment account. A week passed by, without receiving anything. So, I called them asking to talk to the person dealing with my request. I was told that that person was not there, neither did his manager, but I was going to be connected with one of the 'directors' of that company. After an extended period of waiting, which I attributed to clarifications regarding my case being made to the director, I heard a loud and irritated male voice: "YES?" My instinctive reaction was as resounding and equally irritated: **"YES"!** His tone suddenly changed, becoming polite, for a change that is!

MY NAME IS ...

A couple of years ago, I started to have difficulty with talking for an extended period of time, as that invariably caused me to cough because my larynx got quickly irritated; I was then referred to an ENT specialist. When I got to that clinic, I was asked to wait for my turn in a small waiting area. Soon after I sat down, the clinic's door opened and a beautiful young lady entered followed by whom I thought was her mother, who was not any less attractive; **both were very tall**. As they sat opposite to where I was seated, I was intrigued by their towering height and couldn't resist the force of curiosity. I stood up, approached them respectfully with a friendly smile and addressed the young lady with: "I am 5 foot and 1 inch **tall**; how **short** are you, if I may ask?" She blushed and said shyly: "six - seven". Noticing that her 'mom' appeared bemused, I continued: "Basket-ball?" She replied: "No". I didn't push my luck any further, and went back to my seat, engrossed in making calculations regarding how much the top of her head was higher than mine and try to absorb the result of that mathematical calculation; the thought wasn't very pleasing!

In few minutes, I was asked to wait in an examination room. After some time, the door opened and someone, I presumed was the doctor, entered; at that, I thought: "Good; no more waiting"! That gentleman left the room after 'visiting' a cupboard without a word, as he did when he entered.

Ten minutes later, the same gentleman came back, and like before, he acted as though the room was empty! As he entered, he turned sharply to his right and went directly to a wash basin, where he started washing his hands. A few seconds later, while keeping a close look at them (his hands), he (without any sort of introduction as etiquette invariably calls for) abruptly and brusquely announced his name in an authoritative voice, with what I perceived as a hint of arrogance: **"Kroddy"** (not real). My answer was short, brisk and not less terse: **"Yes, I know"**. (I would have thought that there were some considerations to be followed when introducing ones' self; maybe I didn't fit that category because of my ethnicity, age or size)! To be fair, however, *he did a good job of detecting the cause of that problem, for which I expressed my gratitude there and then.*

THE TODDLER AND THE CARTOONIST

A few days ago, I saw our Chinese neighbor's two year-old toddler with her nanny. She is about a foot high, shy and has an angelic face (as all babies and toddlers do), truly an adorable tiny little creature, not that I am big by any standards! I had a few casual words with that lady complimenting the kid and telling her that she was 'huggable' (the kid, that is, and here I must make it clear that there was no misunderstanding on her part). Yesterday I had a chance to see the toddler's father, while he and his family were preparing to leave their home, and a funny/cartoonist picture jumped to my mind.

After saying "hello" to him, I continued: "Do you know what happened? The other day, I saw your daughter with her nanny and asked the kid if I may have a hug; she said 'NO!' He smiled and commented that she was a shy kid. I continued: "So, I said to her 'just a 'liiiiitle' bit, please; the kid then emphatically said: '**I said no! Go away, or I call**

my father'. He went: "ha, ha, ha, ha", whole-heartedly; I love making people laugh.

THE HUMAN BALL

One day I was visiting my nephew's family in Denmark. It was during a mild afternoon, and some of us were congregated in the garden; the rest were inside preparing supper. The family have three cute children, whose ages fell then within a range of *eighteen months* and *five* years; the oldest two were playing joyfully close by. I watched them for a while and then wondered about the third, the youngest and quietest (nothing bothered him); I couldn't see him. For a few seconds I was somewhat concerned, but then I got a glimpse of him through a shrub separating me from a play-house. I moved around the shrub and saw a 'ball' clothed in white, somehow attached to the lower wall of a playground structure at a height of about two feet above the ground; I saw neither arms, nor legs! I had had then some wine, but I wasn't drunk, not at all, Sir; what I saw was real!

I hurried towards him only to assure myself that he actually had all the rest of his body parts with him. Nothing was missing, and he was holding tight to a bar attached vertically to the structure! As I got close to him, I saw his right hand move up the bar and hold tight, then his left hand did the same above the other. After that his legs went up and landed right in front of his chest; in that position, his form became spherical (almost). By that time, his grandfather (my cousin) sauntered carelessly and, noticing my excitement, said that the kid had done that before more than once. When that kid got up to a ledge, his grandpa picked him up and put him on the ground. Without losing a precious moment (life after all is so exciting), the kid now started to go up a ladder; that was a piece of cake!

His mother later said that one day at the kindergarten/ day-care unit, she went out for one or two minutes; by the time she re-entered the room, he was dangling from a window's ledge with one hand! That kid could hardly take a few steps on solid ground without falling down, but he never complained!

THE BIG POLICEMAN AND I
(No relation to the movie "The King and I")

A couple of years ago I had a minor accident resulting from improper driving, whereby I bumped into a parking car as I backed my car; I couldn't then turn my body to properly watch what was behind my car, *on account of a damaged back, honest and cross my heart*. My daughter and I made inquiries regarding the owner of the other damaged car and spoke to him; he assured us that there was **'no problem'!**

Regardless, my daughter and I decided that the accident should be reported to the police. She took photographs of both **'hitter'** and **'hitee'** cars (mine and the other's, respectively) on her cell phone. We then went to the nearest police station and explained to them. The policeman taking care of this issue, brought a camera and asked us to lead him to my car 'the hitter'. He took a few relevant photographs and asked us to go back with him, in order to prepare a report.

My daughter, being ahead, entered first and kept a heavy towering glass-door open for me. I took over, held it open and, out of an entrenched habit, indicated to the policeman behind me to go in first. He refused, held the door above my head and emphatically asked me to proceed. I couldn't help my humouristic way of thinking and, in a veiled serious tone, asked him: **"Are you afraid I might attack you from behind?"** My daughter burst laughing at that unanticipated remark, while he **seriously** replied in the negative. He had a 7 foot-'long', 300 pounds body; mine humbly stood at only 5-foot, 1-inch" 'long' and 110 pounds in weight! **As if I would, or even could for that matter; a sense of humour, Sir!**

IS LARGER BETTER?

The answer to that is: Not necessarily. Around 1979, while visiting London (the big town, not the one in Ontario), my brother and I saw strawberry being sold on the road; coming from the Middle East, we got excited, since we had never seen any before, except in pictures! Those strawberries were small, deep-red and fragrant. I bought one kilogram to take home. We walked just a couple of minutes farther and found more strawberries being sold. Those, by contrast, were huge but not as deeply red as the previous ones.

Having limited resources, I was dismayed and wished I had seen the latter first. Anyway, I couldn't resist the temptation; after all, we used to say 'money goes, money comes'. So, I bought a kilogram of the larger ones too. I couldn't wait to go back home to eat strawberries. I tried one of those magnificently large strawberries first; it hardly had any flavor, so I ate another one, only to get the same result! I became disconcerted, thinking the other batch of strawberries would be even worse. I think the reader guessed the rest of the story! Being wrong, that time, was a welcome outcome.

BETWEEN ONE METHOD AND ANOTHER

It is a well-known fact that the English people are tea-lovers; at least they were as far as I know. They add tea, often good quality, to freshly-boiled water in a tea-pot, after which the latter is enclosed with a thick and tightly-fitting tea-pot cover; the tea then is left to brew for a few minutes.

Where I came from, we boil water, transfer it to a teapot, and put the latter on top of a kettle, where water is boiling. Tea leaves (sometimes with ground cardamom) are then added to the tea-pot and left to brew for about ten minutes; that is what I am drinking now! Using samovars, the Russians apply a comparable technique, where upward-moving hot air is used to brew tea in a tea-pot placed directly where hot air flows out from a tube inside the samovar.

Soon after arriving at AGOCO to start a new job, I, together with others, were invited to have tea at one of the local work associates' home. There, we sat cross-legged on the floor, forming a circle. That associate brought a small stove, which he placed on the side of that circle. He then added a substantial amount of tea and many spoonfuls of sugar to water in a kettle; he boiled the water, with its content for quite some time, which I found astoundingly outlandish! Then, he poured the content, now a **thick, foamy black liquid**, into another teapot while holding the former about ten centimeters above the latter and then re-transferred it to the former; he repeated this action several times, before serving it!

The first time I heard about green tea was when a new Chinese acquaintance asked me if I wanted to have green tea, instead of the regular dark Ceylon/India tea. I accepted the former out of curiosity, which he soon served. I looked, with anticipation, at the cup he brought me; there was no tea in the cup, but slightly murky water. As he moved back to his chair, I asked: "Where is the tea, Jo?" By contrast to their method

of brewing dark tea, Libyans make excellent green tea, which
they import from China. As soon as the tea is ready, they add
a few fresh leaves of strongly fragrant mint.

FROM HERE TO ETERNITY
(No professed relationship to the movie)

During the first year of my arrival in Benghazi (1988),
the Expats were truly spoiled by a Portuguese kitchen staff,
in terms of tummy and mind-satisfying 'yum-yum' food.
After a whole year of such indulgence, it was time for my
first physical exam, after which I had the displeasure of being
informed that I had had high blood pressure and unhealthy
elevated levels of cholesterol and other bad fats. That revelation
meant that I stop eating anything and everything which was
grouped as delicious, or even tasty, with the exception of
fruits and vegetables; oh, yes, I could eat as much spices as
my stomach could hold!

With time, our family physician, who is generously
humanitarian at heart, insisted on lowering the levels of both
causes for medical concern to those worthy of a twenty-year
old man, and he did so! During another annual physical-
exam episode two years ago, he looked at the test results and
gave me the relevant numbers for blood pressure and bad
lipids. Then he said that the results were excellent, and good-
naturedly declared that I '*might live up to two hundred years*';

at that I would then be competing with "Gagool", in **Sir H. Rider Haggard**'s *'King Solomon's Mines'*.

At this junction, the reader might have guessed that this is an introduction to something else, which is correct! A week ago, I went to a store specialized in the sale of eye-glasses, in order to replace the aging pair I have been using for the past one hundred and fifty years, and I was in one of my happy talkative moods. The older saleswoman taking care of my order and I chatted for a quite some time while going through finding a new pair that fitted my face very well. She noticed my excitement for having one that I liked and had to let me know that it will take three weeks for the eye-glasses to be ready, and then asked me if that was all right with me. In response, I told her I had no difficulty there and that I was prepared to wait three months, even three years, after which I related to her my present state of affairs regarding health. Then I added: "So, you see, even if I had to wait that long, I still have many years left to enjoy using those glasses", to which she expressed full understanding with merriment and protracted laughter.

This story reminds me of another. There was a middle-aged dentist, who had the greatest of esteem and admiration for his own princely self (at least that was what he firmly believed). This honorable caretaker of human mouths fell in love with a young bird-like lady, to whom he went with all expressions of happiness and expectation and asked for her hand in marriage. That confused heavenly creature, who wasn't by any stretch of the imagination thinking of matrimony (definitely not to him), tried her best, with profuse expressions of apology, citing various reasons to decline his marriage proposal without daring to refer to the miserable state of his bald head, and wishing him all the best in finding someone else. Stunned by that rejection, this gentleman flares up: *"What; you refuse my offer, a dentist and driver of a Ferrari! You are making a biiiiig mistake. If you stuck with me, your teeth would have lasted you a thoooousand years!"* (That is even better than my projected 200 years!)

PART NINE: PERTAINING TO SPORTS

OF KARATE AND THE UNBELIEVABLE
(The Karate Section)

One Friday afternoon, and right after we had had lunch at AGOCO's guest-house's cafeteria, four of us expats decided to play bridge in one of the ground-floor's rooms, with Kays (who graciously tolerated my frequent failure to play right) and I forming one of the two opposing teams. One of the 'opponents', whom we only knew casually, carried a couple of large fresh oranges offered at the cafeteria; as we sat down, he put them down carefully on a coffee/end-table close by him.

At one point during the game, my partner (typically reserved and quiet) and I won the "contract"; I had to play that particular game. As "dummy" (a term technically related to that game), my partner leaned back on his chair for a second, and then stood up, seemingly restless. He moved about, then came back; as he reached the coffee table, his right arm lifted in the air and quickly and sharply came down with both adroitness and precision, and at the same time unexpectedly roaring **"hayah"**; one of the poor unsuspecting oranges broke in half. Its rightful owner froze in his seat without saying a word, perhaps wondering where the *next "hayah" was going to land*; the rest of us laughed uncontrollably.

(THE UNBELIEVABLE/BELIEVE IT OR NOT SECTION, MORE LOGICALLY THE LATTER)

And now for the second part of the heading, above. On another occasion (about 2002) and on the same table, four of us sat to play bridge after having a hearty supper at the guest-house; once more Kays and I were partners. All were in a good mood and that probably was what prompted us to decide to get a new deck of cards. One of the opponents rose and went to his room to bring one, which he promptly did. He opened the brand new box, and drew the cards out. After removing the jokers, he shuffled and shuffled the cards several times. He then placed the deck of cards in front of my partner, who *'cut'* it. As the cards were new, someone suggested jokingly to have it 'cut' again. The cards owner didn't hesitate and placed them in front of me, and I gave the deck the same ceremonious treatment.

He dealt each player thirteen cards, which we picked up; looking at my cards, I was stunned! After a moment's silence, the dealer bid **seven diamonds**; I jumped into the fray with **seven hearts**, soon to be followed by **seven spades**. We looked at each other in amazement, then one of us laid down his cards, face up, and the rest did the same. Each of us had thirteen cards of the same suit! (An almost impossible, albeit true, story to be *believed, or not believed)!*

UNPARALLELED SPORTSMANSHIP!

An international football game (as in European) is taking place. One of the well esteemed, internationally-recognized players had set his mind on scoring, whatever the cost; but, alas, even after trying his very best, he just couldn't! Anger, preceded by prolonged frustration, finally took control of that player; as a result, fate gave him the opportunity to be physically in contact with the shoulder of one of the adversaries, who had the misfortune to be close enough. After a split-second decision, and as they both were forming one 'intertwining' mass during a simultaneous jump, that player, who was stout and had a remarkably pronounced and large teeth, bit it (that is the other's shoulder!) Then, sure enough, good Earth's gravity brought both of the players slamming on the ground.

Both gentlemen started to protest vehemently and simultaneously: The "**Bitee**", jumping in the air and howling, disgustedly uncovered a shoulder with reddish, immaculately-imprinted teeth-marks reminding one of the *'fleur-de-lis'* emblazoned on Milady de Winter's shoulder in Alexander Dumas' *'The Three Musketeers'*. The "**Biter**", in his turn, had his mouth wide open and a finger pointing to his seemingly perfectly-intact front teeth. When asked, the former indicated that he was rudely bitten, in plain contravention of the most sacred rules of the game. In his turn, the latter, who decidedly was the more vociferous of the two, *claimed pearly innocence and complained that* **the other guy's collar bone struck his mouth, and that it was very hard too; it might have broken his tooth**, *he said over and over, again!*

On a different note, another 'innocent' incident took place during boxing. This tough champ was challenged by another, who proved to be equally tough and an even more proficient boxer. After several bouts, during which the **champ** gave the fight *more than his very best*, he became overwhelmed with mind-blinding frustration and anger. He came to the irreversible conclusion that if internationally-accepted boxing rules and regulations were not the right way to deal with his 'challenger opponent', so be it; if he couldn't beat him with fists alone, he should employ an additional tool, but he needed to be in a very close contact with him.

When the opportunity presented itself, he placed his face very close to that of the challenger's, an act which some people hailed, as they thought he was going to kiss his opponent, in brotherly forgiveness for all the crushing punches the other had so rudely (without even asking: may I?) landed upon him. That facial contact lasted almost three seconds, but may have seemed an eternity to the challenger; instead of expressing appreciation as some may have expected, however, he (the challenger) jumped half a metre in the air, howling! Those spectators advocating the kissing assumption, as everyone else, were shocked to see blood on the arena canvas, together with a sizable torn piece of the challenger's ear-lobe. Consequently, the Referee stopped the boxing match abruptly, an action that caused the "Biter champ" to wonder if he had actually won the contest by means of **technical 'ear-biting' knock-out**, but disappointedly realized that it wasn't the case, at all; and, worse than that, he had to abide by it! (Both of these stories are from the inexhaustible actual reality shows of life's theatre)

ASKING FOR SUPPORT FROM GOD!

Just before the start of a recent (July 2015) game of football (soccer to some) between Canada and Brazil on Canadian soil, the camera showed the Brazilian goal-keeper kneeling on the soccer field's turf ground and half raising his arms towards the Heavens, where he was fervently looking. Latinos tend to be expressly religious, so I plausibly thought that he was praying to God to keep the ball as far away from his goal as possible; his wish appears to have been granted, since the Canadians failed to score in that game!

The camera then momentarily focused on another Brazilian player. The latter, one of the strikers, was in the middle of a similar posture; my thought then was that the guy was praying to God to give him goals (on the other side of course) **lots and lots of goals**.

PART TEN: ANIMALISTIC

WAWEE DID IT!

My granddaughter was about two years old then; she was lying on her back on the kitchen's island-table, with my wife having the kid's pampers changed. Lying in that position, the kid was facing the ceiling above her and looking at a small patch where white paint had peeled, due to water damage. All of a sudden, she points to the ceiling and says: **"Wawee broke it"**! (Wawee was what she called our big German Shepherd-Rottweiler dog, Louie).

Then, after a moment's contemplation, possibly pondering the complex physics involved in that 'heinous' deed, and explaining what had actually happened, she exclaimed: **"He jumped higher and higher"**. (That was one scientific dilemma solved).

Five years later, the same granddaughter, now a sensitive beautiful kid who knew I was her mother's father, asked me (at age 70) how old I was, to which she got the following answer: "Forty." To that she responded in amazement: "Oh; you are the same age as my mom!" I then said: "Yes, what a coincidence!" At age seven, her brother asked me the same question and got the same answer, to which he made no reply, but only gave me a probing look. After apparently consulting with his grandmother (the home engineer), he later came back and talked about something irrelevant, after which he said casually: "Haney, I know how old you are; you are seventeen." I sensed a mocking tone in his voice and had to say that that wasn't correct, only to get this response: "Yes, I know; you are forty". So, I happily said: "You got it!" Following what appeared to be a 'grace period', he went: **"You are seventy-five; aren't you sad?"** After guessing what was going on in his mind I nevertheless asked him why I should be sad, he went: *"Because you are going to die soon?" (I was so happy until that last encounter)!*

Today (first week of December, 2015), our home chief engineer went to the church accompanied by both of her grandchildren. She had in the past complained about our grandson as being talkative during mass and thus wasn't keen on taking him in particular, but agreed to do that after I told him firmly that he should be quiet there. Two hours later, they came back; as she entered the house, she told me that unlike previous instances, he sat quietly during the mass; then it was time for the preacher to give his sermon. He had come recently from sub-Saharan Africa and had a heavy accent and thus was difficult to understand. As such, the church, usually full, was very quiet in an effort to catch every word he pronounced. Today's sermon was longer than usual and our kid was quiet throughout. However, as the parson finished his sermon and started to turn in the middle of silence and contemplation, our 7 year old grandson drawled: **"Finally"** in a quite audible voice. Embarrassed, my wife instinctively turned around, only to see several heads turned towards him. *But, he was quiet 99% of the time, wasn't he?*

DENDESH AND THE UNWAVERING AGGRESSOR

I was around twelve year-old. It was early evening when my Dad and I went on top of the roof, where our beds were (we had then flat roofs, so it was convenient for people to sleep there during summer nights). There was no television and, out of boredom, some people went up there to catch a puff of cooler air. I remember that on one such afternoon, I was with him there at dusk when we both heard the two consecutive cannon-like booming sounds of, presumably British, jet-fighters pass low overhead as they landed at the Basra airport, which was only a couple of kilometers away. We never had any such experience before and were definitely startled. As those jets passed by, my father called his friend on his roof, two houses away and asked him if the war had started again. The other, an electrical engineer, was better informed and was able to explain. The very next day we walked to the airport to see the two planes; I remember that they were light gray and had what appeared like two parallel tails.

Our duplex building had an open area, as large as the building itself, behind it. The latter functioned as a square in front of a small Assyrian church serving the Assyrian (Ashuriyeen) people in al-Ma'qal. Also, it was a convenient 'football ground' where my brother and I played with the neighbours' kids, using a tennis ball. Also, we had door-to-door salespeople announcing what they had to sell passing through there; of those, I remember a woman calling the residents to buy eggs, and another, Ilyahu, a Jewish merchant who sold fabrics. When the latter passed by calling potential buyers, sometimes my mother would open the backdoor and ask him what he had. He normally carried a whitish cloth within which he had several fabrics, each wrapped around a flat wooden plank; he unfurled without hesitation those patterns, which my mother showed interest in for better exposure. On leaving, he rewrapped everything and carried it on his back.

Now, back to our house's roof; our dog, Dendesh, once accompanied my father and me there and was as happy with the cooler air as we were. While there, however, he sensed the presence of another dog on the square's ground below. He went on the ledge and did see a dog there, which, in his mind, appeared as a sinister monstrous aggressor with nefarious intentions against him personally (or, in this case, doggedly). Dendesh was not the most valiant among his peers, but in defense of his inalienable right to reign supreme on that ledge and, considering his physically inaccessible elevated position, he felt comfortably safe and could afford to **show as much indignation and daring as the occasion called for**! There was no way he would relinquish supremacy of his majestic lair!

In his turn, the dog 'downstairs' likewise believed that the existing column of air (also defined as a measurable distance, in this case **height** above a **rigid** ground surface) **was not something the dog on the ledge would ponder sailing through** (not if he was in his right mind), and therefore paid no attention, not even an iota. That nonchalant attitude was considered by the defender upstairs as provoking and unpardonable; it only poured fuel on fire that already existed, something that drove him utterly furious.

The defender's location was strategic, but also precarious; Dendesh, however, out of inexcusable ignorance, wasn't aware of **Isaac Newton**'s Law of Gravity. Nonetheless, envisaging imminent danger, although from far down below, and not foreseeing a potentially injurious outcome posed by that law of physics, he barked so loudly and vehemently that eventually his **center of gravity wandered out of its allocated ledge area**, resulting in the loss of his cherished balance. And there was Dendesh flying in the air and falling on top of the unsuspecting would-be aggressor underneath him. Screams of agony, but more so of fright, emanated from both dogs. Screams were followed by panicky retreat and hasty escape in two opposite directions; both survived the ordeal and were happy to see that they could still leave the scene of that encounter intact, with every limb accounted for, though somewhat physically hurt, but certainly with bruised dignity!

MY CHAIR AND MY CAT; WHO CONTROLS WHAT!

I had a comfortable chair in my office at home; that was a blessing, since I spent most of my time during the day there. That office also had another chair, to which I attached a stool. Both were covered with a soft blanket; they were also topped with both comfortable and cushiony circular cat seat. The latter arrangement I lovingly prepared for my 22-pound male cat, a gray stray 'who' my daughter found in our backyard; when we 'found' him *(my daughter said it was more like **he found us)**,* this cat was athletic, then weighing less than12 pounds. He attained the difference in weight, and thus loss of his former graceful form, after I mistakenly brought him several kinds of treats and food, some of which even appeared fit for sandwiches (not for cats, but humans).

All of these comfort-oriented preparations weren't satisfactory to him, and he often chose my own chair to sleep on. Every time I found him there, I had to ask for his permission to take him to his own chair, only to find out that if I left the room for any reason (to answer a door bell, for example), I would see him back on my chair when I returned. I move him to his allocated place and go to make a cup of tea, only to find myself in the same state of affairs, later. After three years of this delicate and unstable peaceful coexistence, I decided to buy a large new chair, this one exclusively for my own 'selfish' enjoyment and comfort (well-deserved at that); after all, that old chair became considerably 'worn out'.

After anxiously waiting several months for the new chair to arrive, the cat took the liberty of sleeping on it too! When asked about the meaning of such transgression, he just looks at me in a way signifying: **"Are you kidding me? That chair is too old; you sit on it! Anyway, it is too small for me now!"** However, during the first few days after we had that lavish chair installed, he (the cat) apparently tried to be nice to me (after all, I was the guy who paid for it) and condescended to give me enough space to sit on the edge beside him while working on the computer. After a while, though, he decided that that temporary complimentary accession was all he had owed me; now, whenever I leave the room, he spreads himself long and wide on the new chair, in order to leave me no space to sit at all. When I come back, there wouldn't not even be a square inch available to sit on! Take this experience, for instance; he used the same tactic then: *Once, returning to the room with a hot cup of cocoa, I found out that there was no chance for me on that chair. So, I accepted my luck and sat down on my old chair. As I did so and took a sip, while forcefully twisting my body, in order to be able to watch*

TV sideways, 'he' woke up and, with slanted half-opened eyes, looked at me in such a way as indicating: **"Now you understand!"** I asked a lawyer if *I could do something about that disagreeable situation; he advised me that there* **was no case** *at all!* This, my dear reader, is the *status quo* at present.

This cat, who in his own right is a boxer, now and then whacks me with right hooks, especially if he thought I was mocking him. He also has to get some of the jam and sour cream I eat for breakfast, **or else**; that is another good reason for whacking! This cat is truly demanding; I am in the middle of typing, and he starts scratching my expensive desk. No matter how many times I tell him that **he is fat** because of eating too much; when he wants food he has to get it, one way or the other. *[There is a concern relative to this name-calling, which sometimes brings certain annoying thoughts. Both of us die and go to Heaven, but before we are allowed in, there are certain routine questions to be answered. The cat goes first and is asked about his previous life and how I treated him, to which he gives a fair account; but in an answer to a final question, he goes: "Yes, he was all right, but he always annoyed me by calling me 'fat'; also there is the matter of the chair.]*

So, I go to the kitchen, where his food is, followed gingerly by him, and then come back to continue my work. After a short while, he comes back licking his lips. So far so good; I am relieved, because he is content now. No so fast; he gets on my desk and unceremoniously pushes me away from the typing board and, while incessantly purring, goes: "Scratch my back, scratch my tummy, squish my ears ..." **I ask you Reader, is this my retirement reward?!**

His attacks, *only when warranted to be fair*, goes further to include cases of facing unwarranted aggression and nuisance, which can be construed as specifically directed towards him! In those cases, usually filled with rudeness, our big dog stands out at being the most prominent troublemaker! This cat has for two years, that is since we got our dog, made it abundantly clear to the latter that they were genetically different, and that he had absolutely nothing to do with him! I tried to convey the same message to the dog, but to no avail. The doggie, in his turn, is angry as to why he gets this unfriendly treatment, since his only objective in approaching the cat is to play and make friends; and on that peaceful intention, he says, he is more than ready and willing to swear. We, *Homo sapiens* understand that very well, but that fine canine creature doesn't appreciate it!

Let me give you an example of what sometimes happens between the two. The cat goes to the kitchen, eats a fishmeal and sits contently, with one of his front legs across the other, on two stools put closely together. The doggie sees him and becomes jealous as to how on earth the cat could jump on stools and tables, which are almost as high as a mountain, whereas he couldn't! Also, there is the small matter of food portions; we give the cat about two spoonfuls of soft, juicy and aromatic fish, chicken and beef food, which comes in plastic containers that are clearly marked as being especially prepared for cats, *not dogs*. This connotation, notwithstanding, every time the doggie hears us giving that food to the cat, he rushes to get what he firmly believes as being his Heaven-authorized allocated portion; when we tell him that this food is for cats only, he replies: "I don't care, it tastes good; give me too!" So, he gets a portion equaling that of the cat. After devouring it in two seconds, he is now angry why we gave the cat more of that yum-yum food than him. When asked why he thought the cat gets more than him, his response would be: "Look at him, he keeps eating and eating". To that, we add: ***"But, sir, what you devour in two seconds, it takes the cat half an hour to eat"***, *only to get this reply:* ***"I don't understand that; there is something fishy going on!"***

Sometimes, this dog builds up all the potent courage inside him, comes and puts his nose in front of the cat and almost hysterically goes: "WOH, wuh, WOH"; all the time though he is wary and ready to retreat at an instant's notice. The cat, acting infuriatingly nonchalant, stares at the doggie momentarily and thinks *how stupid that canine is, and whether all members of that species are that dumb too*; he then wonders, for some obviously viable reasons: why doesn't he go somewhere and forget to come back? Then, he turns his head sideways to look at anything else that is of any interest, no matter how trivial. If after five minutes the dog is still barking his head off just under his nose, he whacks him with a left, or a right hook, depending on how he is sitting. As the highly anticipated blow is initiated, he (the doggie) jumps backward just in time to avoid it. At that juncture, the cat resumes his comfortable heedless posture, and the dog moves away, with raised head, thinking that he heroically did what had to be done!

The Belligerent Cat Pushing Away
The Rightful Owner from Chair

THE MYSTERY OF THE VANISHING CHICKEN!

At about lunch time today (August, 2015), my son was in the kitchen happily holding a drumstick freshly cooked in the manner of Kentucky Fried Chicken that his mother had just bought. As he was going to have a bite, the front doorbell rang, and he moved in that direction to answer; I had at the moment headed to the bathroom. When I finished washing my hands and left the bathroom, I heard my son and wife talking about the dog; my son was saying something about the possibility that the dog might choke. I looked at our dog, who was all right and listening to the small discussion between the two. From their talk, I understood that as my son was opening the door with his left arm, his right arm was dangling with the chicken still in his hand. As my son was engaged in talking (just a few words) with the person who rang, **that chicken drumstick disappeared** like a strike of lightning.

We bought this dog as a large three month-old puppy two years ago; a few months later he tripled in size. We had then to be careful about what we put on the kitchen counter and island because he could **reach almost 'everywhere' and strike at any time**. One day, my wife brought a barbequed chicken, as was her habit every week. I had a small piece and, since she had already prepared a couple of dishes that morning, she told me that she was going to use the rest of the chicken in preparing a spicy 'biryani' for the next day. She went upstairs and I walked to my 'den' to watch a TCM's film noir and listen to/watch international news on the internet.

Half an hour later, she came down and went straight to the kitchen to start her next dish; then she came to the 'den' and asked me where I had moved the chicken, to which I replied: "I didn't touch it". She looked in our two fridges in the hope that she might have put it in there and forgotten. No chicken! Both of us looked at the doggie and asked him if he had taken it; we got this solemn reply: **"I don't know where the chicken is, cross my heart; if I had eaten it, where are the bones? And one other thing; why do you come after me; how about the cat!"** (As if; the chicken was as big as the cat itself!)

He had a point, though; there was no trace either of meat or bone to be seen! I thought it was a 'Bizarre, Perfect Crime!' I wish there was a way of sending this plot to both **Arthur Conan Doyle** and **Edgar Allan Poe**.

The Author (checkered sweater) and doggie (four legs)
(not to confuse)

TO 'POO' OR NOT TO 'POO'
(Apologies to Shakespeare)

Here, it is worthwhile to relate a relevant story regarding that cat, which may also fit as an epilogue to "a tale of two doctors", above. Once, our cat had a problem; out of ignorance, we had fed him dry cat food only, which apparently was too dry for regular bowel movement. One day we at home noticed that 'he' was stressed out and trying to hide. We soon realized that 'he' had a bowel problem; there was about 1 centimeter of dry 'poo' sticking out of his rear end, and he couldn't get the rest out. All of us were concerned, and my two daughters took 'him' that night to a '24-Hour' Vet Hospital. There, they gave him something to make him relaxed, together with a laxative, and said they would wait up to the next day to see what happens.

The next day, my daughters went to that hospital and brought the cat back, without 'poo,' and we were happy. Out of simple curiosity, I asked what had happened. They said at first they (the clinic) **took an X-ray of his rear end** and the result showed the presence of 'poo' (hurrah for technology), then they removed that 'poo', which was so unambiguously and irrefutably identified, manually. I could easily understand the necessity of having the latter 'operation' performed, **but an X-ray! To show what, the rest of the 'poo'?** That 'poo' 'operation', including the X-ray, cost us about $2,000!

THE RUDE UNPRINCIPLED HORSE

One day around 1974 I was walking with my brother-in-law, a masculine guy, in al-Ashar open-air vegetable market; the greens and fruits there were lush and fresh, in a way calling to by-passers "Buy me, buy me". That was exactly what he did; he bought two large bunches of shiny flat-leaf (Italian) parsley. He was so happy with what he bought (after all he was, like myself, an 'addict' fresh-vegetable eater), he held one in each hand above his shoulder.

We went only a few feet back towards the entrance of that market in order to go back home; on the left side of that open market, I noticed the presence of an old cart, to which a huge brown horse was tethered (they are all big anyway, aren't they?) As we passed by the horse, I perceived a sudden jerky movement to my left and instinctively turned my head sharply in that direction. I saw then a huge horse's head holding a bunch of parsley in that part of it known as 'mouth', move unhurriedly but determinedly away from my brother-in-law, who was walking on my left side. At that point in time, the latter still had both arms up to his shoulders just like before, but he was holding one bunch of parsley in his right hand, while his left hand was wandering up in the air empty and wondering where the parsley went. I couldn't hold myself but laugh and, turning to him, I said: **"The horse didn't even say: 'excuse me, or thank you, Sir'!"** He made no answer, but went back to buy another bunch; this time we walked on the right-hand side of the market.

In retrospect, and considering the quality of that parsley, which I still remember very well, I must say that I would certainly have done the same, if I was that horse; I do love fresh vegetables grown naturally, without the use of chemical fertilizers! You name them: any kind of onions, garlic, chilli, parsley, mint, basil or radish, which I usually eat in bunches, often using them to make veggie sandwiches. After all who am I to attempt discrediting the diagrams of that greatest of all scientists, Charles Darwin, Esq., depicting that humans have ultimately developed from such creatures as fish, frogs and kangaroos?! *[https://en.wikipedia.org/wiki/ Tree_of_life_(biology)]*

ANIMAL NOMENCLATURE

When animals were created, Archangel St. Gabriel was given the task of giving them names, so they could be distinguished individually. In a huge gathering including all animals, the lion goes first to the counter, where St. Gabriel is sitting. The Saint says: "Your name is 'Lion', go". The next animal gets the name 'Elephant', the next: 'Tiger'; 'Giraffe', and so on.

Now, it is the turn of the animal we know as 'donkey'; Saint Gabriel gives him a name (unfortunately not mentioned in the Book of Animal Names for our reference). The donkey starts to go, but then turns and asks: "What did you say my name is?" St. Gabriel gives him the same name again. The donkey takes a few steps away and turns to ask the same question. The Saint becomes irritated, but says it again. The donkey nods, indicating unfailing acknowledgement. But, as he goes away a little distance, he comes back and says: "I keep forgetting it; what is my name again?" St. Gabriel, by now furious, yells: *"Get out of here... you ... you 'Donkey'!"* *(Folkloric)*

OF SMALL ANTS AND BIG ELEPHANTS

In a jungle in Africa, there was a large ant colony, where everything was organized and peaceful, until, one day, they heard loud thumping. All they saw after that was destruction and dead ants; an elephant had just unwittingly roamed through the colony. They did their best to repair the damage. A week later, however, the same elephant came again trampling on ants and wreaking havoc, perhaps without even realizing; such an assumption is based on the absence of any apologies, or even explanatory clarifications. The ants' ruler soon realized that what had transpired posed existential danger to his flourishing ant community. It was a problem that had to be resolved, the sooner the better; so, as *'head of state'*, he decided to have a meeting of his top army generals; they unanimously voted to attack the elephant and kill it, once and for all; just to go ahead and do it! [*No place for threadbare red lines lacking credibility* (as those discarded in Syria), or toothless *'all options' are on the table* (as those wasted on Iran)]

So, they formulated an iron-clad attack plan, whereby the ant army would lay in hiding along the route the elephant had taken earlier, before he reached their colony. After a while, there he comes sauntering towards them. Sure enough, as soon as he approaches the colony, the elephant is attacked simultaneously from all sides, and within a short time many ant soldiers were scrambling up his legs and crawling all over his back.

One of the ant soldiers who was late, because his war fatigues weren't quite ready yet, came running to the battle scene, while still pulling his trousers up and buckling, and at the same time yelling: "Wait for me; wait for me". As this *bona fide* fighter was in the process of climbing the elephant's foot, he raised his head to find an easy route up. When he was in that process, he recognized his ant-friend, Fawzi, on top of the elephant's neck*! He got very excited to find him in that strategic and controlling attack position, and shouted as loud as he could "Fawzi; Fawzi, put him in a chokehold; strangle him!"* (Folkloric)

WHEN CALCULATORS ARE WELCOME!

A few days ago, my daughter brought an illustrative book on sloths, bearing many beautiful photographs of those cute, but definitely lazy and shiftless animals. One of the images showed a grown-up sloth hugging a tree trunk and looking upwards, while still sitting on the ground. I turned to my daughter and said: "This sloth is thinking: if I wanted to climb all the way up to the top of this tree, how many years would that take?"

Then I read something about sloths fighting, which I found somehow surprising, and I expressed my thoughts to her; she laughed and said that they actually do, and the winner of a fight is the one that stays awake until the end of the fight!

TOM AND HARRY

Once upon a time in the countryside, there was a chicken yard ruled by **Tom**, the **Rooster**. Tom was young, strong and agile, and he had a large number of 'Harem Chickens' to *'take care of'*. As time passes by, however, the owner notices that Tom is becoming rather sluggish and more tired than ever. Being an experienced breeder, he made the inevitable decision.

So, one day he brought young Harry home. He gathered all the chicken and introduced **Harry**, the **Rooster**, to them, after announcing Tom's retirement and thanking him for the many chicks he helped produce. Harry dutifully talked about himself and *boasted about his age and agility*.

Next morning, Harry asked everyone for a meeting to explain his way of doing things. ***His first job every morning was "inspection".*** To show them what he practically meant, he asked them to form a line, side by side, facing the chicken-wire fence. Then he hopped the closest chicken; after he was done mating, he got down saying: *'Thank you ma'am.'* Then he started to go faster and faster about his business, attending to the next chicken and the next... Being exceptionally fast, the compliment went like this: *'Thank you ma'am,'* *'thank you ma'am'*, *'thank you ma'am'*, *'Oh... sorry Tom'*, *'thank you ma'am'*, *'thank you ma'am'*. Reportedly **not** a true story, but this one is: At the end of a hotly contested Bundesliga football game, the scorer of the only and decisive goal was so ecstatic, he was hugging, with widely stretched arms accompanied by an elated smile, whomsoever of his team players who was close by. Then he was unexpectedly confronted by a player, so far obstructed from view by others, who was wearing different T-shirt colors; his arms, which were still high up in the air, dropped beside him like they were made of lead and all vestiges of that happy face disappeared leaving disconcerted drooping features; what anticlimax!

WALKING THE DOG
(Variations exist)

Reportedly, a gentleman was flying from London to Dubai straight. Because of a technical problem, the plane was diverted to Rome. The flight attendant explained that there would be a one-hour delay, and if the passengers wanted to get off the aircraft they could do so but had to re-board in time. Everybody got off the plane, except for an older gentleman who wasn't able to discern his surroundings as well as others; a guide dog lay uncomfortably, but quietly, underneath the seats in front of him.

The pilot approached the gentleman asking him if he liked to get off and stretch his legs. The dog's owner said: "No thanks; but maybe someone can help my dog". Soon after, some of the plane's passengers saw their **pilot, who was wearing sunglasses (**most of them tend to do that anyhow**), walk off the plane with a guide dog**! *Some not only tried to change planes, but airlines altogether!*

'TINY' BIRD BRAINS, INDEED!

During one rather hot and dry summer morning, sunny and bright as usual, my geochemist colleague, Haci, and I arrived at geological-laboratory offices compound. As we entered the open grounds through the gate and walked towards our offices, I noticed a sparrow at a distance flying in a circle and landing on a cement building-block that was directly under a faucet (used for irrigation) which was about a foot above the bare ground. The bird stood there for a few seconds, while looking up towards the faucet's spout; then, I thought: "Poor bird; it is, perhaps, wishing that the faucet was turned on (those selfish humans)!"

All of a sudden it flew towards the spout, made another circle in the air and came back to where it was standing a few seconds ago; again, it waited for a short while, then performed the same manoeuver. It did that one more time before we approached that location. As we got abreast with it, I looked curiously at the faucet; then I noticed a drop of water forming at its end. As it grew in size, I could see the sun's ray going through it; then it became 'fat' and dropped on the cement block! That bird, with its 'tiny' brain (compared with ours illustrious humans, of course) was smart enough to wait until the drop was fat enough, using the sun's ray and caught it just before it fell! *[Tiny brains, indeed! They do not kill each other, like a certain species (110 million people in two World Wars); at worst, they (the birds) might fight over one of their females and that, in my humble opinion, is perfectly natural and in a way chivalrous.]*

Staying with the same geological compound, we (the 'educated' expats), as well as the less educated technicians, had sizable offices with large windows assigned to us individually. Mine was at the very end of the laboratory building, four rooms away from Erhan's. Both of us expats were working under the "rotation system" (1991 - 2000), an arrangement that was actually a jewel of a job! Since we did the same work, we had to take those vacations alternately. This guy, being a person who appreciated the presence of all those animals around (we, *'Homo sapiens'*, being so fortunate to have), he was in the habit of feeding a group of local sparrows on a daily basis. Their diet consisted of dry bread soaked and softened with water; the feeding process was limited to having the 'meal' on a tray placed on the windowsill (on the outside that is, since they objected to having it placed inside; "Redefining the term thrust", below). A day before his departure, he asked me to perform the same ritual, which

I was more than happy to oblige, since I love all animals, big and small (not including mosquitos, though).

The next morning I did the same and put the 'meal' outside my window, since the other room was now locked. First day, there was no bird, second day also no bird; the birds, used to the other location, found nothing there. I was both sad and disappointed. On the third, however, well into the morning, a sparrow landed at my window, as it saw the bread. That bird didn't eat right away, but I heard it **screeching its head off to attract others' attention** and telling them that he had found a treasure and inviting them to come and share! (How very unselfish like some humans)!

I have had the habit of giving seed to sparrows in our backyard in Calgary three times a day, starting with one serving in the morning before I took breakfast. One day, though, I woke up late and, as usual, went into the backyard to feed the birds. I am light-footed, and it appeared that I didn't then make enough noise to alert the birds standing on a shrub in the neighbor's yard waiting to be fed; they couldn't see me either, because of intervening shrubs and trees. As I approached them, I heard one them say: "Where is he; it is almost nine o'clock!" I found, then, that some sort of an apology was due.

On a different note, last year I visited my sister's family in Denmark for a couple of weeks, during which this group of sparrows were not fed, and it appears that they still remember that 'catastrophic' event. Yesterday, the clock was officially set back by one hour. So, there was no practical reason for me to wake up the same time I did earlier. Additionally, the day before I had spent a lot of energy (on the front yard that is, nothing else; cross my heart, being a man of honour and integrity), so I stayed in bed much longer than usual. Following an 'honourable' established habit, I went outside directly, in order to feed those sparrows before having breakfast. As I approached the feeder quietly and cat-like, without any inherent adverse intention on my mind, of course, I heard one of them asking others: **"Do you think that he went to Denmark again?"** (The last part of this story is admittedly fictitious)

THE UNBLESSED BIRDS 'DROPPINGS'

On a more amiable side of birds, I find it necessary to relate this narrative. Kays and I, together with an Arabic-speaking friend, were once in the center of Benghazi heading towards the nearby shops. *We first had to cross a fair-sized park studded with huge 'banyan' trees which were densely foliaged with comparatively thick, flat, medium-sized and deep green leaves that were bursting with life; those trees had **huge roots, often sticking out of the ground close to tree trunks**.*

It was about sunset, and at such a time, that area was buzzing with thousands of *dark birds flying round and round in compact, dynamic and **incessantly changing surrealistic forms of wave-like swarms*** before settling down for the night on those trees. We watched them in wonderment, but one of my two companions (the other Arabic-speaking friend), who had very short hair, expressed loudly a genuine concern about the potential of unholy excrement descending on us from the skies; he said he had just taken a shower. Within just a few seconds of that statement being pronounced, **one such fairly huge 'mass' landed square on his forehead**, right at the 'hair-line' where his hair grew on top of his head! After some swearing, he was told that he shouldn't have made that remark about the birds' poo so loudly!

OTHER STORIES ON ANIMAL BRAINS!

Several years later, I received a musical clip showing a sulphur-crested cockatoo, a white bird with a yellow crest, standing quietly and dejectedly alone on a perch outside his cage. Then, Egyptian music is heard, and the bird starts to shift. Egyptian music, mostly in the form of love songs, is often an invitation to belly dancing. As the song goes on, the bird shifts from one leg to the other, then shakes its shoulders, turns its head sideways, then the wings become active moving up and down and sideways. That bird could beat any belly dancer any time!

Starting a year-long geological training visit to London at the start of 1972, my family and I had just arrived to the country and lived next to a street studded with small shops. One day, as we were enjoying the new environment by strolling leisurely where the shops were, we saw a large dog walking briskly towards us, but all of a sudden stopping and facing the road; that location was at a zebra crossing! It waited no more than two seconds before we noticed that cars moving in both directions had stopped. The dog then crossed the road, and traffic resumed. For us, coming from the Middle East, that was an enlightening experience. How many people in this world now enjoy such treatment out of consideration and respect! I know, for a fact, that there are millions who beg just to be left alone!

I recently mentioned this story to my sister, and she laughed. She said two years ago, while taking an afternoon walk with her husband in Berlin, they saw a large dog walking with his owner; the dog was carrying a basket holding food items his master had just bought. That was, so far, an interesting spectacle. Then, all of a sudden, the dog stopped, lowered the basket to the ground and strolled sideway towards a fence. After peeing there, it returned to the business of helping his master with the grocery!

PART ELEVEN: GENERAL

REDEFINING THE TERM 'TRUST'!

A long, long time ago, somewhere in the Middle East, there were two rulers who abhorred each other. One day, their enmity came to open conflict. Their respective armies, comprised large numbers of horsemen and footmen, all with sharpened curved swords and spears, met at a wide open plain, which was suitable for warfare in those times. Each ruler had his own consulting 'wise-men'/'Shoura' with him.

It so happened that before the start of any serious belligerent action, those 'wise-men', on both sides of the conflict, were inter-communicating between themselves and with their respective rulers, in the hope that they might be able to avoid an undesirable battle by finding a middle of the way solution that might be acceptable to both of the contesting rulers. After some discussions, the leaders of the two warring factions agreed to select a **representative 'wise-man'** from each army, in order to meet and discuss a possible solution without any blood being spilled; both rulers solemnly vowed, upon their honour, to abide by any decision that the 'wise-men' came out with.

So, a 'pow-wow' tent was erected in the middle of the distance separating the two armies; soon, two such 'wise-men' were chosen and sent to the tent for talks! After agreeing whole-heartedly on the futility of having those two rulers accept any peaceful resolution to the conflict, those two **'wise-men'** settled on having both rulers **replaced** by others who are not so hostile to each other. In order to convey their decision to the two armies, they would go out of the tent and each 'wise-man' would raise his hands to be seen by all soldiers from both armies. Then each had to remove a solitary ring from his finger, while saying loudly that he is *'removing his own ruler the same way he is taking his ring off his finger!'* Then, they discussed the tricky matter of who goes first! *One of them, a 'super-wise-man' (more like super conniver) asked the other to go first, since he was older!* ***After all, there was complete trust between them!*** The other, who wasn't 'wise enough,' agreed to do that whole-heartedly!

The not-so-wise-man goes out first, mounts a platform that had been erected mid-way between the armies and does the deed, exactly as agreed upon. Now, it is the super-wise-man's turn; as he starts climbing the platform, he inconspicuously removes the ring from his finger before reaching its top. When he is on top of the same stand, he shows his ring to everyone and hollers as loud as he can: **"I**

reinstate my ruler, the same way I put this ring on my finger!"

[This is an actual historical narrative deserving somber thought and an appropriate comment: Moral: Do not forget; always **inspect and verify; if that means anything at all***! This is said with reference to the recently concluded nuclear agreement, 2015. The latter left all Iranian nuclear infrastructure and facilities intact, but (do not hold out your breath too long) with a* **'solemn' promise and whole-hearted understanding** *that the latter (Iran) may continue its infamous activities, albeit at a slower pace, subsequent to the signing of an* **agreement** *(not even an international treaty, mind you)! This 'arrangement' between what has so far been conceived a "supreme power" (in collaboration with other powers that are deemed 'less supreme') and a regime that has, in the past, proved itself persistently untrustworthy and a cheater is an example of a blatant* **tragic comedy** *forced upon the countries in the Middle East. It is a shameless tacit approval allowing what a very high ranking American official once qualified as a "Rogue Nation" to develop nuclear weapons (not now, but later: as in few years, instead of few months, while keeping 5000 powerful new-generation centrifuges, instead of 18000 old ones!)! Wasn't* **prevention** *the* **whole idea** *behind those negotiations? The latest development in this file, as I am preparing this manuscript, is that the US and its friends in the P5 Package have* **agreed** *to let the* **Iranians inspect their most secretive installation by themselves** *(on the understanding that they must* **report their findings** *to*

the Package members! Do they think that people in the 21ˢᵗ Century are stupid? The answer to that is a blatant "No"; they never were, even thousands of years ago!

*And as far as inspection and verification are concerned, there is no problem, as long as the **Grand Permanent Five+One** (more humbly: P5+1) gave a cautionary **notice** before their personnel arrived at any nuclear facility. That is give the Iranians enough time (say twelve days; let's be generous and make it twenty-four, just in case) to properly hide any such activities as those prohibited by the 'Agreement' (after all, and logically, if they are prohibited, they shouldn't be found out)! Such a scenario is a foretold recipe for the opening of a flood-gate to a runaway nuclear armament race in that region, a recipe paving the way for a potentially uncontrollable holocaustic state of affairs: Befuddling, to say the least! Or, is it an ominous sign of what is to come next?)*

*The latest development in this tragedy, at this stage of writing this book is that a high official of the 'Supreme Power' came out lately with the following 'fatwa': **"The entire world has approved this agreement, except one country".** But, Sirs, Iran did swear time and time again, even from the United Nations' podium itself, and in front of official delegates of the whole world including those representing the P5+1, that it vows, and was determined, to destroy that country (only that country in particular, not any other). The statement put in bold, above, is either naively ridiculous, or misleadingly disinformative! With regard to those negotiations, I would* *like to add that recent history does unfailingly remind us of such great personalities as* **Winston Churchill** *and* **John F. Kennedy***; not that there are viable grounds for comparison with the present!*

A wise note to those who are intimately and existentially concerned is due here; the Godfather, cautioning his son not to trust anyone, said: "Son, I always keep a close watch on my enemies, but have a closer watch on my 'friends'!" (How true in some cases)! *Those of us, who are old enough and have followed Middle East politics in recent history, remember that when the Shah of Iran was pressed (by 'friends') to leave the country in 1979, he begged his 'valued and noble friends' to* **keep him safely there** *by accepting him as a cancer patient, if not the previous head of the country. His pleas were rejected, and he ended up in Egypt where he died in miserable abandonment and obscurity! Again, I say: watch it!*

A TALE OF SUPREME COURAGE

Native Americans, forming many tribes, like the Shoshones, Apaches, Cherokees, Pawnees and Kiowa at one time spread over the Great Plains of North America, have all been but wiped out.

Both of the Native Americans and Plains buffalos have coexisted for thousands of years, with the latter surviving there for millions of years before. Since the mid-eighteen hundreds, both of those species have drastically been reduced in number, and as for the latter, estimated in tens of millions, they have all but been wiped out (30 million, according to Andrew Isenberg in: *The Destruction of the Bison: An Environmental History, 1750-1920;* higher still by other accounts).

Buffalos/bison are, in general, equated with cows, due to a wide spectrum of similarities in size, food preference and overall appearance. So, without delving into scientific details (since I am herein only interested in general analogy), I have a strong inclination to consider them (buffalos) as such (cows).

The annihilation of buffalos took place, or was ordered, in order to destroy the Native's subsistence and their irreplaceable lifeline. Stepping away from the **'reason'** to eliminate a species *(kill the buffalo and the Native dies, rendering his land available to be overtaken)* to **'how'** they were decimated takes us to the subject of method. **Courageous** buffalo **'hunters'** were hired to carry out the massacres. They came by their thousands, fully ready with guns, and here I don't mean 'hand guns', but long rifles, in order to kill those Plains cows from a long distance away; after all, those monsters are 'dangerous' **grazers**. As though that wasn't enough protection for them, those 'heroes' hid in train compartments and shot those animals through windows, just in case the latter have some cows on the lookout, that is 'spies' or guards. The duel between the hunters and cows was never equal, since the cows were deprived of possessing any firearms, even after applying for permission to carry defensive types. *Such one-sided skirmishes, all being characterized by stories of **ultimate valor**, ended in the undisputed victory by the 'hunters' and **assured demise of the cows**.*

Recently, I watched *"The stalking moon"*, one of the best of Hollywood's western movies showing the plight of a woman who wanted to return to the world she knew as a kid before being kidnapped by Native Americans. During the course of the show, viewers had a chance to catch a glimpse of forceful removal of "Indians", or "injins", as some called them, from their ancestral lands in the American Midwest. A wider scope of the plight of Native Americans, as they were forcefully expelled, can be found in **Mari Sandoz**'s *Cheyenne Autumn*.

As I watched, I couldn't help but make an analogy with the ethnic cleansing of Iraqi Feyli Kurdish population during the late nineteen seventies and eighties. Feyli Kurds, who are natives of the Zagros Mountains in northeastern Iraq bordering Iran, were deported, in their thousands, to Iran on the premise that they were alien Persians.

NOT THE MOST *'PROPEREST'* WAY OF USING THE ENGLISH LANGUAGE
(Definitely un-Shakespearean)

Clarence and Leon sat chatting over a cup of coffee at Tim Hortons'. After a period of silence, Leon says: Hey, Clarence, listen, this is interesting! My brother was watching a football game on TV in his house, yesterday, when he heard a big **amount of noise**, something like a bang, outside, and thought that there was a car accident. At first, he did not pay much attention, because of the game, but then, he heard a small **amount of shouting** that grew louder quickly; so, he looked out through the window and saw a **large amount of people** outside, standing near two damaged cars. Anyway, the drivers, becoming aware of the rapid build-up of a **large amount of cars**, apparently decided that they were both at fault, exchanged information and left on their different ways.

Another good one: A commentator on a major television broadcasting network, relating some particulars of an incident, advised viewers on TV that since a certain crime had taken place in a highly-frequented open space, there must have been a **'ton' of witnesses**; really?! Taking an average of 80 kilogram per male, that figure can be translated into approximately 12.5 males, and 70 kilogram per female accounts for approximately 14.3. This analysis, however, is flawed when those persons are variably represented by a mixture of both male and female components of the human species; absolutely interesting!

Another example: After the game, my brother wore his heavy coat, as it was **cold temperature** outside (what is the scientific description of a cold temperature, or a hot one, for that matter?). He drove a **large amount of distance** to get to that vegetable store on 11th Street; the vegetables and fruits there are so fresh! As he was browsing, he found green and black figs that had just arrived from overseas, so he bought a large **amount of figs**. He was so happy to find them he decided to celebrate. So, he stopped by the Italian Pizzeria on 12th Avenue, ate delicious spaghetti and drank a big **amount of wine**; I wish I was with him! (These excerpts are not jokes, but intended to be a reflection of the sad state of affairs the English language finds itself in during these enlightened, 'modern' times).

AS LUCK WOULD HAVE IT!

An eight year-old kid leans too far out of a veranda of an apartment on the third floor of a residential building; his 'center of gravity' shifts outside the edge of a ledge and he falls down. After a free downward flight of two stories, accompanied by a shattering scream of fear, he luckily lands on an outward-drawn shade curtain erected by a vegetable-shop owner on the ground floor. The curtain acts as shock absorber; nevertheless, it gets torn, and the boy tumbles onto a cushion of stacked fresh tomatoes and then softly lands on solid ground!

The owner of the store screams, both in shock of that extraordinary happening and because of the financial loss incurred in the form of crushed tomatoes. Consequently, the boy, after a miraculous escape from an assured bone-breaking fall, is confronted with another nightmare. Fearing for his life for the second time in three seconds, he runs away, across the road hoping to reach the other side quickly, only to be hit by a car! He, somehow, survived all three perils!

GOVERNMENT CONTRACTS

Three contractors from Baghdad, Mosul and Basra were in the process of bidding on the building of a bridge, with strict building-material specifications, across the Tigris River, just south of the capital; a proper and intelligent decision on awarding the relevant contract, however, rested on such unquantified criteria as 'appearance', since material wasn't an issue. The Basrawi contractor (from Basra), a rather naively honest entrepreneur, submitted a fair bid of $20 million, with an anticipated profit of $3 million. In turn, the Mislawi contractor (from Mosul), a clever guy indeed, submitted a bid of $50 million, with an anticipated profit of $10 million, in spite of the smaller Basrawi bid; he was counting on bribing a few high officials he knew.

The Baghdadi contractor (from Baghdad), a businessman who was immersed in the intrigues of that singularly corrupt environment, submitted a bid of $100 million, with an anticipated profit of $30 million. He faithfully depended on knowing people who knew the Minister for Constructions! This bidder won the contract to build the bridge, based on *'better appearance'*, the indisputably winning factor.

OF ILLEGAL RICHES

During the 'rebuilding' of Iraq after the 2003 invasion, there have been a multitude of projects, which made some influential people there very rich; substantial sums went into private pockets through untold corruption-related tactics. The 'strangest' of all is that government auditors found out that of the 1.25 million-strong salaried army personnel, only two hundred and fifty thousand were actually accounted for. Iraq a year ago canceled a $4.2 billion deal to buy various kinds of weapons from Russia, citing possible corruption in the contract.

As this story is being written, some of the accused are to be tried in absentia, since they are not to be found anywhere, and believed to have fled the country. A large number of officials have been taken to court with corruption lawsuits. And it only gets better with time; like they say: "The more, the merrier". Early this month (November, 2015), international Arabic TV stations reported that "in eight years,

Iraq sold about $550 billion dollars' worth of oil; $350 billion of that amount has not been accounted for".

EXERCISE FOR PEOPLE OVER FIFTY
(Variations exist)

For you old people (some, including myself, may prefer to use the word older), who are keen on exercising (for general or sexual health purposes), this particular exercise may prove to be excruciating. So, all due diligence should be followed; and please do discuss this plan of exercise with your doctor before you embark on such activity (*heart status should be checked*; this is imperative). Also, better have someone with a cell phone around just in case emergency medical help is required). Begin by standing on a firm, but comfortable surface, where you have plenty of room at each side (front and back, as well, just in case you experience an unforeseen fall; space and ease of movement are of the essence). With a 5-kg potato sack in each hand, extend your arms straight out from your sides until they are flush with your shoulders (this is crucial) and hold them there as long as you can. Try to reach a full minute, and then relax. Each day you'll find that you can hold this position for just a bit longer.

After a couple of weeks, move up to 10-kg potato sacks. Then try 25-kg potato sacks and eventually try to get to where you can lift a 50-kg potato sack in each hand and hold your arms straight for more than a full minute; I am at this level now. **After you feel confident at that level, put a small potato in each sack and exercise!**

WEIGHT-LOSS CLINIC

An overweight guy, wandering around, saw this sign: "WEIGHT-LOSS CLINIC", thought about it for a few minutes, and decided to try it. Entering the clinic, he saw a large sign on the wall, outlining two packages, one losing 7 pounds costing $50, and the other losing thirty pounds for a $500 fee, each within a 'one-hour workout'. He went to the receptionist, quietly opted for the less expensive one and set a starting date.

When he came back, three days later, he was asked to enter a room containing exercise instructions. The last of those instructions required him to take all of his clothes off; he wondered about that, but followed them, anyway. Within a few minutes, an instructor enters. After his weight was taken, he was directed to a door opening to a large gymnasium. There, he saw a beautiful girl, completely in the nude! The guy was curious to know what all that meant, but soon everything was explained to him. The instructor said: *"She is going to run around here; you chase her, and if you catch her, **you can have your way with her!**"* The guy ran and ran and ran. At the end of an unfruitful, longer-than-usual hour and, being exhausted, he left the gym. Upon weighing again, he found out that he had lost seven pounds; notwithstanding his failure in catching the 'beauty', he was thrilled with the result he had achieved!

After giving this experience a serious thought and remembering how beautiful the young girl was, he wondered what kind of beauty is offered for $500! So, he decided to take it! He tried his best to get in shape, so as to be prepared, and went back to the clinic. He went through the same procedure; the instructor came in, had him weighed, and then led him, full of pleasant thoughts and anticipation, to the same gym. When the gymnasium door was opened, he saw standing there a young muscle-bound African American, grinning roguishly at him. *The instructor turned to him and said: "You will have to run as fast as you can, because he will chase you, and if he catches you, he will have his way with you!"* This guy lost more than 30 pounds that day! (Semi-Folkloric)

THE HUNTER AND THE LION

A hunter-traveller, alone and on foot, is on an African Safari. Emerging out of a jungle-bush on the plains, he notices a movement within a clump of shrubs, about a hundred meters away. He treads cautiously, with his eyesight never leaving it; nothing happens, so he walks farther on and at relative ease. However, as he puts a fair distance from the bush he just left, a lion appears from those shrubs, now situated on his right. It does not take him long to realize that he is in trouble; there is no chance he could make it safely back, but thinks that he may have a chance reaching another bush to his left, where several large trees are standing. He makes a quick decision and goes for it.

Knowing that the lion is chasing him, he runs as fast as he can. But, he soon realizes that the lion has overtaken him, and is right on his heels. All he could do was to drop on the ground, crouch and starts praying. Within a split-second, the lion is on top of him. Clinging to dear life, he throws his arms and legs in all directions, trying to keep the lion away from him. All of a sudden, everything becomes quiet and, by some miracle, he is still alive. As he opens his eyes, he finds the lion lying quietly sideways beside him, and wonders what is going on. *He realizes, then, that his hand is resting on the lion's groin and understands what happened. So, he gently massages that area, but keeps looking around to find a way to make an escape.*

He picks one of the trees he saw in the bush he was running towards, a tree that has several stout branches not too far above the ground, and thinks: 'If I can only reach it'. So, he goes on with his comforting strokes and, all of sudden, makes his move. Alas, he is only a few feet from that tree, when the lion is on top of him, dropping him on the ground. He crouches, with arms covering his head, and prays again. Seconds pass, a minute passes by and nothing is happening;

no terrible bites, nothing! *He opens his eyes slowly and sees the lion lying down sideways beside him and looking at him, **with one paw supporting his chin and the other pointing repeatedly at his groin!** (Semi-Folkloric)*

BY GOD, THIS IS A TRUE CURSE!

A long, long time ago in Mesopotamia, the Wali (governor) of a town had an urgent need for money. He ordered his guards to bring in three rich citizens, a Christian, a Muslim and a Jew to his palace right away. After a short search, three such esteemed, but manifestly trembling, men were taken to a room opening to the palace's grand hall, where the Wali managed the daily town's affairs. He ordered his guards to admit the Christian first.

As this honoured man entered, he saw the Wali sitting on a huge chair, with ministers around him; there was also a donkey in the room! The Wali asked the Christian what that animal was; the latter, shaking with fear, was perplexed, but managed to say: "Mawlana (your eminence), this is a donkey". The Wali said irritably: "A donkey? This is a cow!" Then, he turned to his assistant and ordered him to charge the Christian 10 dinars ($1000, in present times). The latter paid willingly and left the hall, not believing he had escaped with his skin unblemished. As he was leaving, two fearful gentlemen still waiting outside asked him what had happened, and what the Wali wanted; he told them everything.

The Muslim was brought in, next, and was asked the same question. He took a deep breath and said: "Mawlana, but of course, this is a cow". The Wali angrily shouts: "Are you stupid or blind; you see a donkey and call it a cow! Charge him 10 dinars". The guy pays quickly and rushes out of the hall. The Jew, waiting outside, got that information, as well; being the smartest of the three, he realized what the Wali wanted right away; so, he relaxed, knowing that at the end, he will leave that hall alive and can enjoy the rest of his life in peace.

Then, the Jew was introduced and asked the same question. He calmly replied: "Mawlana, this animal is neither a donkey, nor a cow; by God, it is unquestionably a true curse; here is my 10 dinars, take it". Without further ado, he paid and left. (Folkloric)

FEELING ETERNALLY COLD

There are people in this world who always feel cold; I am one of them. There was this Iraqi guy who exulted in summer, when temperatures hovered around 50° Centigrade (around 120° Fahrenheit); anything substantially below that and down to 30° Centigrade he considered as rather cool, and cold or freezing below that.

One day, he reached that stage of life on earth when he had to be summoned for the **"ultimate trial"** that everyone has to go through. There, he was told that he had committed several evil acts in his life and, as consequence, duly shown the gravelly road to Hell; on the way there, he pondered his new situation: "Well, that sentence might not be too bad after all; at least, it is not cold there". On arrival, he was given a space fairly deep in that eternal furnace (a reference here to **Dante Alighieri**'s *"Inferno"* is due), based on his copious previous contribution of evils during his life.

Sometime later, a new consignment of the 'Condemned' arrived, and it was a large batch of evil-doers. The gates of Hades were then unbolted and stretched wide open, in order to allow the latest crowd to be appropriately welcomed into that scorching kiln. The induction of that procession, however, took quite longer than usual, as it was lengthy and everyone so excited (the hosts, not inductees). Also, *some of the brand-new tenants were not overly keen on entering that horrifying cave-like, flame-whipped and howl-filled enclosure, and thereby needed some encouragement and 'friendly persuasion' in the form of a nudge or, at times, a shove in there, accompanied by screams of displeasure amounting to indignation and substantial levels of rebellious resistance.* As such, the gates were left agape for quite a long time, allowing huge gusts of cool air to be sucked in.

Then from deep down there, someone bellowed as loud as he could: "Who is the 'son-of-a-bitch' who opened those gates and forgot all about them? Somebody there close them; **I am freezing here**".

THOSE DAMNED BREEDING SAUCEPANS!

A long, long time ago, in a village somewhere in the Middle East, a guy who was known for his cunning came up with a devilish idea, one that did not lack humour, either. This guy, whose name was Juha, went to his neighbour's house and knocked on the door. The door opened and the neighbour came out. After exchanging customary salute, Juha asked if he could borrow a medium-sized saucepan for a day.

After some hesitation, knowing Juha's bad reputation and deviousness, he assented out of traditional courtesy. He went back in the house and came out with a medium-sized saucepan. After thanking him, Juha took it to his house. A day later, he put a small saucepan inside the one he had borrowed and headed to his neighbour's house.

As he knocked on the door, the neighbour appeared and was happy to see his saucepan again. They chatted for a little while, during which time, the neighbour removed the cover of his saucepan out of habit, only to be amazed in finding a small saucepan inside. When he asked Juha about it, he responded: "Oh, I used it last night, cleaned it and put on the table to dry, in order to bring it back to you the next day as I promised. Today, however, I found out that your saucepan had **given birth** to a small saucepan". The neighbour was incredulous, but happily took both of them; why not!

A week later, Juha went to the same neighbour again and asked for a large saucepan. With due expectations, the neighbour was more than happy to oblige. Once more, Juha promised to bring it back the very next day. Next day, Juha did not appear, and not on the next, either. The neighbour now started to become apprehensive and, after a week, he went to Juha's house and knocked on his door. When Juha opened it, he asked him about his large saucepan. Juha, now showing deep grief, replied: **"I don't know how to tell you this, neighbour; but your saucepan died"**. The neighbour said: *"Died?! Do you think I am a fool? How could a saucepan die?! I don't believe you!"* Juha said: "For sure they do; you believed me when I told you that your other saucepan gave birth; didn't you?" The neighbour contemplated him for a few moments and then turned and left, without uttering another word. (Folkloric tale)

VARIOUS CATEGORIES OF ELECTIONS

During a round of American presidential elections, an American happens to be visiting China. One day he finds himself discussing matters of day-to-day significance with a Chinese acquaintance. The American tries his best to keep both of them understand each other comfortably, thereby maintaining a friendly discussion flowing as smoothly as possible. Both were doing well, notwithstanding commonly encountered difficulties regarding the **letters "L" and "R"** on the side of the Chinese gentleman; such difficulties, especially when it comes to pronunciation, is known to be a characteristic that is fairly common to Chinese people.

They talk about different topics, including cuisine, culture and others, and then revert to politics. The American enthusiastically talks about the democratic electoral process in the United States and the freedom that the American people enjoy in choosing their own government; he talks about the campaigns, primaries, and discussions, and how exciting those times are. Then, as an afterthought, he turns to the Chinese and asks him: "Do you have **elections**?" *With a roguish smile on his face, the latter replies:* "**Evly day, evly day!**"

MORE OF ELECTIONS!

Today, as I am about to finish writing this manuscript, I went out with my son, who was taking me to a store. Outside, we saw several elections placards, and exchanged a few comments, regarding the political parties involved. My son mentioned the present province's recently elected premier, and said that he actually is doing a good job of balancing the budget, to which I mistakenly mispronounced that word while saying: "Yes, newly erected". Luckily, he didn't seem to have caught that mistake.

AL-DHERRATT IS BACK!

Shakir grew up in a Middle Eastern village community. One afternoon, he was with a congregation of men, a daily ritual in that part of the world, especially where friends meet daily at 'cafes' to drink tea, gossip, and play backgammon and dominos. One such afternoon, Shakir saunters into his favourite café and sits with his friends, two of whom were playing backgammon. After a while, one of those friends says something funny, and everyone laughs. As luck would have it, Shakir had eaten a lot of cooked beans during lunch, a delicious dish that his mother new how to cook very well. As he joined the laugh with a lot of mirth, a gigantic fart escaped with tremendous force. Being one of the most shameful things in such societies, everyone at the café, who heard it, was shocked and embarrassed, but more so the 'culprit' himself.

In the coming days and weeks, kids would laugh every time they saw him; they run around and shout to their friends: "Hey, look, guys, al-Dherratt (the Farter) is here". As months passed by, this horrible humiliation became worse and worse to a degree pushing Shakir to decide to leave the village, altogether.

After twenty years of self-imposed exile, and knowing how people in those societies are deeply attached to family and cousins, he couldn't bear homesickness any more, and decides to return, thinking that what had happened was long forgotten. Alighting from the bus at his hometown, he is happy to have taken that decision. He heads towards his old home, a little uneasy at first, but found that nothing much had changed in the village, and he starts to take deep sigh of relief. Then, as he reaches his home, he hears a shout: "Hey, Ahmed, do you know what happened? **Al-Dherratt is back!** He is back, tell everyone!" (Folkloric)

THE HASHISH SMOKERS

Somewhere in the Middle East, and not too long ago, two friends were smoking hashish in a small hashisha-café. The room had a few elongated, narrow wooden chairs arranged close to each other and back-to-back. They sat there smoking and chatting intermittently. As a matter of habit, as one of these two guys sat, he had one leg underneath him; it was not long before that leg went numb.

After some time, one of the two, the one whose leg grew numb, audibly said to his companion: "Abu Jasim, you know what? My left leg is not there". After a while, his companion responded: "What?! What happened?" After another while, the first said: "I don't know, Abu Jasim; I think someone stole it."

Then, from an adjacent chair, a whisper is heard: "Abu Ali, did you hear that?" "Yes; someone stole that guy's leg". After another while, during which the issue was probed in depth, the other goes: "Abu Ali, I think we should leave right now before someone blame us." This short exchange was soon followed by the sound of shuffling feet hurriedly heading towards the hashisha-café's door. (Folkloric)

ABU AL-QASIM AL-TTANBOORI'S SHOES

In Baghdad, there was once a man called Abu al-Qasim al-Ttamboori. He was fairly well-off, but exceptionally frugal, for which he was very well known; but, with time he became exceptionally famous for wearing the same green shoes for years and years on end. Whatever happened, he wouldn't spend money buying new ones. As they were made of leather, every now and then they got cracked and developed holes; but he always had them repaired. So, after many years of everyday use, the shoes became covered with leather patches and their soles were continuously fortified with extra leather.

The time came when people celebrated their birthday, so Abu al-Qasim decided to have a bath, a bath that he rarely enjoyed one, because he had to pay for it. So, he went to the nearest Bath-House. At the door, there, he took off his shoes at the doorway, paid the bath attendant and went in to one of the rooms where they had hot water. He took his clothes off and slid into the tub. Meanwhile, the attendant, feeling embarrassed to have those faded, old patched-up shoes be seen by the bathers who regularly came, hid them behind the door where he was standing.

After enjoying the comfort of a rare bath, Abu al-Qasim al-Ttamboori prayed and asked God to give hive him a new pair of shoes as a present. As he was leaving at the door, neither the attendant, nor his old shoes were there, but he saw a pair of brand new blue shoes. He thanked God for granting his wish, wore them and went back home. After having his bath, the owner of the blue shoes, a rich Baghdadi merchant, started to leave, and was perplexed as to where his shoes had gone! After inquiry, the attendant told him that there was only one other bather there that day and showed him the old shoes. Both agreed that Abu al-Qasim al-Ttamboori must have taken the merchant's shoes.

A few minutes later, there is a knock on the latter's door. The merchant, holding the battered green shoes, is angry and demanding ten dinars for his shoes in the presence of curious neighbours. It was then that Abu al-Qasim al-Ttamboori decided to get rid of those tattered shoes. Next day, he went to the Tigris River and threw them away as far as he could. The river was known to have abundant fish, and still does; one afternoon, thereafter, a fisherman drew in his net and was surprised to see that, in addition to fish, he had also *caught* Abu al-Qasim al-Ttamboori's shoes. He took them to him and asked for a reward.

The very next morning, he rode his camel out of town and threw the shoes several miles away. That afternoon, some travelers on their way to the town saw them, and in amazement wondered what Abu al-Qasim al-Ttamboori's shoes were doing there; they took them to him as soon as they entered the town!

That night, he took a lamp, together with the old shoes, and went into his garden; he dug a hole and buried them, there. A nosy neighbour saw him digging and hiding something. The next day, Abu al-Qasim al-Ttamboori woke up hearing noise. As he looked through the window, he saw a horde of people digging all over his garden. He had to pay them each one dinar to leave his garden. That very same day, he went to the court, took the shoes off and said: "I, Abu al-Qasim al-Ttamboori, solemnly declare that from this moment on, **these infernal shoes do not belong to me, and I disavow having anything to do with them.** From now on, I will walk barefoot." (A folkloric tale)

ALOHA CALGARY!

Calgary, thirty years ago, had one of its usual winters, with the temperature sticking at minus thirty degrees Celsius for a whole month.

One day, the announcer on the radio, knowing that most people were disgusted and tired of the cold, came on the airwaves and in jubilant, but mocking, voice said: *'I have good news for you, folks; it is warming up! Actually, in the last seven hours, **the temperature skyrocketed from minus thirty to minus twenty-nine!**' Then, he finished with 'Aloha, Calgary!'*

THE UNITED NATIONS COMPLAINT

I was in the middle of resolving the status of a sudden influx of geological projects, and my work-days' time at the company was severely over-stretched, since all of those reports were 'urgently' needed. The pile of projects I had to deal with included a comparatively very large one, requiring several days of work, which I could not afford! As that large project was sent to us by the company's main office in the U.S., I had several requests from management to have it finished and sent out. Being the supervisor/geologist at the time, I saw it more proper, however, to work on several pressing small projects, requested by other companies, instead, before the approaching Christmas holidays.

One day, the president of the company personally asked me to have that large project done and sent to the parent company as soon as I could. That request I couldn't ignore! I called our company's junior geologist to discuss the matter. As he entered, I said: "You are aware of that big project for the parent company". His answer was rather slow, but in the affirmative. In an innocent tone of voice, but pretending to be as serious as possible, I said: *"The parent company is so upset that they wrote to the United Nations complaining against us, and that the matter might be transferred to the Security Council, itself!"* **He looked at me with glassy eyes, and managed to utter: "Huuuh?"**

THE DIFFERENCE BETWEEN
WESTERN AND ARABIC CHESS

By Western rules, a chess game ends when the *king* is checked and there is no place for it to move to safely. In the Middle East, a king (in this case the *ruler* of the country), facing a similar situation, may be checked and checked, without the possibility of being removed; the same game keeps going on and on until he is checked out of this life, one way or another!

THE THREE STEEL BALLS
(Variations exist)

There are three convicts, an Englishman, a German and 'Another', each held in a separate jail cell. The jail's superintendent decides to help them get busy during those long days they have to spend in their cells, instead of sitting there brooding. After some thought, he gives each convict three small, but solid, stainless steel balls to play with.

A couple of days later, he decides to check on those convicts. He goes into the Englishman's cell and finds him sitting at his table and moving the steel balls back and forth and sideways. He asks him what he is doing. The Englishman diplomatically says: "I am trying to invent a game using these balls". The superintendent is pleased, and he wishes him good luck.

When entering the second cell, he finds the German convict sitting at his table and gazing intently at his three steel balls; he is deeply absorbed in thought. He asks him what he is doing. The German says with haughtiness, but emphatically: "I am thinking how I can make a calculator, using three balls". The superintendent is thrilled and he wishes him too good luck.

In the third cell, the Superintendent finds the 'Another' convict lying leisurely on his bed smoking and sipping tea. On the cell's desk, there is only one steel ball. In response to his query, the latter indicates that he had only one ball left. The Superintendent asks: "What happened to the other two?" He answered: **"One of them is lost"**. With evident amazement, the Superintendent asks: "Lost? You only have a bed, a chair and a desk here; how could it be lost? The prisoner responds with: **"I don't know; I cannot find it"**. The superintendent says: "I see; well, if you cannot find, then it must be lost! He takes a deep breath and continues: "All right; what about the third ball?" He replies: **"Oh, it broke."** (Broke? A steel ball, broken?!)

THE SPERM SAMPLE

A guy visited a sex-health clinic complaining of difficulty having children. The sex therapist gave him a small jar and asked him to bring a semen sample back. Three days later, he comes back with an empty jar.

The doctor had a look at it and asked him: *"where is the sample?"* The guy replied wearily: *"Doctor, I tried several times, but all efforts were futile; my wife tried her best to help, so did our young female helper at home; we could not do it. Even our middle-aged neighbour, who has a lot of experience, tried too; she even used her teeth and put it between her legs, all to no avail. We all tried, but **no one could open the jar!**" (Folkloric)*

COPYING DOES NOT ALWAYS WORK

Three men awaited execution by firing squad in the condemned cell, from which the site of their forthcoming ordeal could be clearly seen. The first, an Englishman, was taken out and stood against the wall. As the firing squad raised their rifles, he suddenly shouted: **"Avalanche!"** at the top of his voice. The soldiers looked about in alarm, threw down their rifles and turned to run. Taking advantage of the momentary chaos, the Englishman scuttled away as fast as his legs could carry him and escaped.

The second condemned man, an Italian, seeing the success of this ploy, when his turn came shouted: **"Flood!"** with exactly the same highly successful effect, and off he scampered. The third man, was impressed by the resourcefulness of his collaborators; so, he determined to follow suit. **As the rifles were raised and fingers curled around the triggers, he shouted "Fire!"**

GHOST SEX

Somewhere in America, a lecturer makes a presentation on paranormal events to a group of enthusiastic students. In order to get his audience involved, he asks: "Who here believes in ghosts?" Many raise their hands. "All right; how many of you believers have actually been acquainted with one?" Fewer hands were raised this time. "So far, so good; has anyone ever had the honor of talking to a ghost?"

Only three or four hands went up in the air. "Fantastic; now I am going to ask you one more question before I start my lecture, and this is truly personal; please feel free not to say anything, unless you are inclined to do so; **has any of you ever made love to one, a ghost I mean?**" An excited listener from the East sitting on the very back bench of the auditorium waves his arm eagerly. Bewildered with the unexpected response, the lecturer says: "Wow; no one has ever before indicated to have done that; this is extraordinary. Kindly come over to this stage and tell us all about that unique experience; by all means do!"

In apparent unrestrained animation, this student makes his way up there, where he is whole-heartedly asked without any further ado. "Please tell us everything about having sex with a ghost; feel free to go into detail?" At that, the student exhibits unfailing indications of bewilderment and says: *"Ghost? What ghost? Back there I thought I heard you say goat; that is different!"* ('Semi-Folkloric')

SHARP AND READY

Gandhi studied law at the University College of London. While there, one of the professors genuinely disliked him; that feeling, which was mutual, probably due to 'personality clash', was openly expressed by both, sometimes leading to heated "arguments". Gandhi, one day, with a food tray in hand, looked around the dining room for an empty seat, where he could sit down and have his meal. The room was then full, except for one table that was partly occupied by that same professor; he didn't hesitate to walk there and sit down beside him.

The professor, looking at him warily and scornfully, said: "Mr. Gandhi; you do not understand... a pig and a bird do not sit together to eat". As he rose to leave, the latter replied: "Oh; I'll fly away, then".

The professor decides to take revenge on the next encounter, which happened to be during a test, coming in only a week's time. When Ghandi's exam sheet got to the professor, he quickly and unhesitatingly marked it with the word **"idiot"** and then returned it to him. The latter looked at it, and after a few seconds of pondering, he went back to the professor and said: **"Sir, there is only a signature here, but no grade".**

DURING THE SIX-DAY WAR

Regardless of the negative images of political chaos and civil disorder displayed recently, **Egyptians are known**

to thrive on humour, even self-inflicted, and for that matter not sparing anyone even during disastrous events!

During the Six-Day Arab-Israeli War, ending with the demise of several Arab armies, notably including the Egyptian, there were 'abundant' and varied jokes that did not spare anyone involved in that conflict. One of the more cleverly humorous depictions published by a well-circulated Egyptian newspaper was in a form of a cartoon. The cartoon showed a car **racing onward**; the Israeli flag was drawn on the back wheel, while the front wheel displayed the Egyptian flag!

This is another one, which is even better. Today, October 19, 2015, an old woman leaving a voting booth in Cairo (Egypt) was asked *whom she had **voted for**; she replied:* **"Haj Ali, God rest his soul,"** after which she was asked who that gentleman was. Her reply was: "He was my husband, God rest his soul; he died eight years ago. I heard on the radio that the government is asking everyone to vote, but I didn't know anyone else, so I voted for him." (Real story)

Today (same date, above) is a Federal voting day in Canada, as well. My wife, daughter and I entered the voting hall together; my daughter went first, shadowed by her mother. Following the normal procedure, I heard the voting official ask her politely to give her name and address, while checking her ID. Next, I moved forward and the same procedure was followed; I was already prepared for it. When she asked me the same question, I produced another ID, held it close to her table and read my name slowly; she smiled and rather apologetically said that that was a regular procedure (humour ma'am, humour)! I then went to the voting booth and opened my voting sheet; *I was shocked, I couldn't find the name of the person I wanted to vote for, nor were there any of the other prominent personalities.* So I marked his party, instead, took it back to that same official and asked her: "Aren't these federal elections?!" she said: "yes". To which I responded: "But where are the **names of the big guys**?" She smiled and gave an explanation, saying something suggesting that voting is not direct! (What is happening in this world? I guess it is ignorance on my side)! As I started to leave, a Chinese voter standing there smiled and asked me if I was all right today?! To which I replied: "Yes, yes; I just had to wake up early!"

'TEMBELS'

Two *super-lazy* men, drinking pint after pint of beer together in the pub, are companionably silent. A few hours pass.

On his 10th pint, the first man raises his glass and says: 'Cheers!' The second man glares at him: *"Look", he says, "did you come here to talk, or drink?"*

MORE 'TEMBELS'

During a hot summer day, two *super-lazy* brothers, Temel and Yilmaz, are relaxing silently on comfortable chairs in their third-floor apartment, with the window open and a small fan working hard, turning this way and that way. Suddenly, there is commotion outside. Without turning his head, Temel says: "Brother ...there is .. noise .... outside." After a couple of minutes, Yilmaz responds: "I heard .. that .....Temel."

Two minutes pass by, and then Temel goes again: "Something is ... happening; .. why don't ..... you .. look ... out of the.. window?" three minutes of heavy utter silence was rudely broken by Yilmaz, who said: "But ..Temel ... I did that ...last week; it is ..... your turn".

PREPARING FOR A BRIGHT FUTURE

An American professor was invited to the Law Faculty in Baghdad to give a lecture to graduating law students. The lecture was lengthy and informative and, in the process, citing many factual examples from home, some of which were outlandishly strange (to the students that is).

After the lecture, sandwiches and soft drinks were served, and people indulged in chatting; of particular, there was a group of five students, who were debating a certain issue hotly. After a while, one of them was heard saying: It is the best job we can ever dream of; solid, and most of the time we cannot lose. He, then separated and respectfully approached the visiting lawyer-professor and asked: "That example you quoted about someone falling down on a sidewalk in your county and suing the owners of the lot for a considerable sum of money, and actually winning his case; don't people there think that strange?" The visitor responded with: "On, no; not at all; it is not as you might imagine; cases like this are fair game."

Directly after that, the student turned to the other four and started speaking rapidly in Arabic. When they finished what appeared to be an exciting discussion, the same student returned to the American visitor and asked if he and the rest of the group were allowed to work in America, to which he responded with an affirmative reply, providing they took several courses in an American Law school. Then he added: "I have to warn you, now, before you embark on any such decisions, that law business, like any other, is highly competitive there." One of them replied: "No, no", **"our job will be easy, just falling down on sidewalks."**

THE ULTIMATE WEAPON

This advertisement was read in the newspapers of a metropolis where mosquitoes have been an epidemic: *"For those who have been harassed by mosquitoes: finally, we have the weapon that works effectively against them; it kills them dead 100 per cent; NO CHEMICALS: 1000 dinars per kit."* Nothing could stop those pesky insects, biting everyone and everywhere; they could even penetrate sleeves and pants.

At that, one of those miserable souls who had suffered eternally from their bites decided to try that remedial solution, whatever the cost. After waiting impatiently, the kit, in the form of a box, finally arrived; at last! Where are you mosquitoes? He excitedly opened it, only to find two bricks with a sheet of instructions; the latter said:

Please follow these steps to the letter, in order to destroy those hated insects:

1. **Catch** a mosquito.
2. **Place mosquito** on one brick.
3. **Squash** it with the other brick.
   4.   *Enjoy life without itching and scratching!*

CHEERS TO ONE AND ALL!

Printed in the United States
By Bookmasters